AT THE
MERCY
OF THE
RIVER

AT THE MERCY OF THE RIVER

AN EXPLORATION OF THE LAST AFRICAN WILDERNESS

Peter Stark

BALLANTINE BOOKS • NEW YORK

Published in the United States by Ballantine Books, an imprint of The Random House
Publishing Group, a division of Random House, Inc., New York.

Ballantine and colophon are registered trademarks of Random House, Inc.

Owing to limitations of space, permissions acknowledgments can be found on p. 333,
which constitutes an extension of this copyright page.

Library of Congress Cataloging-in-Publication Data
Stark, Peter, 1954–
At the mercy of the river : an exploration of the last African wilderness / Peter Stark—1st ed.
p.   cm.
Includes bibliographical references.
ISBN 0-345-44181-8
1. Lugenda River (Mozambique)—Description and travel.   2. Lugenda River Region
(Mozambique)—Description and travel.   3. Wilderness areas—Mozambique—
Lugenda River Region.   I. Title.
DT3410.L84S73   2005
916.79'9—dc22   2004062379

Printed in the United States of America

www.ballantinebooks.com

2 4 6 8 9 7 5 3 1

First Edition

Book design by Kris Tobiassen

*To my rivermates—Cherri, Clinton,
Rodney, Steve, Josh, and Lance—
and to the people and wilds of Mozambique.*

ACKNOWLEDGMENTS

Beyond the Lugenda River itself, this book attempts to explore the adventurous nature of the human spirit and its need for wild places. I had an unfailing guide in these intellectual explorations in the form of Christopher Preston, professor of environmental ethics, a commercial fisherman, and all-around wilderness buff who pointed the way through the great body of literature about human attitudes toward the wilds. I also feel fortunate to have the friendship and help, as well as companionship on various whitewater rivers and steep, snowy mountainsides, of William Bevis, retired professor of English literature at the University of Montana, who likewise is extremely fluent in the literature of the wilds. I owe a debt to his brother, Richard Bevis, whose important work *The Road to Egdon Heath: The Aesthetics of the Great in Nature* helped inform this book. I used two seminal works on wilderness as if they were maps: *Wilderness and the American Mind* by Roderick Frazier Nash and *The Idea of Wilderness: From Prehistory to the Age of Ecology* by Max Oelschlaeger.

Ever since I moved there nearly twenty-five years ago, I realized that in Missoula, Montana, I lived in one of the world's epicenters of wilderness issues. Not only is it surrounded by millions of acres of wilderness—both officially designated and not—but in the University of Montana's Environmental Studies program and Wilderness Institute it offers abundant resources for the study of wilderness. I would like to thank Wayne Freimund, Laurie Yung, and Nicky Phear for their helpful suggestions, likewise the staffs at the University of Montana's Mansfield Library, the Missoula Public Library, and the International Wildlife Film Festival.

Among those who helped me understand the significance of miombo woodlands, the Niassa Reserve, and African ecosystems in general, I would like to thank Kate Newman of the World Wildlife Fund, Rolf Baldus and Rudi Hahn, community-based conservation advisors for the German Technical Corporation.

At the Niassa Reserve, Baldeu Chande and Anabela Rodrigues were both informative sources and generous hosts. Halvor Astrup did much to make the reserve and the Lugenda expedition a reality.

Jamie Wilson and Derek Littleton of Luwire Camp contributed greatly to the success of the Lugenda River expedition, not to mention provided plenty of extra moments of thrill, and Necky Kayaks generously donated the boats that we paddled and that performed wonderfully on the river in very difficult circumstances.

This book started in the most unexpected manner, with a phone call on a Friday afternoon. Thank you to Laura Hohnhold, former editor at *Outside,* who thought of me when the Lugenda expedition first came to her attention and gave me that first phone call. Leslie Weeden saw the assignment through and shepherded the original story through editing. I'm grateful also to Hal Espen, Ki Bassett, Mary Turner, and the other editors at *Outside* who helped launch me down the river. Nobody realized quite how intense a ride it would be.

The editors at Ballantine Books saw the potential of the idea and how the river adventure itself could be expanded to address the larger issues. This book wouldn't have been possible without Dan Smetanka, who initially signed on to the idea, and to Allison Dickens, whose intelligent and deft editing and enthusiastic support brought the project to fruition.

Josh Paul, my kayak companion on the last part of the river, provided many of the beautiful, atmospheric photographs that accompany the text in this book, and Cherri Briggs generously lent her photographic collection. Heather Ellis, and the rest of the staff at Cherri's adventure-travel company, Explore, of Steamboat Springs, Colorado, expended countless hours arranging travel logistics for the Lugenda expedition. Jane Ragsdale contributed her considerable research skills to compile the book's bibliography.

Finally, I can't express enough gratitude to those in whose company I journeyed down the Lugenda River—my companions both in fact and in spirit—through what was for me a very difficult and ultimately very rewarding time: Cherri, who made it all happen, Clinton, Rodney, Steve, Josh, and Lance. And to Amy, Molly, and Skyler, all of whom, in some way, accompanied me every paddle stroke of the river.

CONTENTS

AT THE
MERCY
OF THE
RIVER

PROLOGUE

MY GRANDFATHER

My grandfather took me on my first overnight canoe trip when I was four. I remember the comforting smell of sun-warmed canvas as I napped in a nest of sleeping bags amidships—my grandfather paddling the stern and my father the bow—the jumping flames of the campfire in the dusk, the twilit river sliding past, the sweet fizz of root beer on my tongue. Propped on his elbow near the fire, my grandfather gestured to the dark, forested, opposite shore. He told me they would soon build a big highway bridge right here.

"When you're grown up," he said, "this will all be gone."

And so my life has been shaped. That statement speaks both to a value for wild places and an underlying sadness that they will someday disappear. For me there is also a visceral fear that these wild places will vanish before I can experience them—a compulsion that has taken me to Greenland and Manchuria, Tibet and Sumatra, and many places between. Now it has led me to one of the wildest and most remote parts of Africa, down a river that has never before been paddled by Westerners.

There are dozens of "reasons" that people give for heading off into the wilds. But their answers seem to float about, knocking into one another like so much flotsam on a sea of mystery that rises from a deeper source within the human spirit.

Nor am I exactly sure why I'm so drawn to seek out these wild places. And what exactly constitutes the "unknown" or the "wilds" or "wilderness"? Is it a place somewhere out there? Or is it something instead that lies within us? I journeyed down the Lugenda River to try to find the answers to these questions. As we paddled deeper and deeper into the wilds, and as our campfire created a tiny circle of yellow light in the vast dark forest, I thought back to my grandfather and those first canoe trips with him. I thought of the explorers who came to Africa before, and of explorers still to come. What is it that connects us? What is it that urges us toward the unknown?

THE CALL

The call came in at 2:30 p.m. on a sunny Friday in April. Very much "between things," I felt like the proverbial private eye with his feet up on the desk waiting for something to happen. The caller was a magazine editor of my long acquaintance. As soon as she started talking, I felt I'd stepped into a drama—one in which I was an actor, a reluctant one, pulled by a dozen conflicting impulses.

"There's this American woman," she said. "She lives in Botswana, and her name is Cherri Briggs. She owns an adventure-travel company named Explore that runs a lot of African trips. Now she's putting together an expedition to make the first descent of an unpaddled river in Mozambique. She's looking for a writer to go along."

Oh, yes! was my first reaction.

I saw jungle rivers. Thick vines hanging down. The trumpeting of elephants. Naked hunters with bows and arrows. Unnamed waterfalls arcing out over rocky escarpments and cascading in clouds of spray to the forest below. In short, I saw the whole African explorer's fantasy nurtured by Hollywood imagery of Humphrey Bogart in sweat-soaked khakis hacking his way through the jungle.

Then I reconsidered in the harsh light of reality.

Whoaa, I thought. *This could be really dangerous!*

I knew of too many kayakers and rafters embarking on "first descents" of wild rivers in far-off lands and drowning in unknown rapids.

Still, I listened while she read passages and elaborated on Briggs's email.

"Five weeks," I heard her say. "Seven hundred and fifty kilometers in sea kayaks . . . African wilderness . . . thousands of elephants . . . lions . . . no rapids . . . leave in a month."

No rapids. The editor explained that no one knew for sure, but the river was believed to be flat water. I felt relieved—and I liked the idea of all those thousands of elephants in the wilds, and the lions, too. Then my alarm rose again. If there were no big rapids, I no longer had such a ready excuse to decline.

"We need an answer by five o'clock today," the editor said.

No way, I thought.

But I didn't say so aloud. It was as if I was looking for a way out of this. Or was it that I was looking for a way *in*? I didn't know, but I didn't want to burn my bridges just yet.

I checked my watch. In five minutes I had to leave to pick up our two children, Molly, seven, and Skyler, four. Time—or lack of it—loomed as a huge issue in our marriage: two children plus two full-time careers, a writer and a professor of modern dance, and each day a mad juggling of who would do what when. Amy, at the moment, was somewhere in eastern Washington performing in a weekend concert with her modern-dance company. She'd be back by Monday to dive into her teaching duties. *Right!* I'd just duck out on my family responsibilities starting next month for a quick five weeks in the African wilderness? I knew that Amy would be especially pleased to hear that I'd be spending those five weeks in the wilds in the company of a woman named Cherri.

"I don't think I can give you an answer by five o'clock," I said to the editor. "And I should tell you that I'm skeptical about my chances of going."

"Think about it over the weekend," she replied. "We can probably give you that much time. I'll send you the email."

Late that afternoon, with my mother-in-law watching the children, I went for a run over the high, grassy hills above the Montana university town where we live. When I want to think things over, this is the route I run, with its soaring view across the tawny hills, the grid of the town below, and the high, snowy mountains beyond, as well as the pellucid spring sky arching overhead.

I panted up the trail, climbing up one grassy rise, then another and another, stepping higher.

Here lay my perpetual dilemma: I was irresistibly attracted to wild places and risky outdoor activities. But I was scared of them at the same time. This, too, was part of the legacy from my grandfather. He sometimes pushed me forward into these things, past the point where I became afraid.

You've been trying to learn to say no, I told myself as I ran up the hills. No one is going to accuse you of being a sissy or a coward. If you don't want to go, don't go! Don't feel you *have* to. Just shelve it. Don't pursue it. Don't even open the email.

So that was that. I came down from the tawny hills, slipped off my running shoes, and played with my children.

The next day was Saturday. As was my habit, I went to my office for the morning. "Office" was only a manner of speaking. It consisted of a small spare bedroom that unfortunately sat beside our only full bathroom. By then the bathroom had quieted down. Instead, I felt the entire house thump as Molly and Skyler played downstairs with a babysitter and two friends. I flicked on my computer to start the morning's work. I glanced at my email account, as I always did first. As the editor had promised, there was the email. It had no title, only a forward tag from the editor.

You weren't going to read this, I told myself. I slowly moved my cursor onto it. *Okay,* I thought, *I'll at least scan it. Then I'll give my definite* no. *I know the answer will be* no.

I clicked my mouse. The email spread across my screen.

Cherri Briggs's well-shaped prose rhapsodized about the vast wild lands of northern Mozambique, about the broad and beautiful and as yet unpaddled Lugenda River, about estimated populations of fourteen thousand elephants, undiscovered wildlife species that probably existed in this largely unknown region, about hippos, crocodiles, lions—possibly some rogue lions—and a stunning landscape dotted with granite upthrusts called *inselbergs.* The lands along the lower third of the river had recently been designated the Niassa Reserve—an area roughly the size of Switzerland—to preserve its wildlife. The reserve would provide us with logistical support in the form of an airplane and a helicopter for at least part of the time that the expedition was on the river. Plus we'd be assisted by a hunting-safari camp located on the river's lower reaches.

"The Lugenda is one of the last important unexplored rivers in one of the last great wildernesses in all of Africa," Briggs wrote in her pitch.

It was intoxicating. I felt my excitement start to rise. *But you were going to say* no, I reminded myself. *You went up on the hills and probed what you really felt, and the answer was* no. But this expedition sounded really intriguing.

Okay, I told myself. Here was a solution: I'd get a second opinion.

I picked up the phone and dialed the number for a certain Super 8 motel in Yakima, Washington. I didn't know whose names the reservations were in. I tried five or six names associated with Amy's dance company. Finally, one worked. The receptionist put me through to a room. One of Amy's dancers answered. She gave me a number to call for another room. This time Amy's father answered. He was a former foreign correspondent and inveterate world traveler, a romantic about faraway places who had taken Amy and her mother to live for several stints in Bangkok, the Philippines, and Cairo.

I knew without asking what his advice would be. I also well knew that his daughter had inherited his love of travel—she had accompanied me to Greenland, Tibet, and Sumatra. More than anything she hated to be left behind.

He said that in a few minutes he was meeting Amy for breakfast. I asked him to have her call me as soon as possible.

She phoned back a short time later.

"Listen to this," I said.

I read Cherri Briggs's email into the phone.

"What do you think?"

There was a brief pause.

"That sounds amazing," she finally said. "If it's really as good as she makes it out to be, I think you should go."

THE WARNING

For the next week I felt good about my decision. The wheels were set in motion. I was signed on to the Lugenda River expedition. The following weekend Amy had another dance-concert date. Without her, I accompanied some friends to a reception for eighty-year-old George McGovern, who had been the opponent of Richard Nixon in the 1972 presidential election. He had received my first vote thirty years before, and recently, in retirement, he had moved part-time to Montana. A welcome party was being held for the McGoverns.

I walked in the side door of a sprawling ranch house in the Bitterroot Valley and found myself standing face-to-face with my old friend and backcountry skiing companion Skip Horner.

We shook hands warmly. A professional mountaineering and river-rafting guide with impeccable credentials on several continents and his own adventure-travel company, Skip years before pioneered the first descent of the tremendous rapids on the Zambezi River that lay below Victoria Falls. I couldn't help bragging to him about my upcoming expedition.

"You're going to do *what*?" said Skip incredulously. "You're going to run an African river in sea kayaks? Are you *crazy*? What about the hippos and crocs? Have you ever seen the size of the teeth on a hippo? They're like this." He measured out the distance from his elbow to his hand. "They're the size of railroad spikes! Do you know what those teeth would do to you if you were sitting low to the water in a sea kayak?"

As an oarsman he had always been partial to rafts over kayaks. He described one of his rafting trips in Africa where two kayakers had quit after the first few days because of the threat of hippos and crocs. They had to be "chopped out."

"A raft," Skip concluded authoritatively, "is the only way to go."

I tried to sift out Skip's partiality to rafts in general in this discourse. Was he saying all this simply because he disliked paddling a kayak compared to a raft, or should I be truly concerned? But even allowing for a partiality on his part, my sense of alarm soared. I looked about for the bar in the hopes of tamping it down. It was in the living room, beyond a circle of people surrounding George McGovern who was holding forth on his latest policy proposals. I got a glass of wine. It didn't help. I still couldn't follow George's policy proposals. Instead of worldwide food distribution, all I could think about were those massive jaws and railroad spike hippo teeth crushing me and my kayak.

When I saw Amy late that night, I told her what Skip had said. I was considering emailing Cherri in the morning to ask her about these dangers.

"I think that's a good idea," Amy said. "The sooner you do, the better—so you won't brood on it."

In the next days there followed a flurry of emails between me, the Steamboat Springs, Colorado, home office of Briggs's adventure-travel company, Explore, and Cherri herself, who lives most of the year in Maun, Botswana—the staging area for the many tourist safaris heading into the wildlife-rich Okavango Delta. Even with these communications I couldn't get a grip either on the depth of the Lugenda expedition's dangers or on the nature of this woman putting it together.

Initially I'd written to her and introduced myself, mentioning that I planned to study Portuguese. Mozambique is a former Portuguese colony;

it has many tribal languages, but its official one is Portuguese. At least some of the people we'd meet would speak it, and it would help a lot to be able to communicate with them, both for our expedition's logistics and for my learning more about the region we paddled through.

She replied that I didn't need to worry too much about the Portuguese. She was more worried about the hippos and crocs.

When I wrote back and said that I'd just talked to Skip Horner about exactly that and he recommended going in rafts, she replied not to worry; she hadn't forgotten the "croc-hippo equation." There were ways to deal with them, although there was no question this trip was a "dangerous mission." She was now more worried about unrest with military types.

I didn't know what to think. Was Cherri for real? Did she really know what she was getting into? Was her vacillation and glib treatment of these dangers the result of the awkwardness of email communication, or was she as uncertain—or even unstable—as she seemed? In other words, was she naive or, worse, crazed in some way to be even proposing this?

Hang on for a while, I told myself. Live with uncertainty and see what unfolds. I didn't have to wait long. A day or two later I received a missive from Cherri, via e-mail, that sternly warned of the "real risks" we'd be facing. We were heading into one of the most remote parts of the African continent, to a region where not much has changed in two hundred years. On an intensity-of-expeditions scale, she gave the Lugenda expedition a 9. Every member of the expedition needed to be very strong and healthy, "and mostly have balls of steel."

Cherri closed by admitting she was nervous about it herself, but also very excited, as there were few expeditions like this left on the face of the earth. We wouldn't forget it. But she wanted to know now if we were "overly nervous" about it. She signed it, "Thanks guys. Cherri."

The email was addressed to the three other Americans besides Cherri going on the expedition—me, Cherri's brother, Steve Briggs, and Josh Paul, a photographer who would fly in by bush plane halfway down the river, where there was a small strip in the forest, and take Steve's spot. In addition to Cherri, there would probably be two African professional guides.

With that last email I really didn't know what to think. My sense of alarm was now fluttering up through my stomach and nearly ringing in my ears. I couldn't help thinking it was a stupid thing to risk my life on so hazardous an expedition while leaving two young children and a wife at home—especially with a woman who couldn't seem to settle on a danger level for the expedition and seemed constantly to jump around about what constituted the most serious risks. And all this risk for what? To satisfy my selfish sense of curiosity? To write a magazine article? Why should I risk so much—and risk leaving behind so much—for that?

Amy had been very generous in encouraging me to go. I thought I should consult her again.

We had put the children to bed and had read them stories. Amy was in the bathroom next to my office brushing her teeth. I printed out the email. I sat on the edge of the bathtub and read it to her.

When I got to the part about needing "balls of steel," Amy paused her toothbrushing and rolled her eyes. She had also inherited from her father a sharp critic's eye.

I finished reading the email.

"I'm wondering if I should bail out."

She took her toothbrush out of her mouth and spat into the sink.

"It's hard to believe what Cherri says about how dangerous it is because it keeps changing," Amy said.

"I suspect she's not really sure herself," I replied, trying to understand it from Cherri's point of view. But it wasn't a point of view that gave me a lot of confidence.

Amy took a gulp of water, rinsed her mouth, and spat into the sink.

"I think you should find out all you can about paddling African rivers and then decide whether to go or not." She turned to me, her blue eyes flashing. "I still think it would be a great trip. But if you let these people push you into doing something stupid and you get killed, I'm going to be really angry."

THE APPROACH

I'd never had a knife pulled on me before. When it happened, I wasn't anywhere near African wilderness. It was a little more than three weeks since Amy and I had talked in the bathroom that night. I had made dozens of phone calls trying to track down people who might have a grip on the dangers we might face. The picture was not a lot clearer, although I did manage to talk to one of the guides going with us. In the end, despite the uncertainties, I could not say no.

So I was on my way. I had flown from Montana to Detroit and then overnight across the Atlantic to Amsterdam, where I was scheduled to wait all day before boarding another night flight to Johannesburg. Instead of hanging around the airport for eight or ten hours, I rode the shuttle train into Amsterdam's Old City. I was curious: For years I had heard about its red-light district. I wanted to see it. What exactly I planned to do there I didn't know.

At 11 a.m. the day's first prostitutes were settling into the viewing windows along the old streets. They looked like immigrants in need of money—Eastern European or Russian or black African—and appeared less desperate or bored than simply forbearing. I hurried past them, suddenly not as curious. I skipped the hashish bars, too, and settled in for a quiet beer and a sandwich at a sunlit outdoor café along a canal.

After a pleasant meal, it was time for me to head back for my flight. On the way to the train station I wended my way through narrow alleys. I'd seen local Dutch people in office clothes using them and assumed they were safe. Not far from the station I arrived at the entrance to a particu-

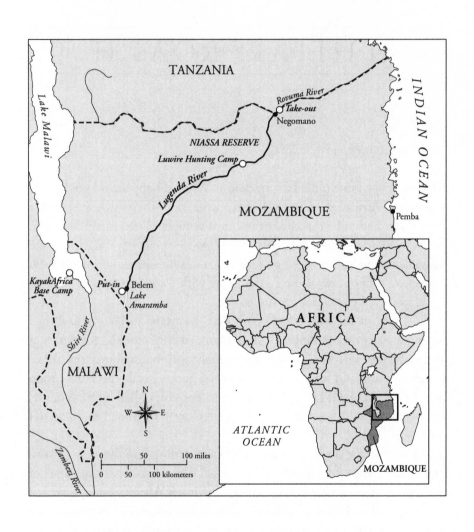

larly narrow alley only a block or two long. I could see cars whizzing by on its far end—the main thoroughfare that led to the station. I hesitated for a moment. There were thin men—most of them black, I assumed African immigrants—in long, stained coats hanging out on door stoops. The main street was so close, just over there through the alley. The Dutch people walked down these alleys, and it was broad daylight—early afternoon. If I was going to paddle an unexplored river in Africa, I had to screw up my courage for dicey situations. Here was a dicey situation. Don't let yourself be scared too easily, I told myself.

I held my camera bag closer against my chest and started in.

Once I had committed myself, I saw word of my presence ripple among the clumps of men and their heads turn toward me. I momentarily considered turning back, but it was too late. Or maybe this was pride. I was heading toward the African wilderness and yet was frightened by a two-hundred-yard-long alley in Amsterdam? I braced myself and walked quickly.

Halfway down the alley one of the thin African men came up to me wearing a long-sleeved canvas coat.

"Where are you from, man?" he asked in accented English.

I kept walking briskly.

"Answer me!" he demanded. "England? America?"

I said nothing. He tugged at the small pack on my back as if to slow me down. I could feel the straps straining on my shoulders.

I spun toward him. "I don't understand!" I said, feigning I didn't speak English. I turned away and kept walking fast.

"I said where are you from, man?" he shouted at me from behind.

Now he was pulling hard on my backpack, on the straps, pulling me back toward him. My reaction was instinctive. Angrily, I spun at him.

"What are you *doing*, man?" I demanded, pushing him hard in the chest, away from me.

I saw his left arm jerk up. His hand shot out from his sleeve. A thin, razorlike knife blade flashed once in the sunlight, his index finger extending partway down its length to hide it. He held it there toward me, letting it hover for a moment as if to make sure I saw it. Then, already rocked back on his heels from my push, he lost his balance and staggered backward.

He recovered his footing. His hand disappeared up his sleeve again. He turned away and walked slowly back down the alley toward his friends. None of them moved.

I quickly exited into the busy street.

Jesus Christ! I thought. *I almost got myself stabbed! Would he really have done that? To me?*

I have to be more cautious, I told myself. That was really stupid. In the hushed air-conditioned comfort of the shuttle train to the airport, I realized what a fat target I must have been—camera bag dangling, daypack bulging. I dripped with the wealth of the West. I had to remember I was now branded with this status, wealthy and Western and white—things it was easy to forget in the United States. He probably only wanted to slit the bag's strap and run off with the camera. But what if I had resisted and he had stabbed me? It would make an ignominious end to my grand plans for an African adventure before I could even get started. The same fate had befallen so many of the grand African exploration schemes of centuries before.

I had taken Amy's advice and read about how difficult the Europeans had found it to penetrate Africa's interior. The continent threw out endless ways to stymie them, usually fatally. Many didn't even make it past the African coast. Some barely made it *to* the African coast. There was an arrogance on the part of many European explorers, especially those on big, well-funded expeditions, and an assumption that they had the sophistication, technology, resources, and intelligence to succeed. It was a kind of macho, I-can-do-anything approach—because God and civilization are on my side—that led them to believe they would just waltz to the center of the continent.

Other Europeans, more humble, arrived on Africa's coast as solo travelers armed only with their incredible daring and adventurousness. I already knew of one such would-be African explorer in the person of John Ledyard. He was a kind of hero or anti-hero at my alma mater, Dartmouth College. Ledyard's father, a New England sea captain of the same name, had died when John was young. With two other children to look after, his mother sent him to live with his grandmother in Hartford, Connecticut. Young Ledyard showed great curiosity about the world during elementary school and was a quick learner, but urged to take up the study of law, he promptly rejected it as too boring. His grandmother dispatched him north in 1770, age nineteen, to the wilds of Hanover, New Hampshire, where a family friend, Eleazar Wheelock, had recently founded a college to give Indians a Christian education. The grandmother's hope was that Ledyard would become a missionary and preach to the heathens.

Ledyard lasted four months at Dartmouth, with much of that time spent mounting his own theatrical productions, before heading out into the forest to learn the Algonquin ways. He returned to Hanover briefly after three months in the wintry woods, hated school even more, chopped down an enormous white pine on the banks of the Connecticut River, and hollowed it out with an axe to make a canoe fifty feet long and three feet wide. He then set off alone down the Connecticut River toward the sea, carrying little more than a bearskin cover and a volume or two of the classics.

Thus began an outlandish series of adventures—first as a sailor on a ship heading across the Atlantic to Gibraltar, then as a petty officer on Captain Cook's third voyage, where he witnessed (and detailed in his memoirs of the voyage) an angry Hawaiian run Cook through the back of the chest with a spear. Cook fell dead in the surf. Ledyard then hung out in Paris with Thomas Jefferson while scrounging up the backing for a sea expedition to America's northwest coast. He had seen trade possibilities of the region on a voyage with Cook. When his subscribers backed out at the last minute, Ledyard decided to walk to northwest America, striding alone and nearly penniless at the rate of two hundred miles per week across Russia and Siberia toward the Bering Strait, where he hoped to hop across to Russian Alaska. He had almost reached the Russian far east when he was arrested as a spy and sent back to Europe.

In London, Ledyard was recruited for his boldness by Sir Joseph Banks. Banks had served as naturalist aboard Cook's first around-the-world voyage and now was president of the Royal Geographical Society. Aristocratic and wealthy, Banks had met with several friends over dinner at St. Alban's Tavern one night in 1788, a year before meeting Ledyard, and founded the African Association, dedicated to exploring for science and profit the mysterious interior of that unknown continent. The first task the association set for itself was to "solve the riddle" of the rumored river known as the Niger.

When could he start for Africa? Ledyard was asked.

"Tomorrow morning," he replied.

Soon Ledyard had landed in Cairo on the African Association's first mission. He laid plans to join a camel caravan traveling south across the Sahara and then bearing west toward what he hoped was the Niger River.

But it was in Cairo, barely past the coast, that the African continent stopped the intrepid Ledyard in his tracks. According to a contemporary's account, the hot Egyptian sun brought Ledyard a bout of constipation. This prompted Ledyard to take a remedy of vitriol. The ever-enthusiastic adventurer apparently swallowed too much; so eager was he to get under way that he tried to hurry the remedy. He suffered internal pain and burning. He then swallowed a tartar emetic to purge himself of the vitriol, no doubt figuring he'd be up and ready to go in no time. Apparently he took too much of this, too. He died in violent bouts of vomiting and diarrhea—certainly not the last would-be African explorer to expire in this manner.

Yes, be more careful, I told myself. *Don't let your enthusiasm run away with you, like stupidly walking down that alley.* But where do you draw the line? If some enthusiasm is a good thing, how much is too much? And, likewise, caution. Where does caution turn to outright paranoia?

"It was a young man's game," said one account about African exploration I had read, "and it virtually assured such young men an early death."[1]

They faced poisoned arrows from tribes who did not welcome strangers, robbery from bandits, predations from large carnivores, drowning in river rapids, dying of thirst in endless deserts, and, most lethal of all, the "disease barrier"—the fevers and other maladies that felled Europeans as soon as they stepped onto the continent. Few European explorers of Africa, I read, survived past the age of forty.

So why did they go?

Why did I want to go?

Or, putting it another way, why didn't I simply turn back from the alley in Amsterdam where the thin African men in the long, stained coats hung out on stoops? It would have been so easy. An extra two- or three-minute walk. But I had framed it as a kind of a test: If I couldn't negotiate this alley, how could I negotiate the wilds of Africa? I could have avoided it all and simply viewed it as a potentially dangerous alley from which to steer clear. Why did I see it as a test? I remembered so many occasions with my father and grandfather that were presented this way—a test. They frightened me at times. They would grab me by the arms and legs and swing me, pretending to throw me into the river. I had nightmares of clouds of little white bubbles closing over my head. I remembered my grandfather prodding me forward to stand at the very lip of a cliff over the Wisconsin River that must have been close to one hundred feet high.

"I've got hold of you," he said, his big, strong hand wrapped around my arm. "Don't worry."

But I was worried.

"River rat," he called me when I met his standards. "You don't want to be a sissy, do you?" he'd say if I was scared and "Einar the whiner" if I complained. I never did figure out who Einar was—a Scandinavian name from his turn-of-the-century Milwaukee boyhood, maybe. Whoever he was, I definitely didn't want to be Einar.

I wondered what kind of family legacy John Ledyard carried. His father and grandfather, both named John, had been sea captains—his father in the New England–West Indies trade. I imagined young John, fatherless, growing up with stories recounted by his mother and grandmother about his father's and grandfather's heroic deeds at sea. He would idolize and romanticize their adventurous seafaring lives. Not for John the dry-as-dust, studious career of a lawyer or a preacher, directions his grandmother had clearly urged. Instead he threw himself headlong into adventure to stand in his ancestors' exalted company.

I could see all this in John Ledyard because I could see some of it in myself.

June 1—Flight to Johannesburg

I mulled this over on the night flight from Amsterdam to Johannesburg, eight thousand miles across Europe, the Mediterranean Sea, and down the length of the African continent. I slept for a while, then woke and read, then closed my eyes again in the dimmed, humming, wide-bodied airliner. I visualized the terrain we were flying over—what a wildly different world from the smooth plastic cabin in which I sat. A decade earlier Amy and I had flown from Cairo to Ghana on the coast of West Africa. The plane had swung in a vast sixteen-hour loop over much of the African continent: first the enormous tawny, rock-and-sand ripples of the Sahara Desert, then the lush green tabletop mountains and cascading waterfalls of the Ethiopian Highlands, then the vast jungly lowlands of the Congo Basin, where we had finally swung back north. I had read that south of the Congo Basin lay a broad belt of dry forest known as the "miombo woodlands," and below that were the plains and steppes and desert of southernmost Africa, tapering down to the continent's tip at the Cape of Good Hope.

I guessed that below us now lay the great belt of miombo forest slung across Africa's lower midsection. The Lugenda River ran through this forest. I tried to picture the river, winding for hundreds of miles through the wilds. I couldn't see it. Instead my mind returned to the cabin—so secure, so comfortable, an electrified jet-fueled time capsule. I tried to forget where I was heading, that vast forest below. This was my moment of calm and rest before diving in. I closed my eyes again and slept.

June 1—7 a.m., Johannesburg

"Gee, I sure enjoyed your book. I read it on the plane over here."

Steve Briggs and I had just shaken hands in the bleary dawn of the Johannesburg airport arrival hall, coming out of customs. His flight from London, the European transfer point to which he had flown from his home in Phoenix, had landed a few minutes before mine from Amsterdam. I thanked him for his kindness about my book. About my age, mid-forties, he was broad-shouldered and muscular with a Marine-style buzz cut. He projected an easy American friendliness.

"I didn't sleep but two hours during two nights of flying," he said. "I stayed up all night last night drinking with an anesthesiologist."

I got the sense that Steve was an easygoing, all-American guy who also liked to party.

Cipo, the driver sent by the hotel, helped us tote our big duffel bags out of the hall. Outside, black drivers tried to hustle us into their cars, but Cipo, who was also a South African black, directed us to a Volkswagen van. Already I felt self-conscious about the division between black and white. We whisked through the damp, chilly morning of a South African winter along a four-lane highway toward the hotel where Cherri waited. From the air I had seen green farms and what looked like gated communities. I wanted to talk to Cipo—who had greeted me with a friendly, finger-popping handshake—to show him I didn't believe in any hierarchy of black and white, but Steve wanted to talk, too. If he was to be my teammate, I figured I should get to know him.

During the twenty-minute ride, no doubt we were both assessing the same thing: Can I live and paddle with this guy in the wilds for weeks on end?

We compared bios. We compared children. Both he and his wife had sons from previous marriages. He and Cherri had grown up "all over" the American West—mostly Nevada—as their family traveled about to big jobs with their grandfather's road-construction business. For a number of years Steve had driven machines such as bulldozers but now worked out of Phoenix as a salesman of precision electronic measuring equipment.

"What do you like to do for recreation?" I asked him, hoping the answer would be something that demanded wilderness skills.

"I like to go four-wheeling," he replied.

This wasn't the right answer at all. The environmental types I hung out with in Montana had nothing but disdain for those who tore around the landscape for fun on 4×4 vehicles and ATVs. Would he and I have philosophical differences? Plus, his preference for gasoline-powered vehicles implied that he didn't possess much in the way of wilderness survival skills.

"I should tell you," Steve added, "that I had never been in a kayak until a few weeks ago."

I already knew that. I also knew that Cherri hadn't, either. She had explained this to me in one of her emails. Their total lack of kayaking experience wasn't too great a source of concern to me, though. Cherri had canoeing experience with tourist groups on the placid Lower Zambezi. The Lugenda was supposed to be mostly flat water, too, which was relatively easy to learn to paddle in a kayak. Besides, we'd be paddling tandem sea kayaks, which are designed specifically for flat water and for carrying equipment plus two people. If necessary, Cherri and Steve could each ride with someone more experienced.

But if there were big rapids, that would present an altogether different problem. I knew from Cherri's report that there were *some* rapids. A few weeks earlier she had flown over a section of the Lugenda River with a bush pilot on a reconnaissance flight and spotted rapids through the forest cover. Mostly she thought they were ones of moderate size and mostly in the river's first section. Of course, what one sees from hundreds or thousands of feet of altitude while winging along at one hundred miles per hour and what actually exists at river level could be two entirely different things. I'd also done my own research, mail-ordering a huge aeronautical map of this region of Africa. Back in my office, squinting hard at the map's topographic lines and at times using a lens, I had calculated that the Lugenda dropped about fifteen hundred feet in elevation over the course of four hundred miles of river, a perfectly reasonable grade for the rivers I knew in Montana. But so much depended on *how* the Lugenda dropped—gradually and constantly or cascading over periodic large rapids and falls. I was very much hoping for the former.

Cipo maneuvered the van off the four-lane onto curving streets. We drove along a small lake—mirror-smooth in the early morning—surrounded by large condo projects. We came to a big steel gate and a guardhouse with dark one-way glass. A uniformed black man stepped out and looked in the van. Then the heavy gate swung open and admitted us into the hotel complex.

That, for the moment, was my total impression of South Africa, or at least Johannesburg.

Meeting Cherri felt like meeting a mail-order bride. My fate was inextricably bound up with this woman, but so far I'd had no more than the briefest contact with her by email and telephone. I was both anxious and excited to meet her.

First, though, I wanted to take a shower. The warm water felt wonderful after nearly three days on airplanes from Montana. Steve had gone off to his room to sleep. Wrapped in a towel, I lay down on the big double bed under the warm covers and began to drift off. The phone rang.

It was Cherri. I sat up on the edge of the bed.

"How were your flights?" she asked.

"Really not bad."

"What are you up to now?" she asked.

"Kind of dozing."

"Sleep, sleep," she said comfortingly. "We have errands to run all day. We'll meet at five. I'm really eager to meet you."

"I'm eager to meet you, too."

"We're in the lobby about to have breakfast if you want to come down and say hi."

"I've been thinking of having breakfast."

"Great," she said. "Come on down. We'll see you here."

I hung up. I felt nervous. I chose my clothes carefully: slender outdoor khakis, a thin black pile sweater, river sandals. I removed my glasses, which I'd worn all night on the flight, and inserted my contact lenses. I didn't want to look too scholarly or too old. I was forty-eight—"pushing fifty," as my father liked to tease me. Older than the average age of explorers of the past. Still, I considered myself in very good physical shape. In Montana I jogged up a small mountain every day.

I looked in the mirror. I laughed to myself. *Yes, what you want to achieve is the dashing adventure-writer look.* I brushed my teeth. I wondered if I'd be attracted to her. I wondered if she'd be attracted to me. I was acutely aware that we needed each other. She needed me as a writer in order for her ambitious expedition to receive recognition. I needed her as the person making the expedition happen. Without her I wouldn't be here. I'd be back home with my feet propped on my desk.

I spotted her easily. She sat on the far side of the breakfast room near the lakeside windows, facing the door. Her hair flowed over her shoulders in brushed golden waves. She spotted me coming across the room and stood up. She was tall and slender, and wore black jeans and a black sweater—in good shape, not stunning in her features but certainly attractive. I guessed she was in her forties, too. Her hazel eyes crinkled nicely around the corners when she smiled to greet me. We shook hands. I could see the same self-conscious preparations in her that I'd made myself. *Yes,* I thought, *here's the dashing-adventuress look.*

"I feel as if I've known you a long time," I said.

She laughed. We sat down. On the table before her was a French-plunger pot of black coffee and a plate of fried eggs. There was so much to say. The conversation careened from subject to subject: my flight, our family backgrounds, the changing situation with the guides.

"Paul Connolly dropped out," she said. "I thought he would. I hope that's okay with you."

Connolly, originally from Rhodesia (now Zimbabwe), had a lawyer's background before turning to adventure. He owned a whitewater-rafting company on the Middle Zambezi that took paying tourists on the big rapids below Victoria Falls. An expert kayaker in his own right, he had completed many first descents of rivers in Africa and the Himalayas. Originally he had agreed to serve as river guide for the Lugenda River expedition, but then, as departure approached, he backed out, according to Cherri. She said something about Connolly wanting a lot of money to rent his kayaks to use on the trip and his concern that the expedition would take too much time if we spent a week exploring the Niassa Reserve at the river's lower end, which was part of her plan. Instead of Connolly, in the last two weeks she had recruited two other unpaid guides to accompany us—presumably rewarded simply by the experience of the first descent. She was also able to obtain free sea kayaks from the Necky Kayak company.

"Our guides are Clinton Edwards and Rod Wilson," Cherri said. "I'm really happy with them. They couldn't be better. They're perfect."

It was hard to tell if she was trying to convince me or convince herself, but they did sound good. I already knew about Clinton and had spoken briefly with him by phone before leaving the States. He was an expert whitewater kayaker and safari guide who had worked for rafting companies, including Connolly's, on the Zambezi. Rod, Cherri explained, was also a safari guide and a wilderness survival expert. Plus, he had training from his mandatory stint in the South African military, which, she explained, included doing things like jumping out of airplanes at thirty thousand feet—at night. Though Rod didn't have much experience with kayaks, Cherri was confident his strength made up for it.

"I don't worry about Rod," Cherri said. "He's so strong he could pick up a double kayak with all the gear and someone in it."

"So there are just the five of us then?" I asked her.

The numbers felt a little thin for so ambitious an expedition. I wished we had one more expert kayaker like Clinton. I counted for something: I had a lifetime of paddling canoes, including a fair amount of whitewater, and a moderate amount of kayaking experience. I knew I'd have no trouble handling a sea kayak in flat water, although if we ran into big rapids, I wasn't so sure about my ability—or anyone else's—to handle a heavily loaded sea kayak. They weren't designed for the tight maneuvering demanded by river rapids.

She now reported that we'd probably reach most of the rapids she had seen during her reconnaissance flight in the first few days of our journey. Also, Cherri now told me, the helicopter support had fallen through. The pilot, based in Kenya, had had a family emergency.

"I have the email," she said as if I might doubt that she had actually lined up helicopter support in the first place. "I'll show it to you."

"That's okay," I said.

The helicopter, or its sudden absence, didn't bother me as much as I would have guessed. We had other safety backups, Cherri assured me: access to a bush plane based in a safari-hunting camp on the Lugenda's lower reaches. Besides, Rod, a reconnaissance and communications specialist during his military stint, had just purchased a satellite telephone for the expedition. This presumably allowed us the ability to call for help if we desperately needed it. I was both pleased and slightly distressed to hear about the sat phone. Though I liked the safety aspect, I wondered if it would feel like hauling along a telephone booth or some other obtrusive hunk of the modern world.

Despite thin ranks and the lack of promised helicopter support, I was impressed by all the last-minute organization Cherri had managed to coordinate. She said she had been working on the expedition for two years. Five weeks earlier, however, when I got involved, the trip still seemed hardly past the idea phase. Now we were all in Africa with complicated plane reservations made, guides lined up, government permissions in hand, and kayaks acquired and being transported via Land Rover to the Lugenda River headwaters. It occurred to me that the prerequisite for any would-be explorer—whether Columbus or Magellan or Peary or someone proposing the first descent of the Lugenda River—was to be a good promoter. That Cherri seemed to be—in abundance. Her alluring first email alone was evidence of that. She told me over our plates of eggs that her grandparents had emigrated from the British Isles and headed to the American West to seek opportunity and founded a road construction company. Clearly, her grandfather had been a talented motivator of people and had been possessed of an adventurous spirit; Cherri obviously had inherited some of his attributes.

"When I was a girl, I always wanted to be an explorer," she would tell me later. "But I remember very clearly the first time I opened an atlas of the world and saw all the places that had already been explored. It was a huge disappointment to me. I've been looking for an unexplored place ever since.

"When I heard about this river, the Lugenda—that it was one of the last major unexplored rivers in Africa—I said, 'I'm going to paddle down that. Whatever it takes, I'm going to do it.'"

Cherri's white South African boyfriend, Richard, showed up looking sleepy. He joined us for a quick breakfast, and then the two of them went off to buy various items of emergency gear for our trip. After sleeping a few hours, I repacked my own gear. I pared my clothing down so it fit easily into two small stuff sacks. Then I removed it and placed it on the big hotel bed in a few neat piles. In addition to my belongings there was a pile of nearly forty pounds of energy bars that Cherri had talked the Clif Bar company into donating and that I'd toted from the United States in a duffel. I also had a huge stack of T-shirts, sweatshirts, and caps bearing the

"Explore" logo that I'd brought to give as gifts and be worn by us. I was sure Cherri, given her promoter's sense, hoped the Explore logo—the logo for her company Explore—on the shirts would appear in any published photos of the expedition.

She arrived in late afternoon to inspect my gear. She flipped through the clothes I'd laid out on the bed. Space and weight in the kayaks would be at a premium.

"You won't need this," she said, tossing a shirt onto a discard pile on the floor.

"Or this." She flung away a pair of my pants.

"Or these." Two spare pairs of blue-striped boxer shorts hit the floor.

"Let me at least keep the boxer shorts," I pleaded. "I might need them." She considered for a moment.

"Okay," she said. "You can keep the boxer shorts. Steve's wife packed about ten extra pairs for him, and I had to discard them all."

It was the books that presented me with the biggest problem. I'd brought six or seven thick volumes and had read as much of them as I could on the long flights. I'd now managed to cull them down to the two lying on the bed: *The Idea of Wilderness* by Max Oelschlaeger and *Wild Africa* edited by John Murray.

"One of these has to go," said Cherri.

I pleaded with her.

"No. One book—and even that's too much."

I chose Murray's anthology of African exploration and nature writing. It was slimmer. Unlike the Oelschlaeger book, I knew I could read it aloud around the campfire. Its stories of explorers and visitors to Africa might even inspire the five of us on the Lugenda River in a dark and difficult hour. *Wild Africa* seemed eminently useful, a literary emergency kit.

Besides, I loved its epigraph. It was from Pliny, writing from the Roman Empire two thousand years ago: "There is always something new coming out of Africa."

June 2—Heading North

"Some people say democracy won't work in Africa," said my seatmate.

An accountant for an international conglomerate, he was returning to his native Malawi from a business trip to France, and his bulk filled the luxurious, leathery reclining seat next to mine. Cherri had wangled an upgrade to business-class seats for herself, Steve, and me on the passenger jet from Johannesburg to the former British colony of Nyasaland, a thousand miles north. Nyasaland is now known as Malawi and borders long, skinny Lake Nyasa (or Lake Malawi), the southernmost of Africa's Great Lakes. En route, as we flew over bright green farm country in Zimbabwe, I was eating beef fillet and drinking red wine. My seatmate, an African black, finished lunch and described to me the deteriorating political situation unfolding invisibly on the landscape beneath us under the leadership of Robert Mugabe, who had helped lead the country to freedom from white rule in 1980 but then turned increasingly dictatorial. Mugabe's followers had been seizing white-owned farms by force and handing out the lands to Mugabe loyalists as political patronage.

"They say democracy won't work in Africa because a leader won't groom someone to succeed him. The leader is concerned that if he grooms a successor, everyone will go to that person before the leader is out of power."

We had left Zimbabwe and were flying over a deeply forested arm of Mozambique. The accountant suddenly pointed out the window.

"There's the Zambezi River!"

It looked huge and broad beneath us, wending slowly through sandbars and forest. I could see no roads or development whatsoever along the riverbanks. And yet the Zambezi was considered crowded by comparison to the river far to the north where we were headed.

Cherri, Steve, and I changed planes at Blantyre, a city in southern Malawi, after waiting all afternoon in the small airport there. In late afternoon we walked out onto the tarmac to board a twelve-seater, single-engine prop plane that looked like a big Piper Cub. The pilot gunned the engine, and we literally jumped up into the air, going into a steep bank even before the end of the runway. I realized that this was the sort of lifting power one needed to fly in and out of the tight, rough airstrips of the African bush.

On board were the three of us plus a Sikh family, with the father in a turban, and a hip young couple, Marzi and Yuri, who were, I believe, from South Africa and Eastern Europe, respectively. With them was the little bundle of their infant boy, Teak, who had been passed up the tiny aisle from the rear door in a basinette. Marzi had come to South Africa to give birth to Teak under modern medical care. Now the three were returning to their home on the shores of Lake Nyasa, where Yuri and Marzi ran a safari camp that specialized in sea-kayaking. We'd use their camp, KayakAfrica, as our base camp and make a test run in kayaks on Lake Nyasa.

I sat quietly. Cherri and Steve were enthusiastically describing our plans for the Lugenda River to Yuri.

"So you really are going off into deep, dark Africa, aren't you?" Yuri said.

The plane swayed and bumped along at five thousand feet over the bush. Black clouds bunched over purple mountains in the distance, trailing misty veils of rain. A few drops splattered the plane's windshield. Dusk gathered far in the east. Directly below, spiderwebs of tawny dirt paths joined thatched villages in the green bush. Somewhere far beyond lay the great forest and the Lugenda River.

Suddenly, I felt sad and very tired. I wanted to be someplace quiet and comfortable. I wanted to sleep. I wanted to be reading a book with Amy, Molly, and Skyler in front of the fireplace in our clapboard house on Monroe Street with the nice view of the park and the burbling little creek. Instead, what I saw was the Great Rift Valley: the bush-covered pans or flat basins, the worn mountains that looked as old as the planet itself, and in the distance the great watery arms of Lake Nyasa.

Ahead, it all looked like so much effort. Already I felt burned out, exhausted by the effort of getting here, by the anxiety of thinking my way through thus far. I wanted to go back and forget about it. I wanted to be somewhere far from this primordial landscape. I thought of Mungo Park and his lonely dusk on the banks of the Niger. I'd read an excerpt from his *Travels in the Interior Districts of Africa* (1799) on the overnight flight. A few years after John Ledyard's death by emetic in Cairo, Mungo Park, then a young Scottish ship's surgeon, made the acquaintance of Joseph Banks in London and offered his services to the African Association. Banks and company dispatched Park by trading ship to the coast of West Africa, from whence he was to strike out overland. His instructions, similar to Ledyard's, were to find the Niger River, trace its course, and locate its principal towns or cities.

It didn't need stating in his instructions that there was the great hope on the part of the African Association that these Niger River towns, including the fabled city of Timbuktu, were the source of the gold that was flowing out of West Africa.

"Gold is there so plentiful," an association member wrote of Timbuktu, "as to adorn even the slaves."[2]

Nor did it deter Park in the least that since its founding seven years earlier the African Association had dispatched three other adventurers to locate the Niger River—John Ledyard, Simon Lucas, and Daniel Houghton—and only one of them, Lucas, had survived, having turned back far short of his goal. Traveling with little more than a few changes of linen, an umbrella, a couple of pistols and shotguns, and a pocket sextant, Park struck off into the interior accompanied by a native interpreter and a servant, the threesome mounted on a horse and two asses.

Months later, after nearly dying of fever and thirst, and having survived numerous robberies and captivity by a Moorish chieftain who enslaved his interpreter, Park stumbled alone onto the banks of the Niger. As it had long been rumored among European and even classical geographers, the Niger flowed east instead of west. Huge dugout canoes were used to ferry people across the river between large towns on both its banks. Park was refused permission to cross, though. A local chieftain feared that the intrusion of a white man might anger the nearby Moors who ran the region's slave trade and might see Park as a possible business rival. The chieftain didn't want to risk the Moors' reprisals for permitting Park to cross the river. Park had to return to a distant village and wait for further instructions from the chieftain.

He had received a great deal of hospitality from strangers during earlier phases of his journey, but to his "great mortification," no one in this village offered him shelter. He sat alone all day under a tree. As dusk fell, the wind rose and a rainstorm threatened. Park was about to climb the tree, out of reach of wild animals, and spend what promised to be a nasty wet night clinging to the branches when a woman happened by and took pity on him.

She led Park to her house. There in its warm confines she lit a lantern and laid out a sleeping mat for Park and broiled him a fish over the coals. The other women of the household stared at him "in fixed astonishment" until they eventually returned to their work of spinning cotton.

"They lightened their labors by songs," Park wrote in his *Travels,* "one of which was composed extempore; for I was myself the subject of it. It was sung by one of the young women, the rest joining in a sort of chorus. The air was sweet and plaintive, and the words, literally translated, were these:

The winds roared, and the rains fell,
The poor white man, faint and weary,
Came and sat under our tree.
He has no mother to bring him milk
No wife to grind his corn.

Chorus:

Let us pity the white man
No mother has he to bring him milk
No wife to grind his corn.

"Trifling as this recital may appear to the reader, to a person, in my situation, the circumstance was affecting in the highest degree," Park wrote in his *Travels*. "I was oppressed by such unexpected kindness; and sleep fled from my eyes. In the morning I presented my compassionate landlady with two of the four brass buttons which remained on my waistcoat; the only recompense I could make her."

Fighting my own mental exhaustion as rain splattered the plane's windshield and dusk lowered the heavy sky over mountains and bush, I longed for my own little family, my own warm house, or simply a song to comfort me.

We were now winging over a narrow arm of the great lake. I saw small wooden fishing boats dotting the smooth water. We flew over green hills along the shore. The engine noise dropped. The plane eased down toward brushy reddish earth. It was dotted with fat baobob trees. Children ran from huts and turned their faces up toward us, pointing. Frightened goats scampered into the bush. I was gliding down through the transition zone between the world I'd left behind and the raw red earth below. I didn't know what lay in front of me. I braced myself. I tried to get excited about our arrival, but most of all I was aware that what lay ahead was going to be hard.

Thump!

We had arrived.

The motor was cut. It was very quiet. There was no airport. The dirt strip had been cleared from the bush. We climbed out. The air felt soft and warm, unlike the cold damp of the Johannesburg winter a thousand miles to the south. An old van waited for us at the strip's edge. Its driver, a young white man who introduced himself as Monet and who was with KayakAfrica, heaved our bags onto the roof rack. We piled in. The seats were old airplane passenger seats bolted to the van's floor. I wondered what had happened to the rest of the plane. I took the rearmost seat, nestling in beside a pile of leafy green vegetables and bunches of onions.

"Strap yourself down tightly in the rear seat," Monet called back to me. "The road is a bit rough in spots, and you don't want to jam your head against the ceiling."

And so we set off—Cherri, Steve, and me, plus Marzi, Yuri, and baby Teak—bumping and rolling through the dusk toward KayakAfrica's camp an hour away, with Monet at the wheel and beside him a pretty young Canadian woman, Nadine, who had come to Malawi to do medical work and ended up a partner in KayakAfrica.

I just wanted to sit quietly again. I wanted to give myself over to someone else's care, in this case Monet's who was piloting us through the soft twilight. The engine was too loud for easy conversation. Dust billowed from the slowly rolling tires. I saw Cherri's and Steve's heads begin to nod. I thought again of Amy, Molly, and Skyler back at our house in Montana. Mungo Park had had a family, too. He had returned from his solo expedition and become a celebrity of sorts in London, although the aristocratic society women, perhaps because of his shyness, found Mungo rather dull and stiff.

Park repaired to his native Scotland to write a memoir of his travels. He angered Banks by turning down a chance to explore Australia. Instead, he married his dear Alison, eldest daughter of the doctor with whom he had apprenticed years before and sister of his best friend, Alexander. He passed the medical exams and took up a country medical practice in Peebles, a small town in Scotland's borderland. He and Alison had two children. But Park soon found his practice dull and laborious, too.

"I will gladly hang up the lancet and plaister ladle whenever I can obtain a more eligible situation," he wrote to Joseph Banks.

In 1805, after he had been back in Scotland five years, Park received orders from the King of England himself to trace the entire course of the Niger for purposes of its "commercial intercourse." He was offered a handsome salary plus a thousand pounds a year in his absence for his "lovely Allie," a generous sum for her brother Alexander, who would accompany Park, and funds to outfit a large expedition of forty-four Europeans.

Park seized the chance, but it was an utter disaster. Held up by contrary winds on the sailing voyage to Africa, Park's expedition started too late from the coast toward the interior. Mired down in the rainy season's mud and fevers, by the time they reached the Niger's banks they had lost all but twelve of the forty-four Europeans. The survivors pushed off downstream, traveling first in small boats and then in a makeshift raft they cobbled together from half-rotted dugout canoes they had purchased from a friendly chieftain. Soon Alexander, Park's brother-in-law, and seven others were dead of fever and illness, too. Only four Europeans remained plus the expedition's contingent of Africans.

At the rocky rapids of Bussa, the local people apparently mistook Park's raft for a party of hostile Fulani, a distant tribe said to be about to wage war, or for a Fulani slave boat. They greeted the raft with a shower of poisoned arrows. Park and his men fired back with repeated fusillades from their muskets, killing and wounding many on shore. When their ammunition was spent, the white men urged their black assistants to swim for shore. According to eyewitnesses interviewed years later by other British explorers, the remaining four Europeans, Park among them, refusing to be taken captive or killed, locked arms and jumped overboard, disappearing forever beneath the Niger's surface.

It was now dark. *Really* dark. I thought how easy it would be to disappear in Africa. Monet drove through a village. There were no lights, just a circular patch of a hut's straw-flecked mud wall caught in the van's headlights, the dim orange glow of a cooking fire or oil lamp within. A streetlight here was as unimaginable as a mud hut would be in Manhattan. Out the window I could see that the night sky had cleared and there were stars—intense multitudes of stars. I could smell the sharp fertile richness of the onions heaped beside me. Despite my sadness, there was something compelling here.

I tried to think of the reasons why Mungo Park might have left his wife and children for Africa. Was it that his work as a country doctor was that boring and laborious? Or had things been going badly with "his" Alison and he had felt burdened by the responsibilities and unceasing demands of two small children? Or was it the promise that if this expedition succeeded, he'd be able to provide for them forever and live in comfort without toiling as a country doctor?

It could have been that after five years returning to Africa simply didn't seem that daunting, that the passage of time had erased the sharp memories of hardship and near death. He had survived one trip to the Niger River. Why not another? Or maybe he was acutely aware of the hazards. Taking on that risk, in one sense, is an oblique form of suicide. The possibility of death on the Niger might have been preferable in Park's mind to the sure suffocation of life as a country surgeon.

I couldn't help thinking that the greatest reason of all for Park to leave wife and children was the intoxicating lure of Africa itself. That despondent moment alone under the tree at dusk, with the wind and rain and the threat of wild animals in the night. The kind woman who took him in and grilled him a fish. The beautiful songs sung by the women as they spun. He had been so moved by it all. This could not be compared to the life of a country doctor in Peebles. Traveling alone in the African interior, stripped of all things "civilized" and European, *was* life—life writ large. One moment you could be utterly desolate and empty and broken, and the next brim with fullness and warmth.

But if my surmise was correct, why did Park have to go to Africa to find this kind of emotional fulfillment? Wasn't there enough at home? I didn't feel any lack at home, but I had left a wife and two young children for Africa just as Park had. Already I missed them badly. Maybe, without really knowing it, this was one reason I had been drawn to Africa: to understand how badly I would miss them. Maybe this was one reason Park had gone, too. Africa—all wild places—in some way taught the lesson of what was important.

Monet stopped the van. Its headlights illuminated a metal gate. The legs of a figure emerged in the headlights and swung it open. Monet drove through and shut down the engine. We climbed out. Through the darkness I heard a generator's muffled throb and water lapping on a shore. Ahead shone the soft yellow glow of electric lights from within a large bamboo-and-thatch pavilion.

"Go on in," someone said.

Steve and I followed a path into the brick-floored pavilion, blinking in the light. The Rolling Stones played over a sound system. A big dining table stood off to one side; a sitting area on the other was appointed with wicker chairs and wooden stools. African artifacts hung from the thick poles that supported the thatched roof. The open-sided pavilion gave an impression of warm, rustic elegance—a complete contrast with the pitch-black villages we had passed through.

Two muscular young whites were sitting in the wicker chairs. Wearing shorts and T-shirts, they hopped up as Steve and I entered and strode with bare feet across the brick floor, beer bottles gripped in hand.

They gave us firm handshakes.

"Clinton," said one.

"Rod," said the other.

"Would you like a beer?"

"That sounds great."

Steve and I took the beers they offered and sat on stools. I felt a little like Mungo Park coming into the kind woman's house—all this warmth and hospitality suddenly blossoming in the dark African night.

Cherri swooped in.

"You made it!" she said to Clinton and Rod. "I'm so relieved! I was worried we wouldn't find you here! How was the drive?"

It hadn't been so bad, they said. With the new sea kayaks strapped to the roof, they had driven Cherri's aging Land Rover from Botswana, where Rod, Clinton, and Cherri all made their homes, across a good part of southern Africa here to Lake Nyasa—three countries, a thousand kilo-meters (six hundred miles), and several days. Meanwhile, Cherri had flown down to meet Steve and me in Johannesburg, the region's major air hub and destination for European flights, and then the three of us had flown north by the passenger jet and bush plane to meet the others here at Lake Nyasa.

"Lance has already driven much farther than we did," Clinton said.

From somewhere out in the darkened courtyard Lance appeared in the pavilion.

"The stew is about ready," he announced. "Four hours ago it was two chickens running around the courtyard. This other 'oke and I had to chase them down. You should have seen it!"

"'Oke" was white African slang for "bloke," I soon learned. Lance had an ample belly and pale skin that contrasted with the hardened outdoors look of Clinton and Rod. He was a friend of Rod's and Clinton's from Zambia who ran "mobile" safaris in Land Rovers with his family's com-pany. He, too, had been recruited at the last minute to join the Lugenda expedition, serving as "backup driver." He had already put in some six thousand kilometers—from Botswana down to Johannesburg to pick up the sea kayaks at a Necky dealership and then back up to Botswana to pick up Clinton and Rod in Maun, the staging town for the many tourist safaris going into the Okavango Delta to observe wildlife. He had then driven across southern Africa with those two and the kayaks to Malawi and Lake Nyasa to meet us. He still had another four thousand or so kilometers to go to deliver us all to the Lugenda put-in point, a good day's drive over a mountain range from KayakAfrica's pavilion; then he had to circumnavigate much of northern Mozambique and its vast roadless forests to meet us at the river's mouth. In a lifetime of making "shuttles" for canoe trips—arranging for vehicles to drop the boats at the put-in point on the river and meeting them at the take-out—this was by a factor of ten the longest shuttle I'd ever known.

Lance disappeared back into the dark to make final dinner preparations. Cherri was sending emails from the computer in the pavilion's screened-off office and bedroom area. Steve and I and Rod and Clinton drank beer and talked. I studied the two of them. They appeared younger than I had expected. They both had the sun-bleached hair and weather-reddened features of whites who had spent years in the bush, but Clinton, despite a slightly balding head, was only thirty and Rod only thirty-two. I had expected grizzled veterans more my own age.

As part of my pre-expedition research to reassure myself, I'd spoken to Clinton by phone at his home in Botswana. I'd immediately felt reassured by him. I sensed that Clinton had plenty of experience in assessing risk in the wilds. He seemed like a straight shooter.

"We're not going to go paddling straight into a pod of hippos," he told me over the phone from half a hemisphere away. "We're going to look where we're going. We'll assess the risk as we go along. The same with rapids."

I'd liked him right away. But now when I saw him in person at KayakAfrica, I had a hard time reconciling my expectation of a grizzled veteran with the guide opposite me who was young enough to be my son. Cherri had told me about Clinton's scars: the puckered circle on his hard belly from a nine-millimeter bullet wound, the huge S-shaped incision where the doctors had cut him open to repair ruptured organs, the smallish scar on his right hand from his first venomous snakebite, delivered by a Mozambican spitting cobra, and on his left forearm the long curving scar where doctors had cut out the putrefying flesh of his second and more serious venomous bite, from a stiletto snake. Tattooed over his left shoulder there was also a set of wild dog tracks.

I realized it was possible to interpret Clinton's extensive body markings in two very different ways—either as the hard-won badges of deep experience and wisdom in the wilds or, conversely, as a road map of recklessness.

"Dinner is served," Lance called out, ferrying in a mounded pot of rice, a chicken-tomato stew, and bottles of off-the-charts Malawian pepper sauce.

I watched Clinton and Rod as they stood up barefoot on the brick floor—their hard muscles, callused feet, quick movements, and eagerness. Maybe youth and quickness did indeed serve one better in the African wilds than age and wisdom.

I didn't know, but I was quite sure I'd have occasion to find out.

June 5—To the River

It was so tight in the old Land Rover that my dusty toes caught the back of Cherri's carefully brushed blond hair. After removing the rear seat, Lance, Rod, and Clinton had crammed our gear in a careful layer of petrol cans, water jugs, spare tires, tents, sleeping bags, tool kits, and hundreds of other items. Lance drove and Cherri wedged into the center seat between him and Rod and various gearshifts. In back, Clinton, Steve, and I lay flat on our backs, feet forward, atop the pile of gear. Overhead, on the Land Rover's roof rack, we had strapped the two cream-colored double sea kayaks and one yellow single, like a load of very strange fruit from some outsized tropical forest.

All morning we worked around the southern end of Lake Nyasa, rolling through dusty villages peopled by African women in brightly colored wraps. At the lake's foot we crossed a long, narrow bridge over its outlet, the Shiré River. From this outlet the river cascaded southward to the Zambezi and then to the Indian Ocean, a total drop of fifteen hundred feet. It had been David Livingstone's great dream to build a British Christian colony in the nearby Shiré Highlands; however, rapids and waterfalls on the Shiré had thwarted the easy access by steamboat from the Zambezi on which he'd pinned his hopes. It was only one of Livingstone's many grand schemes that had gone astray, one more spot where his iron-tipped ambition had run head-on into the granite wall of Africa's reality.

We followed a dirt road over the green mountains that rimmed Lake Nyasa's eastern shore, marked on some maps as the Livingstone Range. Pausing near the top, we gazed back down the way we had come. The mountain slope bellied out into the wide pan across which we had driven, the far side of the plain filled by the bright blue foot of the lake like a giant puddle in a road rut. The lake extended out of sight to the north nearly four hundred miles—as long as Lake Superior but much narrower. Across the lake, only a few dozen miles away, we could see a further range of hills.

We were looking across the entire Great Rift Valley. When the two huge plates of the earth's crust began to slide apart thirty-five million years ago, the crack spread all the way up and down East Africa. The narrow slice of crust between the plates simply dropped, creating a trough that geologists call a *graben,* while mountain ranges lifted along its edges. When parts of this graben filled with water, it formed the fjordlike Great Lakes of Africa, such as Lake Tanganyika and Lake Nyasa. The latter is believed to have formed only about two million years ago.

Two days earlier, the morning after our arrival at KayakAfrica's pavilion, Steve and Cherri, paddling together in one double kayak, and a guide from KayakAfrica and I, paddling in another double, had kayaked through choppy waves ten kilometers out to a group of islands in Lake Nyasa where KayakAfrica maintains a safari-style encampment in Lake Malawi National Park. Monet then had motored out to the islands in an *African Queen*–style launch, bringing scuba gear. With Monet guiding us, Steve and I had scuba dived at a depth of ten meters, circumnavigating tiny Jumbo Island. We flippered among huge tannish blocks of rock, some as big as a house, that rose toward Nyasa's wind-churned surface. The bottom slanted away beneath us toward the lake's darkening turquoise depths, which, I learned, reached the lake floor two thousand five hundred feet—half a mile—below the surface. Here was the very bottom of the Great Rift. Because the lake's surface sat at an elevation of one thousand five hundred feet, the bottom of the Great Rift lay nearly a thousand feet beneath the level of the sea.

It was along this great crack in the African continent that scientists believe our earliest hominid ancestors evolved. The oldest positively dated fossils of hominids—human ancestors after they split off from the ape line—are about five million years old. They were unearthed by archaeologists in or near the Great Rift Valley in Ethiopia and northern Kenya, which were then antelope-rich grasslands.

By 3.6 million years ago a hominid called *Australopithecus afarensis* used humanlike hands, possessed a chimpanzee-sized brain, and walked fully upright. Mary Leakey discovered the footprints of this creature fossilized in volcanic mud along an ancient riverbed of northern Tanzania, about a thousand kilometers north of where Steve, Monet, and I dove down into the Great Rift. The footprints consist of two sets, one smaller and one larger, walking parallel about ten inches apart. Nearby were fossilized tracks of elephants, rhinoceroses, giraffes, a saber-toothed tiger, and antelopes heading to watering holes.[3]

The first true humans, *Homo erectus,* appear to have evolved around two million years ago. Powerfully built, *H. erectus* possessed a long, low skull that housed a comparatively large brain and made stone tools, crude at first but increasingly sophisticated. These choppers and scrapers for butchering animals are unearthed in caves and extremely ancient campsites on old lake beds and river courses along the Great Rift Valley and its edges.

I swam onward through the sun-dappled water with air bubbling up from my lungs, Monet guiding me from behind. Electric blue and orange cichlid fish darted among the great tan primordial blocks of stone. The turquoise depths slanted fathomlessly off to my right. Gliding along, I thought about how I was floating through the basement of our own creation. The water felt soothing against my skin, not sharp like the lakes I knew from the Northern Hemisphere. It was almost tepid, as if this was the temperature at which I belonged, at which I could flourish. Ten meters beneath the surface of Lake Nyasa, deep in the Great Rift Valley, I felt strangely at home.

Now we were on our way to the Lugenda. The racist jokes started as we drove on the far side of the crest of Livingstone Ridge. The dirt road dove down the eastern slope of the range, which, instead of draining into Lake Nyasa, spills into the vast Lugenda River basin. As we lost altitude, the terrain appeared drier and the forested slopes opened. The dusty villages were populated by similar brightly dressed women holding babies, but now some of the men wore fezzes and we spotted small, mud-built mosques. In mid-afternoon we finally reached the border post—two Mozambican officials playing a board game at a table in the sun. They led us into a crumbling building, took our entry fees, and stamped our passports.

"Is there a place to change money?" I asked in Portuguese.

There were no banks. They pointed to a money changer who waited outside. We traded Malawian kwacha and U.S. dollars for fat wads of Mozambican meticais which, after heading into the nearby village, we used to buy a wooden crate of beer.

We cracked open the big bottles, passed them around, and jounced on down the road.

"What's green and has one hundred eyes?"

A tree in Mozambique!

"What's the difference between a tourist in Africa and a racist?"

Two weeks!

"Guys, you'd better tell them before Josh shows up," said Cherri. "He's from New York and probably Jewish."

The off-color jokes and indicative attitudes of the white Africans—Clinton, Lance, and Rod—made me uncomfortable, as they obviously did Cherri, too. The previous evening Lance had restrained me from getting out of the Land Rover and opening the gate to KayakAfrica.

"They'll get it," he had said to me of the black staff. "This is why we live in Africa."

Should I say something? I asked myself with every like comment, every dismissive slight they showed to the black African villagers we asked for directions along the road. It seemed almost a reflex to them, a form of joking among themselves, an ongoing conversation, as if they wanted to assure themselves that they were superior to these black African villagers. But it was more complex than simple black and white. Back in Malawi, when we had stopped at a road construction project and asked directions of a road engineer who was clearly highly educated and also black, Clinton was very polite and even deferential toward him.

Now the debate rang on in my head: By speaking up, would I be able to change them? Probably not. Would I alienate them before we even got on the river? Probably yes. Was I complicit in racism by not condemning it? Maybe. What would I accomplish by speaking up—beyond establishing my own moral superiority.

And on and on.

I held my tongue.

The rutted dirt road ran through tall savannah-like grasses and patches of forest. We passed only one other vehicle, an SUV bearing what appeared to be, in the quick glance I had from my berth lying wedged on my back, a World Health Organization seal. We both had to inch to the edge of the dirt track to pass. A while later we came to a truck tipped off the road. A crowd had gathered to extract it. We slowly squeezed by. As we passed, a wizened black man in a white fez wildly waved his arms at us. We stopped. With fevered excitement he told us in Portuguese that he was the mayor of the town just ahead, Belem, and he would take us to the *chefe*. Belem was our goal. And the *chefe* was exactly the person we needed to find.

"I love beer!" Ismail exclaimed with a heavy accent.

It was the only English I heard him speak; the rest was all Portuguese. Ismail was the *chefe*, a portly, friendly Mozambican in a gownlike white shirt who served as the administrator for the Belem district. Translating "Bethlehem" in Portuguese, Belem itself was an outpost in the bush consisting of a scattering of lichen-covered Portuguese-style bungalows and small administrative buildings that might have been attractive fifty years before, shaded as they were by large trees. Having been informed by letter from the Ministry of Tourism of our arrival, thanks to Cherri's logistical preparations, Ismail had greeted us warmly—*"Cleen-ton! Beel Cleen-ton,*

Rod, Clinton, and Steve after portaging the falls.

presidente!"—and gave us a spot to pitch our tents between his bunga-low/office and a corn patch. He and the mayor then guided Cherri and me through the orange and purple dusk to the Belem market; these were small stalls covered by thatched roofs where we purchased onions, garlic, sweet potatoes, batteries, and extra beer for our hosts.

When we returned, Lance was preparing dinner on his big camping stove. Ismail's assistant brought out a small table from the bungalow and spread it with a white cloth. Cherri offered Ismail a beer and invited him to dinner. While the others attended to gear and dinner preparations, I sat down next to Ismail, and since I spoke a bit of Portuguese, I took up the role of host.

"See what you can learn about the river," Cherri said to me.

I unfolded the big aeronautical map that I had brought from the States and spread out the sheaf of slightly more detailed topographical maps that, after months of trying, Cherri had managed to obtain from the Mozambican government. By candlelight Ismail confirmed the few spots on the map among the thousands of square miles of forest where it was possible to resupply by bush plane.

"What about the people along the river?" Cherri asked Ismail in Span-ish, which he could more or less understand. "Are they friendly?"

She had heard that there was a tribe somewhere in the forest called the Mikuni who liked to file their teeth to sharp points.

"Gente nao problema," said Ismail.

"Ask him about crocs and hippos," said Clinton.

"Crocodile e hippos—sim," he said. *Yes.* "But no problem."

And if there were problems, Ismail said, he had a gun that could deal with them. Mention of a gun instantly brought Clinton and Rod to the table.

"What kind is it?"

"Ask him if we can buy it."

A gun had been an issue all along. It was illegal to purchase a gun in Mozambique since the seventeen-year-long civil war had ended a decade earlier. Nor did we want to risk smuggling one across the border. Cherri, on her reconnaissance visit to Mozambique, had heard it was possible to buy a gun from the police, but she had also heard this may be a sting oper-ation that could land us in jail. So we had no gun, but Ismail gave us hope.

I put Clinton's request to Ismail in Portuguese.

"Buy a gun? *Nao,*" Ismail replied, curtly dismissing the idea. "But if you take me along on the river, I will bring my own gun, and I will shoot any crocodile that makes problems."

He raised his hand and aimed his finger down toward the imaginary river surface. *"Pao!"*

"We don't have room in the boats for you," said Cherri.

And that ended that discussion. I felt myself sliding down the food chain from predator toward prey.

DAY ONE

"Okay," Clinton called out to the four of us gathered around the kayaks. "Before we go, here's the safety talk. The front person paddles, the rear person steers. If your boat hits an object such as a log, don't lean away from it, lean into it. If a hippo bumps your boat just once, keep paddling. If a hippo knocks over your boat, swim away from it. Forget about the paddle, forget about the boat, just get away from it. It wants the boat, not you. If a hippo knocks you over and a croc bites you, you're having a bad day. If a croc swims at you and you're in your boat, wait for it and hit it away with your paddle. If a croc bites your boat, hit seven colors of shit out of it. If you're knocked into the water and there's a croc about, try to get up on top of your boat. If you can't get on top of it, wrap your arms and legs around the boat from underneath. You don't want them dangling down."

"And don't drag your hands when you're paddling," added Cherri.

"And if you're trying to get away from something, don't panic-paddle and knock your blades together," said Rod. "Make strong, steady strokes."

Everyone had something to add. It was like some group ritual acknowledging our smallness in the face of the great unknown that lay before us on the Lugenda River.

"What if a croc gets hold of you in the water?" I asked in turn. "Is there some technique to fend it off?"

I was thinking of Livingstone's account in the journals I'd read of his porter prying himself loose from the jaws of a croc during a river crossing by gouging out its eyes. Mungo Park told a similar anecdote.

"Sure, you can try going for the eyes," Clinton replied heartily. "Or if you can jam your arm down his throat when you're underwater, he can't close his breathing passages and you can drown him."

"Okay, thanks. I'll try to avoid the need," I said, managing a nervous laugh. Somehow I hadn't expected an answer quite so *vivid,* but looking at the topography of scars winding about his bare torso, I should have known better. It was as if his body was a magnet for animal bites. Only a couple of evenings earlier, back at Lake Nyasa, a scorpion had hidden in his jacket, and when he slipped it on against the evening's coolness, it stung him on the belly. Fortunately, it was a relatively minor sting.

"Any more questions?" Clinton now asked.

"I guess that about does it," said Steve.

"Okay," said Clinton, "let's go."

With Lance's and Ismail's help, we dragged the loaded kayaks over matted grass toward the riverbank. The Lugenda looked peaceful here, even bucolic; it was only about sixty feet wide as it wound quietly between grassy banks and patches of forest. Above us was an old bridge with a dirt track leading through the bush to Belem about ten kilometers or so. Seventy or eighty of the local people now stood on the bridge. They had emerged from somewhere out in the bush and watched silently as we had loaded the boats, jamming our waterproof bags containing tents, sleeping bags, clothes, food, and cook pots into the round cargo hatches.

Steve and I were sharing a tandem kayak. It felt beastly heavy as we dragged it to the riverbank, at least two or three hundred pounds. Steve and Cherri had originally hoped to paddle together in a tandem—brother and sister who hadn't seen each other for a long time—but our trial run to the islands out in Lake Nyasa proved we had to adjust our plan. A stiff southeast wind, the *mwera,* swept the lake and kicked up two-foot waves. Cherri and Steve had to work hard simply to stay upright. It was then decided—I didn't really have a part in these deliberations—that Cherri and Steve would paddle in separate boats. Clinton, truly an expert kayaker, would be our scout, paddling alone out in front in the single yellow kayak. Somehow—just how I don't know, or maybe it was an arbitrary choice at first—Cherri ended up paired in a tandem with Rod, and Steve with me.

We all gave our assent. I knew from years of canoeing about the delicate and sometimes volatile chemistry when pairing two people in a single boat. So, apparently, did Clinton.

"We can always switch off," he said.

Rod was our de facto head of security and wilderness survival expert. Besides his training with a reconnaissance unit in the South African military, he had also trained as a paramedic and had veterinary experience (his father was a veterinarian), in addition to his current work as a freelance safari guide in Botswana. While we didn't have a gun, Rod had made sure we carried just about everything else. On the banks of the Lugenda as we finished loading the boats, he handed Steve and me a heavy wooden club with an iron spike projecting through one end—something like a medieval troll would carry. He had commissioned a village craftsman at Lake Nyasa to carve it. We called it the "croc axe." He had lashed a similar club beneath the bungee cords on his rear deck. Clinton's boat sported a big machete bungeed to its front deck. Rod and Clinton also had been looking around to buy a certain type of African throwing stick shaped from a hardened root-ball and used to knock down game. Their military connection that was supposed to supply us with flash grenades intended to scare off intruders had fallen through. ("We don't want to kill anybody if we can help it," Clinton had advised me over the phone.) But they did manage to secure a supply of flashbomb/firecrackers, although the fun-loving trio— Lance, Clinton, and Rod—had apparently detonated all these for their entertainment during the long drive from Malawi by dropping them out the back of Cherri's Land Rover as they drove past unsuspecting villagers.

Rod also carried a sturdy orange waterproof case—the Pelican case, as

Clinton gives the safety talk at the put-in.

Unloading the kayaks from Cherri's Land Rover at the put-in.

it was known. This was lined with thick foam in which he had assembled the tools of his trade. These included an infrared scope (to spot intruders at night), a flare pistol ("We can always rig the flare pistol to a tripwire around camp. It's quite simple, really"), a Global Positioning System device to pinpoint our location, an emergency radio that could communicate with high-altitude jetliners, and the satellite telephone with which he could ring up just about anyplace on the planet that had a telephone ("for emergency use only," he stipulated).

"I have all sorts of goodies in that case," Rod declared.

A huge sheath knife also dangled on a thong around his waist. It swung between Rod's legs with manly abandon as he lashed the orange Pelican case to the deck in front of his cockpit.

I sported my own little "river knife." I nervously moved its black plastic sheath back and forth, clipping it first to the right side of the elastic waistband of my blue river shorts, then to the left. I couldn't decide: Which would give quicker access if a croc seized me in a "kill spin" and I had to stab out its eyes? The knife that had looked so shiny and lethal when I'd purchased it a few weeks earlier at a Montana kayak store now looked merely puny here on the Lugenda's bank. I felt as if I was going into a sword duel armed with a letter opener.

Clinton removed his river sandals and clipped them with a carabiner to the bungee cords on his rear deck. I copied him. Both he and Rod were now barefoot and bare-chested, as if to meet the river mano a mano. Clinton slid down into his cockpit. Rod held his tandem steady along the bank while Cherri slid into the bow seat, wearing a straw sun hat that brought to mind Katharine Hepburn. Cherri had told me with some pride that a fashionable lifestyle magazine, *Town and Country,* had once referred to her as "The African Queen." Now, sitting in the bow wearing her sun hat over her golden hair and with bare-chested, muscle-stacked Rod in the rear, she definitely looked the part. Steve, who had strong arms and shoulders himself from weight lifting, stepped into our bow cockpit wearing black neoprene river booties. These contrasted with his bare white legs to project that caught-unawares, boxer-shorts-and-black-socks look. I dipped my muddy feet in the water and nestled down in the stern seat. I gripped the paddle. I tried hard not to think that this was the jumping-off point, that there was no turning back, that with the first paddle stroke I was diving headlong into the unknown. I focused instead on the minutia of getting myself situated in the boat.

Maybe the knife would be better on my right *side. . . . No, I can reach across better with my right hand if it's on my* left *side.*

We shoved off, paddle blades sinking into the mud-and-grass bank. Steve's and my kayak bellied heavily into the river. We all bobbed awkwardly for a moment, tensely. It was as if we expected some large animal to leap from the water and devour us or the sharp-toothed people to leap from the forest.

Nothing happened.

Clinton took a stroke. We all took a stroke. The kayaks glided slowly toward the bridge.

"Look how low you are in the water," said Rod.

He pointed his paddle toward my stern. The rear deck was almost underwater. With two heavy men plus so much gear, our kayak was very heavily laden.

"You're pretty low, too," I said, not wanting to be the heaviest boat on the river.

"Send me messages as you go along the river," Ismail called out in Portuguese.

"*Sim, sim,*" we called back.

I knew we wouldn't.

We slid under the bridge, taking care to avoid its pilings. The bridges in Mozambique had been set with mines during the civil war, from 1975 to 1992. We looked back. The people had now gathered on the downstream rail, watching silently.

We lifted our paddle blades in the air.

"Good-bye! Good-bye!" we shouted.

Arms lifted from the bridge in salute.

We then turned the first bend of the Lugenda, and they disappeared.

At first, not much happened. Around the bend Clinton pointed out a fat squiggly line in the sand where a croc had bellied along, dragging its tail. After all the buildup, the stories of killer animals, and the tribe of needle-toothed people, the Lugenda at first appeared almost monotonous. In some ways I felt right at home. The Lugenda here, only a few kilometers from its source in the swamps of Lake Amaramba, reminded me of the southern Wisconsin rivers of my youth where silver maples drooped over greenish sun-dappled water as it twisted between banks of mud and grass. Here the trees were called waterberries, but other than the name, they and so much else looked the same.

"Is this how you hold it?" Steve asked, raising his paddle overhead so I could see it.

It was at least the third time he'd asked me the same question, starting back on Lake Nyasa.

"Maybe put your hands a little farther apart," I replied.

It wasn't difficult to be patient with Steve because his requests were so genial and trusting, and he was trying. But I could already see he wasn't a natural at kayaking. He would need plenty of help—maybe more than I knew how to give—if we encountered difficult water where one has to think and react very quickly.

We paddled onward. Now he was paddling too fast, overeagerly. As the paddler in the bow, Steve was the boat's metronome, setting the rhythm for both our strokes. A fast rhythm always bothered me; I preferred a meditative, long-haul stroke. I instructed him how to keep a slow, steady rhythm that could carry us for days on end.

"Like this?" he said, easing his hyper stroking.

"Yeah, that's good."

We settled into the rhythm, paddling our white tandem between Clinton's yellow boat out front, seeking the best way down the river, and Rod and Cherri's tandem, taking up the rear, as if Cherri wanted an overview of the whole operation.

No one said much. About twenty minutes and five bends past the bridge I had a sudden and distressing thought: *What if it's like this for 750 kilometers? What if nothing else happens? What if we paddle for three weeks around one quiet bend of the river after another with only one another to distract us?*

Being trapped with these people for weeks on end in the wilderness suddenly looked far more daunting than the threat of crocs and hippos and sharp-toothed people. Steve, needing lots of help; Cherri, whom I sensed could be bossy and manipulative when I watched her issue orders back at Lake Nyasa to a quietly bristling Clinton; and Clinton and Rod, close friends who were distant from us and full of macho. And how did they see me? What stereotype had they drawn for me? Worried and withdrawn? We had hardly started, I reassured myself. I should give my teammates and the river a chance. But I still couldn't completely escape my fears.

How much of this had been Cherri's hype? Make it sound dangerous and romantic to lure me—to lure all of us—on what was going to be a long, hard, boring paddle so she could seize the prize of "first descent" of the Lugenda River?

But here I was. There was no turning back. I had a sudden flash of Sartre's famous play about three quarrelsome people locked in a small room that is Hell: *No Exit.*

"Pull ov-*ah* to the bank," Clinton called out in his Rhodesian accent. "Right he-*ah*!"

Clinton hacking a passage with his machete.

Ahead, the river was spanned from bank to bank by a picket fence–like barrier of logs and woven branches, the current sieving through frothing gaps and spilling down a foot or two to the pool below. This was a "fish trap" erected by local villagers to corral fish. Cherri had spotted them from the air during her reconnaissance and warned that we'd encounter many in our first few days.

Clinton paddled up to the fish trap, yanked at a limb here and a limb there until he pried one loose. He wrenched open a gap just wide enough for a kayak.

"Lift your rudders," he called to us, "and paddle through this opening he-*ah*!"

Rod and I reached behind our cockpits and pulled the cords that lifted the steering rudders on our sterns. River kayaks, designed for quick maneuverablility, usually don't have rudders, but sea kayaks are fitted with them to help "track" in a straight line in the long distances of open water. The mechanism is operated by two foot pedals under the cockpit.

After lifting our rudders so they wouldn't bang into submerged logs, we aimed carefully and shot our boats through the opening in the fish trap, splashing down into the pool.

"All right!" we called out, congratulating one another.

It was our first obstacle on the Lugenda River. It felt good to overcome it.

A fisherman was watching impassively from the bank as we broke through the structure. Clinton reached under the deck of his kayak, extracted an energy bar wrapped in its shiny silvery package, and tossed it up to him. Then Clinton, too, paddled through the gap.

Around the bend lay another fish trap. Clinton couldn't pry loose any of the thick limbs and had to chop through with his machete.

Thwack . . . thwack . . . thwack!

Here was the very symbol of the European explorer attempting to penetrate into the African interior. *Thwack . . . thwack . . . thwack!* Sharp steel on tropical hardwood, on thickets of vegetation, on these barriers that native people built for their livelihood, the sound of the machete said *Yield to me!*

"Stop right there!" I called out to Clinton. "This looks great! We need a photo!"

Clinton paused while I pulled out my reliable old manual Nikon from a small dry bag I had lashed to the deck. I maneuvered our kayak next to his and clicked off photos as he raised the machete over his head and swung it down on the woven thicket. I sensed Clinton warming to the part. I had a sudden flash of self-consciousness. I was taking pictures of us looking like African explorers. Were we real African explorers? Or just playing at being African explorers and making it look good for the folks back home—the photo-album version of African exploration?

The fish traps now came steadily, one after the other. Clinton pried and macheted our way through. We sensed villages somewhere back in the forest. The smell of wood smoke was in the air, but we saw no one except a few fishermen poling along in canoes. These they had shaped from sheets of tree bark, sewn together with root fibers, and strengthened with shaved sticks that served as thwarts. The canoes reminded me of pea pods. The sinewy, sure-footed fishermen poled them along standing upright and then crouched to drop their nets woven from vines and bark fibers. The

A small canoe fashioned from tree bark and sticks, stitched with fibers.

only sign of the modern world was the ragged T-shirts, some of which had probably made their way to Africa through a long chain of charitable organizations, hanging loosely on their black, lanky limbs.

"*Bom dia,*" we called out in Portuguese.

"*Bom dia,*" the fishermen politely replied.

They stared at us and our bright plastic boats. Had they learned centuries ago to keep to themselves when strangers appeared? Or had they heard we were coming? Cherri had contacted the American ambassador to Mozambique, who had contacted the minister of tourism, who had contacted the governor of the enormous and thinly populated Niassa Province, who had it broadcast over the provincial radio station that an American group of boats was coming down the Lugenda River and to help us out. But who knew if these fishermen even had access to a radio? Or if they had heard, did they await our expedition like some convenient American shopping mall about to float past their villages from which they could help themselves to pricey and otherwise unavailable consumer goods?

We saw birds, lots of birds, winging down the river and over the forested banks. Clinton and Rod deftly identified each one. The vivid names made a kind of poem as I wrote them in my notebook:

Malakite, kingfisher,
open-billed stork, long-crested eagle,
brown snake eagle,
little bee eater,
green-headed heron,
African fin foot.

On we went—a rhythm of birds, sunken logs, low limbs, and fish traps.

"There's a big croc he-*ah* ne-*ah* the bank!" Clinton called out. "Now he's disappea-*had*!"

We kept paddling, watchfully. Clinton and Rod pointed out the deep, well-like hippo footprints. Clinton very much hoped to avoid running into a hippo in this narrow section of river—there was so little room to flee or maneuver past it.

I already knew a little about hippos. Before leaving for Africa I had seen a wildlife film about them. Its underwater photography showed how hippos literally run along a river bottom. Behind the hippos swim schools of fish that suck up clouds of dung discharged into the water after the hippos' nightly intake of nearly one hundred pounds of land plants. In the wake of the fish swim crocodiles, snapping them up.

A hippo is a one-animal ecosystem, but it is also widely acknowledged as the most dangerous animal to humans in all of Africa and kills more people on the continent than any other animal. Not only will a hippo on land trample down anything or anybody that blocks its path back to the water, but the males are extremely territorial. A big male possesses a certain section of river, and if another male enters the territory, he'll fight it off with tremendous, crashing bites of those railroad-spike teeth. The problem is that these big male hippos tend to mistake native canoes for rival males. Thus, the overturned and crushed canoes, and the mangled and drowned occupants.

A hippo had overturned a canoe on Lake Nyasa just a few weeks earlier, and eleven or twelve people had died. Clinton himself had seen some of the damage a hippo could do on the Zambezi. He now kept up an intense watchfulness as he paddled out in front of us and between the narrow banks where hippos could be hiding in deep pools.

"With a hippo," said Clinton, "it's over before it starts."

We couldn't breach one fish trap even with the machete. We dragged the kayaks up on the grassy bank and portaged around it. Clinton, trying to launch himself and his kayak off the three-foot-high bank into the deep pool below the fish trap in a flashy kayaking move called a *boof,* dropped his bow into the water and then inadvertently rolled the boat over in slow motion, spilling out into the river.

He splashed about, trying to crawl back into the flooded cockpit.

"Get to the bank, man!" Rod shouted in alarm.

Clinton hefted himself on top of the kayak and straddled the cockpit. The swamped boat slowly rolled over again, dumping him.

"Get out of the water!" Cherri shouted. "Get out of the water!"

I could see Clinton resist Cherri's shouts. He deliberately took his time swimming the kayak to the bank, casually spitting water, as if to say to her, "Don't tell me what to do."

"Well," Cherri said, watching as he hauled the kayak onto the shore and poured the water from the cockpit. "I guess there are no crocs in this stretch of the river."

We stopped for lunch where a rib of granite pushed open a sunny, grassy clearing in the forest. Clinton and Rod quickly kindled a fire of dried sticks and set a cast-iron pot of river water on a small iron tripod, in the cooking style of the African villagers. As we waited for the boil, Rod unstrapped his orange Pelican case from his boat, extracted the GPS, and punched it on. Its signal locked onto satellites thousands of miles above us. The numbers flashed on the screen. Our position lay just south of the fourteenth parallel. Rod and Cherri studied the maps. They compared our location on the map to the list of rapids and other landmarks Cherri had spotted during her aerial reconnaissance. Using a GPS while on the bush plane, she had marked these by latitude and longitude coordinates.

"We're about forty-five minutes from the first set of rapids," they agreed.

"Oh, good," said Clinton.

Faster water meant less chance of encountering hippos or crocodiles, which prefer lazy current.

This all seemed too easy to me—these GPSs, satellites, aerial surveys, the list of rapids and landmarks with their coordinates, typed and laminated. How could this possibly be "exploration" when you already knew what lay around the bend? You had spotted it from the air and marked it by GPS. How could you call this *the unknown* when the mystery was gone? Part of me wanted the reassurance of knowing what lay ahead while part of me resisted, wanting to be left in the dark. After all, wasn't the mystery part of what we came for?

We downed a lunch of instant oatmeal, stirred up in our blue plastic mugs, and a few handfuls of nuts, and climbed back in the boats. Eight or ten children suddenly appeared from a village that must have been back in the forest and chased us, screaming and laughing, along the riverbank. I felt like some rock star gliding along in a long white limo—the elaborate plastic kayak in the mud-and-thatch landscape—pursued by throngs of screaming fans. We finally outdistanced them.

We paddled on. The rapids didn't arrive—not after forty-five minutes, not after two hours. Just the winding greenish river under the drooping waterberry trees as we stroked along dodging low branches, sunken logs, and snags. I began to question Rod and Cherri's navigation and their placement of the rapids on the map. Cherri, meanwhile, continued to shout orders at our boat from behind.

"Watch out for that log!" "Go right!" "Go left!" "Turn *now*!"

"I see it! I see it!" I finally called back in irritation, giving her a contemptuous toss of my head.

"You were playing with your rudder again," she said to me.

My sticky rudder had been kicked up by a log, and I'd been tugging on the cords to pull it down while she thought we were about to plow into a low-hanging tree branch. But I'd paddled hundreds and hundreds of miles on rivers just like this and didn't need her to tell me how to steer. Up front, I could hear Steve muttering under his breath. It sounded like curses directed at his big sister.

We paddled quietly for a while, well ahead of Cherri and Rod.

"I didn't want to paddle with Cherri because she keeps giving me orders," Steve confided.

He lifted his paddle out of the water and turned his head partway back to talk.

"That's the thing about Cherri," he said reflectively. "She's a natural-born leader, so she'll lead whether she knows what she's doing or not."

"She should look after her own boat, and we'll look after ours," I said.

We resumed paddling.

I tried to be considerate and calm in the instructions I gave Steve as we maneuvered through the hanging tree limbs and logs.

"Okay, paddle two or three times on the right . . . now switch to the left."

But I brooded, wondering if I should say anything to Cherri. Again, it was a question of whether speaking out would disrupt the harmony of the expedition. On the other hand, by not saying something I felt my resentment simmering about her bossing me around, especially with that alarmist tone as if I were about to crash the boat when I knew way more about canoeing and kayaking than she did. Would this only get worse? I knew from personal experience how the close confines of small boats, propelled by either paddle or sail, brought out both the best and worst in people. Likewise, Africa. So many of those early European expeditions had deteriorated into near chaos under the strain of heat, fever, and countless other hazards that laid bare the sharpest edges of one's personality and intensified petty disputes into major crises. I recalled one infamous instance—the running personality clash across the southern Sahara Desert between Major Dixon Denham, Hugh Clapperton, and Walter Oudney.

The start of their dispute was in a perverse way the peace that arrived with British victory in the Napoleonic Wars in 1815. Suddenly, thousands of soldiers, seamen, and officers who had manned Britain's enormous military force were left unemployed. They dispersed in a hundred ways, but the most adventurous headed north to struggle across the ice and make a name for themselves as Arctic explorers; others went south to plumb the interior of Africa and spread British might across the globe.

Like Mungo Park who had preceded him to Africa by some twenty years, Walter Oudney was a doctor and a Scotsman. He had served as a surgeon's mate aboard a man-o'-war, returned to Edinburgh, took the medical exams, and set up private practice. As with Park, this apparently was too tame a life for Oudney. After reading Park's *Travels* he decided he, too, would explore Africa. He mentioned his plans to his friend and fellow Scotsman Hugh Clapperton, who had commanded a schooner in the Royal Navy. He asked Oudney if he could come along. Oudney agreed, and with instructions from Lord Bathurst, secretary for war and the colonies, the two friends departed in autumn 1821 for Tripoli on the coast of North Africa. Their hope was to penetrate south across the Sahara to establish British trade with the African interior.

At the last minute, however, another member joined the party. This was Major Denham, a Londoner who had distinguished himself for bravery as an officer in the Spanish theater of the Napoleonic Wars and then earned an appointment in the Royal Military College. He was known to be, as one account put it, "opinionated and excessively managing."[4] He, too, wanted to explore Africa. He approached Lord Bathurst, offered to serve without pay if he received a promotion, and was given permission to join Oudney and Clapperton in Tripoli and take command of the expedition.

Instantly, Clapperton and Oudney took an intense dislike to the rigid Englishman, and he to the two chummy Scotsmen. They hated his imperious orders and military decorum. He, in turn, found Clapperton "vulgar, conceited and quarrelsome," as Denham wrote in a letter to his brother, and flatly dismissed Oudney as "utterly incompetent."

They worked their way south from oasis to oasis, sometimes traveling together, sometimes in separate caravans. Oudney and Clapperton suffered from fever, and everyone struggled with thirst, heat, and exhaustion. In places their camels literally stepped on the brittle skeletons of slaves who had perished in the desert on their way to the markets.

By January 1823 relations between Clapperton and Denham had deteriorated to the point where they communicated in writing rather than by speaking. Clapperton wrote to Major Denham after the latter ordered him yet again to take sextant readings at regular intervals:

> Sir, I thought my previous refusal would have prevented repetition of your orders. . . . You must not introduce Martial System into what is civil and

scientific, neither must you expect from me what is your duty to execute. . . .

I have the honour to be, Sir

Your most Obt. humble servant,
Hugh Clapperton

Things deteriorated further from there. Clapperton and Denham began to dispatch reports to Lord Bathurst on each other's reprehensible conduct, including one in which Denham reported rumors of Clapperton's having a homosexual relationship with one of the expedition's servants. This was later proved unfounded and was dismissed by Lord Bathurst. Despite their mutual dislike, the explorers did manage to traverse a good deal of the uncharted regions of west-central Africa around Lake Chad, often traveling in separate parties. Oudney, finally so weak he was tied to a bed frame lashed to a camel's back, died of fever. Both Denham and Clapperton, traveling separately, returned to England, only to set out again—independent of each other—for further ventures in West Africa. From these neither would return.

I decided not to speak out unless Cherri's orders continued.

Around 3:30 p.m., as we rounded a bend, a wiry older man suddenly stood up on the riverbank where clearly he'd been waiting for us. We paused in mid-stroke, wondering if this was a setup. He waved a folded white piece of paper. We pulled over.

Clinton unfolded the paper, his paddle resting across the foredeck as he bobbed near the bank.

"It's in Portuguese," he said. "I don't read Portuguese."

He thrust it at Cherri. She took it and studied it.

"It's from Ismail." Using her Spanish, she haltingly decoded Ismail's Portuguese. "It's addressed to 'Mr. Clinton.' It says to wait here for Ismail. He will return soon. Do not go on until he comes here. There is danger ahead. There are big *cataratas*"—this was the Portuguese word for rapids or waterfalls—"big *cataratas* like Victoria Falls!"

She looked up at the man on the bank. She didn't hesitate for a moment.

"No problema," she said to him. *"Cataratas no problema."*

He looked back at her, confused. She was bold—I had to hand it to her.

"Maybe we should wait for Ismail," I said. "Maybe he knows something we don't."

"That could be hours and hours," said Clinton impatiently. "Tell him we know about the rapids, and let's go."

And so we did.

An hour or so later, around 4:30 p.m., the light began to fade. The sun drops early and fast during winter—known here as the dry season—just below the equator. Clinton paddled to an inside bend on the left bank, surveyed it from his kayak, and consulted briefly with Rod. To me the bend looked swampy and low, overarched by waterberry trees and matted with thick grass. I wouldn't have chosen it.

"We'll camp he-*ah*," Clinton announced.

We unloaded the boats, hauled gear up the bank, and tramped out tent sites on either side of the big waterberry tree that grew from the bank. We each had our own tent, except Rod and Clinton who shared one, the four structures forming a line like four cocoons—blue, green, and yellow—along the riverbank. Mine, a light blue two-person tent, sat at the upriver end, slightly removed.

We regrouped under the waterberry tree where Rod and Clinton had started a campfire. Rod boiled water and opened packets of rice and sauce for dinner. The flames jumped in the dusk. After the rush, rush, rushing of gear selection, transatlantic flights, customs, driving the Land Rover, packing the boats, and each night a session of beer-drinking joviality, it felt so peaceful out here on the Lugenda.

I suddenly thought of my younger brother, Ted, who was nineteen when he and I paddled the length of the Mississippi River together one summer, standing beside our single tent in the midst of an empty mile-long sandbar with nothing but lonely woods and water for miles around.

"So where's the party?" he had asked the forest at large.

It was an existential remark to which there was no reply.

Now, on the Lugenda, there was only the faint hiss of the flames, the burble of boiling water, and the quiet scraping as Rod poured rice in the iron pot and stirred. I heard the faint singing of women from a village somewhere in the forest across the river, the distant cries of children, the far-off bark of a dog. It was as if we were outlaws lying low in the sadness of the African dusk.

Rod carefully poured out a canteen capful each of the Jack Daniel's we carried in a water bottle, dumping it into our blue plastic mugs. We sipped our grog ration sitting under the waterberry tree. Rod took out his GPS from the Pelican case, took our bearing, and located it on my big aeronautical map. He marked it with a spot of my pen. Then he marked the bridge near Belem where we had put in.

Against the length of the Lugenda, the distance we had paddled today looked tiny, minuscule. Rod punched the buttons to get a reading of the straight-line distance we had traveled since the bridge. Fourteen kilometers as the crow flies (about 8.5 miles) in an entire day of hard paddling. That was nothing. We had at least 400 kilometers as the crow flies to reach the Lugenda's mouth, some 750 kilometers by the winding course of the river.

I believe we all experienced the same thought in that moment: *What are we in for?* From our familiar world of instant results, of distances and times truncated by emails, jet airplanes, and four-lane highways, we had suddenly stepped into the realm of the eighteenth-century explorer. The sheer geographical magnitude of our undertaking—of their undertakings—settled heavily over our camp. It was as if they spoke to us from the past: "Isn't this what you wanted?"

We served ourselves plates of rice, spooning over it the sauce of Indian shrimp curry that Rod had stirred up from a package. We ate dinner quietly, metal utensils clicking on blue-enameled plates. Cherri told some croc stories, as if to liven the conversation or inject an element of danger and adrenaline in our undertaking—some of the *romance* of adventure at least. One was about an Israeli couple on their African honeymoon who insisted on having their photo taken on a riverbank despite their guide's warnings against it. An eighteen-foot-long crocodile lunged from the water and swallowed the groom whole.

"I swear it was as wide as my Land Rover," said Cherri. "I saw it with my own eyes after they had shot it."

"When I saw that small croc this afternoon," Clinton said, "the reality of the situation came home to me. I was in front, and a big croc could be twice as big as my boat. For an hour after I looked right, I looked left."

He twisted his head back and forth, pretending to scan for crocs.

We got up, switched on our headlamps as we left the circle of firelight, and stepped down the bank to the river to wash our plates with water and handfuls of sand as scrubbers.

"Crocs probably really like these new LED headlamps," I said to Clinton as we descended the bank.

"They just love them," he replied.

He and Rod instructed us how to keep a lookout for crocodiles at night when you're near the water's edge. One person sweeps a flashlight or headlamp beam across the surface. The eyes of a stalking croc will reflect back bright red in the lamplight.

Dishes done, we stood awkwardly around the campfire as if unsure what to do next. It was only seven o'clock or so. Clinton, still full of energy, wanted to tell stories and talk. Rod, always the quieter of the two, interjected comments at times. I asked Clinton about his experience as a safety kayaker for tourist rafts on the Zambezi. He described with relish the huge rapids and enormous standing waves below Victoria Falls. There was a bit of swagger to his tone. I wondered how much was for my benefit as the official chronicler of the expedition.

But even though I had prompted him to recount his deeds, I was too tired to participate with much enthusiasm. I wanted to be alone with my thoughts.

I excused myself, clicked on my headlamp, swished through the grass to my tent, and crawled in. There is something especially empty about a two-person tent with only one person in it. I blew up my inflatable pad and pulled my sleeping bag from its stuff sack. I felt a soft lump at the bag's bottom. I'd forgotten it was there.

As I was about to leave home, Amy had asked four-year-old Skyler and seven-year-old Molly, "Can you give Daddy something to remember you when he goes away to Africa?"

Skyler rummaged through his airplane collection. He handed me a stuffed airplane, velvety green and spongy and roundish, about the size of a grapefruit.

"Don't you have a smaller airplane you can give me?"

"No. You take this one."

I could easily pack the bead bracelet from Molly and the jade hippo amulet from Amy, but the stuffed airplane was a problem. I figured Cherri would cull it if she knew about it, and I surely didn't want Clinton or Rod to see it. *A stuffed toy? And you want to be an African explorer?* I'd considered leaving it behind in Johannesburg. Finally, while packing in my hotel room, I'd pushed it down into the very foot of my sleeping bag and jammed the bag into its stuff sack. When Cherri culled my luggage, I knew she'd never find it there.

Now, as I slid into my sleeping bag, I felt the soft stuffed airplane pressed secretly between my bare feet. I was pleased I'd brought it.

Propped on my elbow, with the headlamp shining on the open steno-notebook page, I wrote up the day's notes. I could hear Clinton and Rod outside, climbing into their tent next to mine. Then I heard soft snoring.

After an hour or so I finished writing my notes. From its dry bag I pulled my library copy of *Wild Africa*. I turned to the first excerpt, "Finding the Source of the Blue Nile." This was written by the eccentric and fiercely proud Scottish nobleman and explorer James "Abyssian" Bruce who had located the flower-covered hillside from which—at least he claimed—the head springs of the Nile gushed forth.

> It is easier to guess than to describe the situation of my mind at that moment—standing in that spot which had baffled the genius, industry and inquiry of both ancients and moderns, for the course of near three thousand years. Kings had attempted this discovery at the head of armies and each expedition was distinguished from the last, only by the difference of the numbers which had perished, and agreed alone in the disappointment which had uniformly and without exception, followed them all. . . . Though a mere private Briton, I triumphed here, in my own mind, over kings and their armies.

I went out to pee. It was very dark outside. Not simply the thick darkness that flows beneath a forest at night but, rather, I was immersed in darkness, suffocated by darkness. Then I spotted two points of light, two candle lanterns that Clinton and Rod had left hanging from a low limb of the waterberry tree. Beneath the candles I saw the dim orange embers of the campfire. I was grateful for this touch of cheer.

I crawled back in and zipped up the tent fly. What was it about Scotsmen? What was it about would-be lawyers and doctors? Bruce, who claimed descent from Robert the Bruce, the Scottish warrior who had vanquished the English armies at Bannockburn in 1314, was born to a wealthy landed family, educated at exclusive Harrow, and then quit the study of law at Edinburgh (as John Ledyard had quit his law studies) to see the world and make a name for himself. After a stint as British consul general in Algiers in the early 1760s and studying Arabic language and native customs, Bruce set himself the goal of finding the source of the Nile.

In many ways he was the prototype and the inspiration—through his enormously popular accounts of his travels—of the British and especially Scottish explorers who followed him to Africa over the next century: the Mungo Parks, the Hugh Clappertons, the David Livingstones. He was fixated on being first, as if being the first European to reach some significant geographical spot of the "unknown continent" was a competition for a school prize or a scrimmage on a playing field. This fixation has endured to this day and has expanded far beyond African exploration to mountaineering—how many different "firsts" have been scored on Everest?—and other outdoor arenas. The five of us, after all, were attempting the Lugenda River's "first descent."

But Bruce, for all his prideful Scottish intensity, sensed the ephemeral nature of his achievement even as he was making it. Camped that night of his arrival at the springs of the Nile, he lay awake in his tent and was plagued by dark thoughts. He realized that he had attained his goal but had completed only half his journey. He still had to travel all the way back home. He thought how unlikely it would be that he'd return safely. He couldn't even get a message to those he cared about. And he was plagued by "some other thoughts, perhaps," he later confessed, "still nearer the heart than those." This was possibly a reference to Margaret Murray, a sixteen-year-old girl to whom Bruce had proposed before leaving for North Africa, and who had pledged to marry Bruce upon his return. For all his suffering and sacrifice to reach its source and his years-long emotional isolation, it now occurred to Bruce that the Nile didn't possess anything in terms of the beauty and cultivation of the river valleys of his beloved Scotland and that the Scottish inhabitants he knew were vastly superior in virtue to the inhabitants of the headwaters of the Nile.

> Grief or despondency, now rolling upon me like a torrent . . . I started from my bed in the utmost agony; I went to the door of my tent; everything was still; the Nile at whose head I stood, was not capable either to promote or to interrupt my slumbers, but the coolness and serenity of the night braced my nerves, and chased away those phantoms that, while in bed, had oppressed and tormented me.

I put down the book. I clicked off my headlamp. At least we didn't have to go back upriver. I gave an imaginary kiss each to Amy, Molly, and Skyler. I felt the soft toy airplane between my feet—my connection with them, an amulet. I knew they were there. The singing from the village had ceased long ago. There was now only the bellowing of frogs, the chirping of crickets, and, from the river flowing silently in front of my tent, an occasional large, soft *plash!* I put my head down on the pillow that I'd improvised from a clothes bag and life jacket. I heard the soft snoring from Clinton and Rod's tent beside mine. I closed my eyes. I felt reassured that they were there beside me.

DAY TWO

At the first dawn light I heard Rod's soft, birdlike whistle outside my tent, waking me. I crawled out, scraggly haired and blinking, after shoving my greasy contact lenses into my eyes.

"Good morning, Pe-*tah*!" he said, echoes in his voice of the chipper-in-the-morning British Empire.

I swished through the cold, dewy grass to the smoking campfire he and Clinton had revived under the waterberry tree. Cherri emerged from her tent looking fresh, her wavy blond hair newly coiffed. Breakfast was quick and Spartan: an energy bar each, a couple of small "biscuits"—cookies—and a mug of instant coffee or tea. We milled about under the tree and gulped it down.

"I feel so much more alive this morning without getting drunk last night for a change," Steve remarked.

"I was trying to do his liver a favor by bringing him on this trip," joked Cherri.

I laughed, but in truth I figured the expedition probably could do my liver some good, too.

Luminous shafts of sunlight filtered through the branches and penetrated the white mist hovering over the greenish river. I was suddenly pleased to be here.

We stuffed our bags, rolled our tents, packed the boats, and dragged them down the muddy bank. Clinton and Rod removed their shirts, preparing to meet the Lugenda with torsos bared. It was 7 a.m. We climbed in. Steve and I took a few strokes.

"I'm amazed that my body doesn't hurt this morning after all that paddling yesterday," he said.

Mine didn't, either. We marveled about it. It was pleasant paddling in the cool, early-morning sunlight and through the lifting patches of river mist. Steve and I chatted amiably about this and that, about our families. We found a nice rhythm. Cherri wasn't issuing orders today—a relief, like the sudden disappearance of a cloud of gnats that had been swarming around your head. I wondered if Clinton or Rod had seen my irritation yesterday and told her to back off. Or maybe they'd been irritated with her orders, too, and took her aside in camp and talked to her about who was in charge where. Whatever had happened to iron out the leadership tangles, it now seemed that Cherri stepped back from an active role in leading on the river itself. On the river Clinton clearly was now the leader while Rod oversaw our security and the camps. Cherri handled logistics and oversaw the expedition as a whole. It was, after all, her expedition.

Whap!

"Whooaa!" I said.

"Did you see that?" Clinton shouted back to us from ahead. "Croc!"

I had seen it, although no one else had. A ways downstream, a long, slim crocodile had launched off a high sandbank in a flat-bellied dive like a racing swimmer, silhouetted in the morning sunlight, landing with a big splash in a deep, quiet bend of the river. It disappeared from sight, the waves rolling to the banks.

"How big?" I asked Clinton.

"Six or seven feet maybe. Its head is as big as your cockpit. It's big enough to eat you."

He squinted downriver toward the pool.

"Follow behind me," he instructed.

We now had to cross the pool of deep slack water. Clinton stroked carefully out front, pounding his paddle every stroke or two against the hull of his yellow kayak to warn off the croc.

"Which side of Clinton's boat do you think will give us the best protection," I joked to Steve as I steered after him, "going to his right or his left?"

The four of us followed across the pool, hammering like banshees against our boats. We reached the far side.

"That gets the heart going," Clinton said.

Two bends later something rose from underwater and snapped at my paddle blade. I saw only the quick splash. Oddly, it didn't frighten me. Whatever it was backed off quickly and clearly wasn't interested—at least not in a piece of plastic.

* * *

I was enjoying being with Steve. The loneliness of the previous night had dissipated along with the forest's suffocating darkness. The morning looked so sparkling and cheery on the Lugenda. I thought about James Bruce's despair that night in his tent at the source of the Blue Nile. How driven he must have been! His expedition itself lasted five years, from 1768 to 1773, but he had prepared himself years in advance of that by living in Algiers, learning Arabic, and studying medicine, drawing, architecture, and horsemanship, all with the hope of reaching his goal.

What a lightweight I was by comparison! The whole Lugenda expedition was expected to take a mere five weeks. I had spent a single month prepping myself by studying Portuguese, reading African literature, lifting weights, and paddling a kayak. Then again, my preparations went far deeper than that. Since I was very young I'd been on countless river trips and other outdoor ventures, and I'd spent the last two decades of my adult life practicing the craft of writing about them. I'd taken an undergraduate degree in English literature and anthropology, and a master's in journalism with this kind of travel and writing in mind. I knew what it was like to take notes while riding on dogsleds and horses, in helicopters and dugout canoes, and on glaciers, mountaintops, and volcanoes.

So, yes, in some ways I had spent a lifetime preparing for this trip without really realizing it. But Bruce's single-minded drive for a very specific geographical destination—the source of the Nile—seemed in the nature of an obsession. It was probably inevitable that the moment of his glory would be accompanied by crashing disappointment. For ten years he had been on the move almost constantly, cutting himself off from friends and family, from home. If he wasn't an eccentric loner to begin with, he was certainly one by the end.

I couldn't help looking to his background for clues to what drove him. I imagined the young Bruce sent from the family estates in Scotland down to Harrow School near London—a young Scottish lad, crude-mannered, perhaps, when compared to the English, speaking in strange northern inflections, who may have been ridiculed and ostracized by his peers. Historians of the subject have noted that many of the greatest African explorers were Celts—Scottish and Irish—and thus "natural outsiders" who were "better equipped" for the task of exploration than the insider Anglo-Saxon.[5] To me that means not only were the outsiders more comfortable with the unfamiliar, adapting quickly to new customs, foreign lands, and strange people, but, I suspect, the outsiders also carried a chip on their shoulders for being considered unacceptable by tight-knit English society. In my few dealings with English society, I quickly sensed its arm's-length impenetrability. I could hear the angry young Scottish lad saying, "I'll show them!"

Surely Bruce was adventurous and risk-taking by nature—he quickly abandoned the study of law at Edinburgh as too boring—but so were countless others who didn't end up exploring Africa. His original plan was to head for India and make his fortune, but that scheme was sidetracked when he met a wine merchant's daughter, fell in love, married her, and joined her family's wine firm. Her death soon after shattered Bruce. Thus began his years of wandering around the Mediterranean, North Africa, and finally Ethiopia.

It was as if, protecting himself from further wounds inflicted by intimacy, he severed any close emotional ties. Early in his wanderings, however, his father died, and Bruce returned to Scotland briefly to settle affairs of the estate. On this trip he met sixteen-year-old Margaret Murray, to whom he proposed with the understanding that the marriage would occur after his travels. When she accepted his offer, surely she didn't guess that Bruce would not return for her hand for an entire decade.

James Bruce carried the legacy of ancestors who battled the English and won Scotland independence, four and a half centuries before. What could he possibly accomplish to live up to that? He decided to choose a different arena altogether to perform noble deeds that would bring him recognition. What better place than a continent that the European world knew virtually nothing about? It would be an arena all his own.

Like Bruce, I had rejected my family's usual arena of accomplishment for one of my own choosing. I was the eldest son in line to be the fourth generation in the family candy-making firm. But to me running a candy factory looked a lot like the study of law had to James Bruce. I opted out, although in doing so I received my own weighty legacy from an ancestor.

"It doesn't matter what you do," advised my grandfather, son of a Prussian immigrant, when I grappled with what direction to take, "as long as you're good at it."

"We're going to have to start calling you 'Team Daisy,'" Clinton said to Steve and me.

We had lagged behind the other two kayaks, talking and taking our time. Now they drifted in the narrow river waiting for us to catch up. We all started paddling again, Cherri putting more muscle into her stroke, too. Clinton had called her a "lily dipper."

We paddled on and on.

Where are the rapids? we all wondered.

Clinton finally pulled his kayak alongside Rod and Cherri's. He badly wanted to get beyond this narrow quiet stretch with its threat of hippos and crocs at close quarters. The three of them consulted Cherri's laminated list of GPS readings from the reconnaissance flight and compared them to the maps. They came to a consensus as to where we were: The first rapids should lie around the next bend or two, right after we passed a tributary named the Luchimua.

"You've been saying that since yesterday noon," I remarked to Clinton as he paddled past.

I had meant it teasingly, but he didn't laugh. There was a kind of competitiveness among everyone but Steve, as if we four—Clinton, Rod, Cherri, and me—were each eager to prove our wilderness skills. At one point, for instance, the four of us were hunched over my aeronautical map debating exactly how many miles or kilometers constituted one degree of latitude. For the most part I'd felt cut out by Clinton and Rod, as if they didn't want to hear what I had to contribute. Now I felt slightly superior at their inability to predict accurately our arrival at the rapids. I think they had mostly paddled on the wide Zambezi. I had so much experience on tightly winding rivers just like this that I knew how huge the difference was between "straight-line" distance on a map and the actual twisting distance the river ran.

"We can't think how far things are," Clinton now said quietly, as if trying to remind himself to be patient. "When they don't arrive, it can do things to our minds."

We paddled quietly for a while. I found it both unnerving and exciting that already, on only the second day out, we seemed to have lost our place in terms of the reference points we carried. I began to realize that whatever lay around each bend was going to come as a profound surprise.

"We'll go past some villages in the first few days," Cherri had told us on the basis of what she saw during her reconnaissance flight. "But after that you won't believe how remote it is. There's nothing but forest."

"There are Rod's relatives!" Clinton suddenly called out.

A troop of vervet monkeys crouched along the riverbank. They turned, stared at us and our bright plastic boats, and then, as a group, ran away along the riverbank, their skinny asses bobbing, throwing glances back. They hopped up into the branches of a waterberry tree and disappeared. The leaves trembled as if a giant hand shook the trunk.

A few bends later we encountered a troop of yellow baboons that fled, grunting as if feeling inconvenienced, and jumped into a waterberry tree, too.

"There goes Clinton's family!" Rod predictably called out.

The weather was perfect in early winter fourteen degrees south of the equator—a warm, blue-sky day. The sun crossed the northern sky before us as the river bore mainly north. No fish traps at all now, whereas the first day we had pried through nearly twenty of them. We spotted many more birds: pygmy kingfisher, hammercop, hadeda ibis, Pels fishing owl, and, high up, a flock of open-billed storks. A bluish mountain rose in the distance. It felt like a good sign.

"The closer we are to mountains," Clinton announced as he stroked toward it, "the closer we are to rapids—and the happier I am."

The villages came less frequently, marked by a whiff of wood smoke or a handful of empty-looking thatched huts. We passed a few fishermen squatting in their bark canoes, draping their vine-woven nets into the water. No sound of jets far overhead or engines of any kind. Already I'd lost track of the days of the week. Only distance mattered now. With every bend the Lugenda felt more remote, isolated, wild. Instead of time I tracked the dwindling human presence along the banks. In some way it pleased me that the human presence lessened. How disappointed I would have been if a car or a truck suddenly drove up to the riverbank and disgorged white people—an intrusion on "our" river. Already I felt possessive about the river, about the "purity" of our wilderness experience, about the "untouched by the West" nature of the region, as so many European adventurers in Africa—James Bruce, for instance—had jealously guarded their "discoveries" before me.

It took Bruce nearly two and one-half years from the time he reached the Blue Nile's source until he arrived back in Marseilles. Tribal wars, suspicious chieftains, illnesses, and the hardships of travel delayed him as he followed the river north into Egypt. On his eventual return to Europe, French aristocracy received Bruce warmly, and he traveled on to Italy to take the mineral baths for his health. It was in Italy that his greatly anticipated homecoming turned sour for Bruce. He learned that his bride-to-be, Margaret Murray, had given up waiting and married an Italian noble-man. Bruce promptly challenged him to a duel, but it was dropped after the nobleman pleaded ignorance of Margaret's engagement.

Back in London, Bruce's Ethiopian stories were listened to in society drawing rooms with "amused skepticism," as one account put it. The En-glish aristocracy found him vain, boastful, and brusque, not to mention a fabricator. Among his greatest detractors was the literary critic Samuel Johnson, who had translated from a French version the travel accounts of Jerónimo Lobo. A Portuguese Jesuit priest, Lobo had traveled widely in Ethiopia (or Abyssinia, as it was known) a century and a half before Bruce. Dr. Johnson, along with many others, doubted that Bruce, due to his wild-sounding stories and contemptuous manner, had even *been* to Ethiopia much less to the source of the Nile.

Bruce, wounded, angry, and proud, repaired to the family estate in Scotland. He married and lived a domestic life, not venturing back to the continent that had once so attracted him. Nine years later, with the death of his wife and the urging of his acquaintances, the cantankerous Bruce finally took out his Ethiopian journals and dictated to a Moravian pastor an account in five volumes: *Travels to Discover the Sources of the Nile in the Years 1768, 1769, 1770, 1771, 1772, and 1773.*

Full of anecdotes and vividly bizarre details of Ethiopian life, such as eating raw steaks sliced from live cows, Bruce's *Travels* became an imme-diate best seller. The work would go on to be an exploration classic that inspired several succeeding generations of African explorers—Mungo Park, Hugh Clapperton, and many more. It was in good part due to Bruce's accounts of Ethiopia, however much dismissed at the time, that Joseph Banks and friends founded the African Association over dinner at St. Alban's Tavern that evening in 1788 and funded the expeditions of John Ledyard and others. But in his African writings Bruce did all he could to discredit or ignore those few Europeans who had gone before him to the "unknown continent." Both Father Lobo and his Portuguese Jesuit predecessor, Father Pedro Paez, had spent considerable time at the Blue Nile headwaters and had visited, many decades before Bruce, the springs on the flower-covered hillside that were said by the local people to be its source. Writing in his *Travels,* however, Bruce attacked Father Lobo as a "groveling, fanatic priest" whose book was "a heap of fables, and full of ignorance and presumption."

Bruce insisted on being first. It was as if for Bruce and those European explorers who followed—which in some small way might even include us—Africa was some great two-handled trophy to be hoisted above one's head.

By late afternoon we still hadn't reached the Luchimua confluence where the rapids were supposed to begin. We came to a few thatched huts on the bank. A fisherman beside the river passively watched us paddle up.

"Ask him how far to the confluence," Clinton said to me.

I put the request to him in Portuguese.

"Two kilometers," he replied.

We paddled a few bends farther. The sun made its quick descent behind the leafy waterberries, overcasting the river with a greenish gloom. Thick forest covered the muddy banks. Rounded boulders and shelves of granite projected from the mud. It felt as if we were entering a geological transition zone, where the earth's bony substructure rose to the surface. If the river ran over this rocky band, the elusive rapids might in fact be near.

"Let's stop here," said Clinton.

We pulled over to the left bank and climbed onto a narrow bench of firm muddy earth overarched by a thick canopy of branches. Underfoot lay a scattering of dried leaves. The spot felt both gloomy and protected at the same time, a riverbank fortress of vegetation. We walked around, checking it out—a ritual that I had performed hundreds of times myself and had watched my father, paddle in hand like a staff or a spear, perform dozens of times before me.

The campsite was not a great one but certainly better than the first night's. Up a short slope the forest opened into a tiny clearing where a few dried cornstalks poked from soft mounds of earth. Amid them lay the charred remains of a mud-and-thatch hut. Whether a land-clearing fire had gone astray or this was a hostile act, there was no way to tell.

We returned to the boats and pulled them onto the bank. From the branches overhead broke a cacophony of baboon howling and barking and grunting and rustling.

"What are they doing?" I asked, wondering if they were trying to convey the message to us: "Get lost!"

"It's just a lot of pushing and shoving going on," said Clinton unconcernedly as he unloaded his boat. "No more than your average family of thirteen children."

We staked down our tents under the trees. Unloading the last of Steve's and my boat, I stood in knee-deep water below the steep muddy bank and submerged one of my dry bags to check if it leaked.

"Watch out for flat dogs, eh, Pe-*tah*?" Rod called out, referring to crocs.

I hopped back onto the bank.

Tent up, boat unloaded, I walked up to the clearing and gouged a hole with my heel in the soft earth between stalks. My stomach had been grinding since we'd stopped for a quick lunch of soup and nuts that afternoon, and now a bout of diarrhea was upon me. For the sake of ecological purity, Cherri had asked that we not use toilet paper while on the Lugenda River. I figured I'd get used to it soon enough. Spilling water on my left hand from a water bottle, I washed myself in the traditional fashion, washed my hand, and kicked dirt to cover the hole. Was this the end of being sick or just the beginning? As I walked back to my tent, I felt almost as if I had vertigo: There were so many unknowns about what lay ahead—so much uncertainty. I knew if I started thinking too hard about what we didn't know and where we were headed, I might find myself awash in anxiety. I pushed it all aside as best I could. Just focus on what's immediately in front of you, I told myself again.

I changed into long pants and a dry shirt, and removed my contacts. With pen and notebook in hand, I joined Clinton, Rod, and Steve at the fire, its snapping tongues of flames cheerfully illuminating the gloomy underside of the branches. It was now dark. In the firelight I saw Rod's opened orange Pelican case nearby, exposing the thick layers of foam that protected the electronic devices hidden within. Then I heard Cherri's voice speaking loudly from the clearing. I saw the beam of her headlamp flashing through the branches.

"Cherri's calling her office on the sat phone," someone said.

It was mid-morning back in Steamboat Springs, Colorado. I could hear her issuing instructions to her employees.

"Tell Josh to bring ten rolls of 200 ASA film for Peter's camera," I heard her say. "We're going through a lot of film."

So much for the satellite phone's "emergency use only" status. As Cherri spoke from the darkened forest clearing in Africa, I imagined the Colorado scene on the other end: hot summer sunlight glinting off big SUVs, air conditioners humming, luncheoners sipping designer water and nibbling baby greens. I didn't want that vision to intrude on where I was. Cherri signed off. The scene instantly vanished from my mind, closed off

Rod and Clinton wait for the river water to boil for soup, Day Two.

by the thick African night, the chirp of crickets, the plashes from the river. Strangely, I felt better. We were here again—alone. Wasn't this what we came for?

We sipped our grog ration, ate plates of pasta topped with a white sauce Rod had prepared from a package using a stirring stick that Clinton had carved and adding a can of crabmeat and bits of sweet potato. We mulled over the day's distance. Rod had measured it by GPS as twenty-eight kilometers as the crow flies. Not bad, we all agreed, and certainly better than the first day. I guessed that meant we had paddled at least forty kilometers by the actual twists of the river.

After dinner I proposed reading aloud from *Wild Africa,* an idea I'd come up with because it had felt kind of empty around the campfire the first night when everyone except Clinton seemed too tired to make much conversation.

We washed our plates and returned to the fire circle, sprawling on the ground. Holding the page to the light of the flames, I read aloud James Bruce's passage about cresting a hill to see a clear stream running over a pebbly bed—"the Nile itself, strangely diminished in size"—and his joy

Rod checks the GPS while Peter writes notes, Day Two.

and despair that night in his tent and finally his acceptance of what he had sacrificed to reach the source springs.

> [I]t was the palm for three thousand years held out to all the nations in the world as a *detur dignissimo,* which, in my cool hours, I had thought was worth the attempting at the risk of my life which I had long resolved to lose, or lay this discovery, a trophy in which I could have no competitor, for the honour of my country, at the feet of my sovereign, whose servant I was.[6]

DAY THREE

"The bag's at my tent site," I called out to Clinton. "Just go ahead and grab it."

"These guys aren't being paid, you know," Cherri rebuked me for not getting it myself.

It was dawn on the third morning. The others stuffed dry bags of gear into the kayaks' cargo holds on the misty, muddy riverbank while, sitting propped against a tree trunk, I was hurrying to finish my previous days' notes. Already I felt I had my hands more than full between paddling all day and writing into the night.

I looked up from my notes. She was as glamorous as ever at 6:30 a.m.

"I know they're not being paid," I replied testily. "I try to keep that in mind."

She retreated. "Sometimes I can't help making a quip. If it gets to be too much, just slap me."

"I'll try to remember that," I said, laughing.

We all shoved down an energy bar and gulped from our mugs as Clinton and Rod called a little conference. They proposed that from now on we stop only once each day—in late morning. That would be "breakfast." Then we'd paddle the rest of the day without stopping for lunch. In exchange we'd get off the river for the evening a little earlier and have a cup of soup as soon as we camped, then make dinner. Instead of our stopping twice, for breakfast and lunch, as we had the previous day, they figured this routine would give us at least one more hour of paddling time daily.

"Is everybody okay with that?" Clinton asked.

We all murmured our assent.

We stepped into the boats. Despite the cool mist, Clinton and Rod

A Makuan fisherman poling a barely afloat bark canoe.

had stripped down to their muscle-ripped bare chests, their usual paddling garb. Instead of muddy or sandy shores, which had been the case upriver, protruding from both riverbanks now were shelves of smooth granite spider-webbed with cracks. Within a kilometer of paddling we passed the mouth of the Luchimua River, flowing smooth and brown out of the forest on our left and emptying into the Lugenda. We spotted a fisherman ahead squatting midstream in his bark canoe, intently setting his nets.

"*Bom dia!*" we called out from afar.

He stood up with surprise, seized his pole, and planted it in the river bottom as if about to flee, then paused.

"*Bom dia,*" he said cautiously.

His baggy cotton trousers were rolled up to his knees, the fabric faded by weather so it nearly matched his white shirt. Like other fishermen we had encountered on the Lugenda, he was sinewy and agile. He had a kind of fibrous quality to his physique reminiscent of the tree bark of his canoe and the vines of his net.

He swung his boat upstream toward us. We stroked downstream toward him.

"Are there rapids ahead?" Cherri and I asked in broken Portuguese as the distance closed.

He looked at us, perplexed, bracing his pole against the river bottom. Then he broke into a toothy grin.

"You must speak English!" he called out.

"Yes!" we shouted in delighted unison.

Our boats bumped together. We grabbed hold of his gunwale. It felt like some kind of homecoming. *Here was someone who could tell us where we were!*

He appeared as pleased to see us as we were to see him. We talked eagerly. He told us he had been trained as a schoolteacher but had moved here from Malawi (where English is the official language) because he couldn't find work. Now he was a fisherman. He picked up a fat fish lying in the bottom of his canoe and held it up.

We asked him again if there were rapids ahead.

"Yes, there are *cataratas*," he said in his thick accent. "Three *cataratas*. The first one is very soon. You can follow a path through the forest past each *catarata*. After the three, there are no more."

We thanked him effusively. Clinton tossed him a pack of cigarettes. He caught it and smiled broadly at his good luck. As we paddled off, I felt a flood of gratitude toward the fisherman. It was as if by simply encountering someone with whom we could communicate reasonably well, we had run into some long-lost relative.

The river remained smooth as far as I could see, to the next bend. Now, after the confluence with the Luchimua, it was twice as broad as before. I hoped the fisherman was right about the rapids, that there were only three. I could handle three. Cherri's laminated list was showing more than that plus a waterfall of sorts. How much to trust a friendly stranger's advice? Was there any reason he had to deceive us? Was there any reason he wouldn't *know* what lay ahead?

I remembered the story of the Portuguese seafarer Vasco da Gama who likewise met a friendly stranger in circumstances not so different and not so far from this spot. The incident with the friendly stranger may have changed the whole tenor of his 1498 voyage searching for a sea route to India as well as those early relations between West and East.

For many days da Gama's three ships, the *San Gabriel, San Rafael,* and *Berrio,* had been blown along by storms in the turbulent and unknown waters in the South Atlantic off southern Africa. The sailors and even his navigators feared for their lives, feared that the small ships would break apart in the huge seas, and pleaded with da Gama to turn back. Da Gama, a "very choleric man," in the words of his chronicler, Correa, replied that he had promised God on leaving Lisbon he would not turn back "a single span's breadth," and he now threatened to throw into the sea whoever spoke of it.[7]

Whispers of a mutiny plot reached his ears, a plot in which his navigators were conspirators. He seized their navigation aids, held them in his hand, and tossed the instruments over the rail into the sea. Then he had the navigators and pilots clasped in irons and locked in a cabin.

"I do not require master nor pilot," da Gama proclaimed, "nor any man who knows the art of navigation, because God alone is the master and pilot."

After finally rounding the Cape of Storms, as it was then known, at Africa's tip, da Gama's ships started up Africa's east coast. At first they encountered no one at all. They then met with some natives in canoes wearing leaves or grass around their middles. One day they spotted a sail. Before they could catch it, the boat disappeared over the horizon, but the crew thanked God for having returned them to a region that knew navigation. Running close to shore, they finally met a cargo vessel at anchor. It was commanded by a Moorish trader wearing a silk girdle and a gold-embroidered silk hat and gold rings dangling from his ears. Da Gama and his crew felt "great satisfaction at having found a man of whom they could ask questions and learn in what country they were."

The friendly stranger guided them to Mozambique. This was a small island off the East African coast that served as a Moorish trading center. Its harbor, to the surprise and delight of the Portuguese, held ships carrying gold and silver, ivory and beeswax from the African interior.

The friendly Moorish trader went ashore to the house of the Sheikh of Mozambique and told him about the Portuguese. Accompanied by ten retainers and dressed in a jacket of plaited Mecca velvet, the Sheikh paid a formal visit to da Gama's ship. When the Sheikh asked what merchandise the Portuguese sought, the Portuguese held out samples of pepper, cinnamon, and ginger.

"The Sheikh, on seeing it, laughed to his own people, and answered that they [the Portuguese] should be satisfied, since he would give them pilots who could conduct them whither they could fill their ships with as much as they pleased."

From this promising beginning, this first meeting of West and East brokered by the friendly Moorish trader, relations deteriorated rapidly—and permanently. Da Gama had promised great rewards to the Moor for his help. The Moor reported to da Gama that the Sheikh had asked him many questions about the Portuguese. This, said the Moor, had raised his suspicions that the Sheikh planned to plunder the Portuguese vessels—in which case, of course, the Moor would lose his promised riches.

On the basis of the friendly Moor's suspicion, da Gama and his men watched for the slightest provocation from the people of Mozambique, whom they regarded as heathens and infidels anyway. The Portuguese soon found it, or thought they did. A local African pilot was guiding their small boat to the mainland for fresh water but apparently had trouble finding the right spot to land. The Portuguese quickly suspected he was actually leading them into an ambush. The Portuguese captain of the boat, da Gama's trusted friend Nicolas Coelho, wanted to kill the pilot. Apparently fearing for his life, the African pilot jumped overboard and swam away underwater as the Portuguese opened fire with crossbows on his surfacing head. They missed, but soon an angry crowd had gathered on shore and showered the Portuguese boat with arrows and rocks.

Accounts vary as to just how much devastation the Portuguese wrought on this first visit to Africa's east coast. Some say that da Gama opened fire with cannon on Mozambique for three hours, mowing down those who stood on the beach, and "weary of this work," the Portuguese "retired to the ships to dine." Other writers of the era report that he finally decided against devastating the port and burning its ships, not wishing to create a poor impression on the first visit. According to these writers, da Gama sailed on peacefully—but not before warning the Moorish pilot he took on board that if the ships hit any shoals on the way to India, both of his eyes would be put out.

We had no reason to distrust the friendly Malawian fisherman, but surrounded by the unknown, surrounded by questions, I realized how much might hang on the advice or misadvice of a seemingly friendly stranger.

Not far past the Luchimua confluence and the friendly Malawian fisherman, the Lugenda split into narrow channels and braided around granite outcrops as if it were spilling across a big shelf of rock. The outcrops formed tiny, willow-covered islands, and the fast, twisting channels between the islands required quick and constant maneuvering.

"Paddle on the left!" I called out to Steve as I steered. "Now paddle on the right!"

He responded enthusiastically to my instructions. But again I could see that while he stroked powerfully and easily on the straight sections—with more power than I did—the knack of paddling trickier water wasn't coming to him quickly.

The braided channels soon rejoined each other. We heard the roar of whitewater. The treetops downstream appeared markedly lower than those nearby.

"Follow me ov-*ah* he-*ah*!" called out Clinton.

We followed his lead to the right bank. Beaching the boats, we climbed the bank on a faint path leading through willowy underbrush. We came to a clear spot. In front of us, the river tumbled over a six-foot-high ledge of granite that spanned its breadth, forming a low waterfall. Midway across, a tongue of water spilled through a notch in the lip. This was the logical place to try to paddle through, except that most of the tongue cascaded onto a toothy rock outcrop.

I didn't like the looks of it, especially the prospect of running it in a boat as top-heavy and tippy as our laden double. Clinton, standing barefoot and bare-chested, studied the drop with his steely blue eyes.

"It's too steep for these boats," he finally pronounced. "It'd be no problem in a river kayak, but it might knock the rudders off the back of the sea kayaks."

He pointed to a rocky islet two-thirds of the way across the river.

"We'll paddle over to those rocks and portage there."

I was relieved at his decision. I went off to squat in the willow bushes. My stomach was no better today.

"You may as well start taking Cipro now," Cherri had advised me the previous night, "because you're definitely going to be taking it sooner or later."

"Let's see how I'm doing tomorrow," I had replied.

Now I wished I'd taken her advice and started a course of the antibiotic, which, among its other uses (such as countering the threat of anthrax), treated troublesome intestinal bacteria. But now my medicine bag was buried deep in the hull, and there was no way to get it until we stopped.

With ropes tied to the kayaks' sterns, Clinton, Rod, Steve, and I manhandled the heavy boats down the rocks and lowered them into the river

Clinton above the first of the Lugenda's many drops, Day Three.

below. Wearing her straw sun hat, Cherri toted the four paddles in her long, thin arms like a bundle of firewood. We climbed back into the boats below the foaming ledge. I noticed that Cherri appeared very pleased. We had just negotiated our first rapid; it was clear that she had assembled a team of strong-backed males who would work hard to overcome the Lugenda's obstacles.

The river gentled into a broad, smooth stretch, and we paddled quietly for a time. The trees now grew thicker on the banks and were hung with vines, dark green shadows lying beneath them. Birds called out, fleeing downriver. No signs of villages. It suddenly felt eerily empty. Maybe what so unnerved those first Portuguese was not people but the *absence* of people. I could imagine coasting day after day along the endless white beach backed by dark green forest, broken only by river estuaries and mangrove swamps. It would have been a great relief to meet the Moors. Friendly or

Lowering the boats down the first rapid, Day Three.

not, these "Mohammedans," these infidels, were a people with whom the Portuguese had been enemies for centuries—a familiar enemy. It must have been a comfort of sorts to slip back into their old hatreds—easier than the unnerving emptiness.

How much of Africa had been explored out of simple hatred? Was this as powerful a motivator as greed? The first Portuguese expeditions to Africa, seven decades before da Gama's, in the reign of King John I, sprang from the ancient enmity between Christian and Muslim. The king's sons, on reaching manhood, wanted to earn their knighthoods in real combat instead of the jousting tournament their father had planned for them, or so the story goes. They thus convinced King John to mount an invasion of the Moorish trading city of Ceuta, at the northern tip of Africa just across from Gibraltar. King John had his own moral imperative for invading

Ceuta: By killing Moors he would be "washing his hands in the blood of the infidel" and cleansing himself of slaying fellow Christians in his previous battles with the Christian king of Castile.[8]

Ceuta fell easily in August 1415—Moorish bodies lay stacked in the streets versus only eight Portuguese dead—and young Prince Henry was appointed its governor. In its lavish houses and twenty-four thousand shops he discovered (and promptly looted) the riches of Africa and India: pepper and cloves, rugs and tapestries, gold and silver. Under Henry's Christian rule of Ceuta, however, this flood of goods that had been arriving by caravan across the desert quickly ceased. Henry studiously applied himself to the problem of how Portugal might profit from this fabulously wealthy trade with Africa and India and at the same time do battle with the infidels.

Returning to Portugal, the reclusive Henry turned away from the life of the royal court and had himself appointed governor of Algarve Province, which included the rocky and remote promontory of Sagres at Portugal's southwest tip. It was here in his fortress on the promontory that Prince Henry established his own small court, attracting cartographers, astronomers, shipwrights, and others pursuing the arts and sciences of exploration. From his high perch at Sagres, Prince Henry—or Henry the Navigator, as he would be known to history—dispatched his expeditions of discovery down Africa's west coast, inspired less by scientific curiosity than by medieval mysticism and religious fervor.

His caravels, a highly maneuverable ship design refined at Sagres, carried a large red cross on their sails in acknowledgment of the crusading nature of Prince Henry's endeavor. When he was twenty-six, soon after setting up his court on the Sagres promontory, Prince Henry agreed to a life of chastity and asceticism in order to be anointed grand master of the Order of Christ. This was the successor group in Portugal to the Knights Templar, the mysterious and powerful brotherhood founded in the early twelfth century to protect Christian crusaders from Muslim attacks.

From the Order of Christ came most of the funding for Prince Henry's expeditions; in effect they sallied forth under the twin banners of Christianity and trade. Where was the legendary Christian kingdom of Prester John? Where was the source of gold that flowed out of west Africa? These were powerful incentives driving Henry, though it took fifteen of Prince Henry's expeditions before one braved sailing beyond Cape Bojador, a slight bulge of Africa hardly a thousand miles south of Portugal and Spain.

Generations of Spanish mariners had held this cape in great fear, reported Prince Henry's chronicler: "For, said the mariners, this much is clear, that beyond this Cape there is no race of men nor place of inhabitants."[9]

Finally, in 1434, on his second attempt, the Portuguese squire Gil Eannes, "despising all danger" and pushing past "the shadow of fear," rounded Cape Bojador. On the following year's expedition, well south of the Cape, Eannes and his men spotted human footprints in the sand, giving lie to the rumor that this region lay beyond the habitations of men. Under orders from Henry to bring back an inhabitant for an interview with the prince, an expedition still farther south to Cape Blanco returned to Portugal in 1441 with two African captives and some gold dust. Prince Henry sent an emissary to Rome to ask the Pope for funding for further African explorations. The Holy Father happily signed on, as he expressed it, "for the destruction and confusion of the Moors and the enemies of Christ" while also absolving of sin all those who took part in the campaign.

Three years later, in 1444, Gil Eannes proudly sailed back to Prince Henry at his fortress in Sagres with a cargo of two hundred humans who would be sold as slaves in the nearby town of Lagos. Prince Henry was reported to be delighted to see the first human captives, not because they promised riches but because he knew that their heathen souls could now be saved.

"[African] mothers would clasp their infants in their arms," wrote Zurara, Henry's chronicler, who personally witnessed the event, "and throw themselves on the ground to cover them with their bodies, disregarding any injury to their own persons, so that they could prevent their children from being separated from them."

According to Zurara, that cargo of African slaves—the first of countless more to come—made Prince Henry a hero among the Portuguese. No more did they criticize him for wasting money on frivolous exploration. They saw there could be profit in Africa, wrote Zurara, "and their covetousness now began to wax greater."

The whitewater roared and sparkled in the sun.

"I don't know about this one," I remarked to Cherri.

We stood side by side on a rock outcrop, part of a long granite shelf protruding across the river, similar to the first drop. A notch indented this second ledge, too, but instead of cascading down onto jagged rocks like the first, the tongue of water funneled into a series of tall foaming waves. Remaining stationary in the river, these are known to kayakers as "standing waves" or a "wave train."

We watched as Clinton hopped into his yellow kayak, paddled upstream, swung his boat around, and aimed carefully at the slot in the ledge. He dropped over the lip, paddled gracefully through the standing waves, and spun into the quiet eddy below. Sidling over to shore, he hopped onto the rocks and clambered up toward us.

"These guys don't want to do it!" Cherri called out to him on my behalf.

"I think it's okay," I said to her.

I wished she hadn't said anything. I wanted to make my own assessment without her interference.

"But one wrong move, and you're over," she protested to me. "Don't hurt yourself this early in the trip."

I squinted again through the bright sun and tossing waves at the line Clinton had taken.

"There's plenty of time to set up," I said to Cherri. I turned to Steve. "Do you want to do this?"

"Sure," he replied, genial as ever.

I slipped into the peculiar frame of mind that I knew from many previous moments on whitewater rivers or steep snowy mountains: a kind of stomach-fluttering nervousness coupled with intense concentration. Though Clinton had shot right through the tumbling cleft, making it look easy, I knew our much heavier boat was a lot less maneuverable than his and thus more difficult to aim into the slot exactly, nor did I have his level of whitewater skill while Steve had no whitewater kayaking experience at all. Most significant, the consequences of a bad mistake here were heightened by its remoteness. It could take days to evacuate someone who was injured. And there was one other factor that added to my nervousness: Half an hour earlier we had nearly tipped by following Clinton the wrong way down a fast, narrow channel. The channel had ended abruptly in a nest of low trees, and our big boat wedged sideways against a limb, nearly dumping. Grunting with effort against the push of the current, we had managed to extricate ourselves. But the incident had underscored again the precarious and top-heavy nature of our laden boat.

Steve and I now strapped on our life jackets, climbed into the kayak, and stretched the spray skirts over the cowlings to seal the cockpits from the splash of the waves. We pushed off from the rocks and paddled upstream in the smooth, fast water above the ledge. I stomped on the rudder pedals and wheeled the kayak around to aim downstream toward the ledge. I pointed our bow at Clinton's upraised paddle blade, which he hoisted from his kayak in the pool below to serve as a marker for the notch. I adjusted our course with rudder and paddle strokes as we neared the smooth green edge.

"Tell me what I should do," Steve called back.

"Just keep paddling," I said, focusing on the lip.

Steve stroked steadily. I steered. The sound grew louder. Suddenly, the river dropped away into a chaos of roaring white. Our big sea kayak tilted lazily over the lip, accelerating rapidly. The rush of wind hit my face, a joyous thrill like all the sled rides and roller coasters I'd ever taken, and we submarined into the waves below. Churning whitewater crashed around Steve nearly to his neck and shook the boat back and forth. He didn't flinch. The boat buoyed back to the surface. The foaming waves flattened into a rush of bubbling green water. I stomped the rudder pedals, steered with my paddle blade like an additional rudder, and swung the kayak alongside Clinton's in the smooth, eddying pool. Steve and I each gave a happy whoop of success. We looked back upstream. Rod and Cherri followed, plunging over the lip, crashing through the waves, exiting in the pool, and whooping loudly.

It was the first rapid we had run on the Lugenda. Our confidence rose.

A kilometer below the rapid we came to a nice sandbar. Clinton and Rod announced that we would stop here for breakfast. "Breakfast" was only a manner of speaking, as it was now around 11 a.m. and we'd been paddling nearly four hours on a single energy bar. Clinton and Rod started a fire and put on the iron pot of river water. As they waited for a boil, they tossed a rugby ball about. Where did *that* come from?

"This would be a lekker place to kip," I heard Rod say to Clinton.

I asked what that meant. He replied that it was Afrikaans slang for "a good place to camp."

I was enjoying sitting quietly on the warm sand, a vacation from paddling. I swallowed a Cipro I had pulled from our cargo hold. I scribbled a few notes. Cherri laid out clothes, wet from paddling, on a rib of granite. Steve came over with two mugs of oatmeal, handed me one, and sat down

Midmorning "porridge" break, Day Three.

in the sand beside me. We gazed upstream at the rapids thumping faintly in the distance. It felt good that we'd run them well. I felt bonded with Steve—boatmates. He stirred the instant oatmeal in his blue plastic mug. Gray clouds hovered overhead, broken by faint patches of sun. The river shone a silvery gray. The forested shores stretched gray-green to the bony white boil of the softly thumping rapids. Something about the scene reminded me of museum dioramas of the dinosaur age, as if at any moment a pterodactyl might come gliding overhead down the Lugenda.

"I think my favorite quote in your book was the one about 'the absolute,'" Steve said.

"That's one of my favorites, too," I replied.

The quote was from Paul Bowles, and I'd used it in my previous book, *Last Breath*. Bowles, the American expatriot writer and Saharan traveler, had tried to address the question about the Sahara Desert, "Why go?"

The answer is that when a man has been there and undergone the baptism of solitude he can't help himself. Once he has been under the spell of the vast, luminous, silent country, no other place is quite strong enough for him, no other surroundings can provide the supremely satisfying sensation of existing in the midst of something that is absolute. He will go back, whatever the cost in comfort or money, for the absolute has no price.[10]

I gestured with my oatmeal mug toward the forest and river.

"We can probably find it out here, too," I said.

I instantly disliked my prophet-of-the-wilderness tone. I felt like some kind of melodramatic pretender to the role. Could we find it out here? Or was it just wishful thinking on my part that we'd experience some profound Bowlesian revelation?

It struck me how different that motive was, Bowles's metaphysical quest for the "absolute," from the Christian fervor and love of wealth that drove the Portuguese and from the "Africa-as-a-trophy" approach of the Scottish explorers like James Bruce.

I now noticed that Rod and Clinton had given up the rugby game. Rod removed the satellite phone from the Pelican case, walked over to the rib of granite, and punched in numbers. He studied the screen. He returned a few moments later to report that he had checked his safari business emails and had received affectionate messages from his aunt and girlfriend.

If we were seeking the "baptism of solitude," would the sat phone deter us from finding it?

At the third drop in the river a big, sunny plate of granite formed a natural dam. The river cut through the plate in a fast S-shaped chute. Clinton hopped barefoot over the rock, quickly scouting. The four of us waited in the boats.

"Go straight down the middle," he called to us. "Halfway down there's a big rock like an island. Paddle left of that, through some big waves, and you're out. It should be straightforward enough."

He jumped back into his boat. He seemed happy. He was in his element—rapids.

"Life jackets on!" he called out. "Splash skirts on! Rud-*dahs* loosened! Follow me!"

I aimed our boat after his bobbing stern and twitching metal rudder, which jerked like a tail as he steered. His bright yellow hull contrasted cheerfully with the emerald-green water and foaming, sunlit whitecaps. He slid into the chute, suddenly accelerating. Then I could feel us accelerating, too, sliding downhill, gray rock banks whizzing past, kayak lifting and falling over the green-and-white waves. *Paddle, paddle . . . steer left of the big rock.* The current whipped us around the final curve of the S-bend, waves pounding into Steve's solid torso. We bottomed out into the quiet pool where Clinton waited.

I gave a whoop. Steve gave a whoop.

"That was fun!" we said to each other.

I could hear Cherri loudly whooping behind us as she and Rod flew down the final curve, her hair flying in the river wind.

They pulled up alongside our boat. We congratulated one another.

"That should be the last big rapid," I noted. "The fisherman said there were three, and that was the third."

Cherri had been consulting her laminated list.

"Guys," she said. "I show that we haven't even reached the waterfall yet, and there are a lot more rapids after that."

We started paddling again. I didn't know whether to believe her reconnaissance or the Malawian fisherman's. I hoped the fisherman was right. I wanted to get past the rapids. I felt exposed running whitewater in a heavy boat with a beginner paddler in the bow and so very far from help. I'd never had as much confidence paddling whitewater as I would have liked. But I had run many moderate-sized rapids in heavily loaded canoes that were in some ways trickier than these sea kayaks because they lacked a waterproof deck and could easily fill with water. Maybe I shouldn't be so concerned after all, I thought. We had run the rapids very well so far.

I had a sudden anxiety: *This is where we get overconfident. This is where we start running the rapids without proper scouting.*

I shoved it down. *I'll try to make sure we give the rapids proper scouting.* I had it in my power to do that. We paddled around the next bend. Still, the river remained flat and peaceful. How to maintain the right level of confidence? That was the trick. I thought of those early Portuguese seafarers and the raw confidence they must have needed to sail those unknown coasts of Africa. What would that word be in Portuguese? In Spanish I knew it to be *confianza,* although I wasn't sure that the concept translated directly—as faith in one's abilities or someone else's abilities. The Portuguese seafarers—at least the leaders like da Gama—required it in giant measure not only for themselves but to convince their sailors that they knew what they were doing as they sailed beyond the map.

Da Gama took one approach: *I've made a pact with God to sail to India, and anyone who speaks of turning back, I'm going to throw overboard.* That was self-confidence overflowing into tyranny. Or maybe this was false bravado, and he was as fearful as anyone but refused to show it, and instead made himself the example of *confianza* to press onward. More likely he truly believed God was on his side. Da Gama wasn't scared of the unknown because he was prepared to die for the cause.

His precursor on the sea route around Africa, Bartolomeu Dias, used a less iron-fisted tact, a consensus, "we're all in this together" approach. Although his achievements rank on a par with da Gama's, this gentler confidence expressed through urgings rather than commands is perhaps why Dias never reached India. He became, in the words of one exploration historian, "the forgotten man of Portugal's Age of Discovery."

By the early 1480s, Portuguese trade with West Africa had grown to where they'd built a castle called Mina ("the gold mine") on the west coast in today's Ghana. In about 1486 the Portuguese merchants working this coast learned that a nearby African chieftain, the king of Benin, had received gifts from another African king who was said to live twelve months' journey into the interior. These gifts bore small crosses. This quickly sparked the rumor that the gifts came from Prester John. For centuries it had been rumored among Europe's Christians that somewhere to the east in Asia a powerful Christian king was ruling. Europeans had been actively searching for Prester John since the twelfth-century Crusades to retake the Holy Land, when Crusaders hoped he could serve as an ally against the Muslims.

Reports of the gifts with the crosses—gifts that had originated somewhere deep in Africa—reached the attentive ears of Portugal's King John II, nephew of Prince Henry the Navigator. John II had an appetite for exploration like his Uncle Henry, who had died some twenty-five years earlier. King John saw two opportunities in Prester John: someone who could be an African ally against the Muslims and someone who might help establish a sea route to India. Recruiting two adventurous travelers, Pero da Covilha and Afonso Paiva, and giving them four hundred cruzados and a map on which to mark their journey, King John dispatched an expedition overland to Ethiopia, thought to be the locale of Prester John's kingdom, and also to India. At the same time he sent Bartolomeu Dias by ship to find a sea route to India around Africa's southern tip.

Dias, superintendent of the royal warehouses and a veteran of earlier African expeditions, departed Portugal in August 1487 with two small caravels and a supply ship. By December he had reached Cape Cross (in present-day Namibia), about four-fifths of the way down the west coast of Africa. Here Dias's ships passed the last of the stone pillars called *padrãoes* erected by Diogo Cão who had twice failed to reach Africa's tip on previous missions for King John. Beyond Cape Cross, Dias sailed south for another five hundred miles. The ships were now nearly four thousand miles south of Lisbon. Still, the coast ran on toward the south ahead of them. Then a great windstorm arose. For thirteen days it blew the ships, their sails only halfway up the masts, far from land. The sailors, according to a chronicler, "gave themselves up for dead."

When the wind slackened, they hoisted the sails and turned east toward shore. They couldn't find land. Dias ordered a course shift to the north. After sailing north for several days they spied tall mountains. Instead of south, the coastline here trended east and west. Bartolomeu Dias knew he had come to the southern end of Africa, a quest that had taken the Portuguese nearly seventy years of systematic effort since Prince Henry sent the first ships down the Moroccan coast in 1420.

Dias anchored his ships off a stretch of coast the sailors dubbed *dos Vaquieros,* "the cowboys," after the pastoralist herders and the cows they saw there. When the Portuguese landed in their small boats, the herders first ran away. When they returned, they hurled stones at the Portuguese until Dias killed one with a shot from a crossbow. The Portuguese sailed on another 250 miles east along the great rounded tip of Africa to an island with two good springs. Here the sailors balked. They wanted to turn back to Portugal. Dias employed persuasion instead of threats. If they sailed onward another two or three days without seeing some compelling reason to continue, he would turn the ships back toward Portugal.

A few days later they reached a large river (the Great Fish River). Now the coastline was trending to the north, confirming that a sea route to India was possible. The sailors and officers, however, refused to follow it.

"Weary, and terrified by the great seas through which they had passed, all with one voice began to murmur, and demand that they proceed no farther."

It was then that Dias, heeding his crew, turned his ships back, first requiring a signed statement from the officers about their desire to return. He sailed away from the stone *padrão* he'd left at his point of farthest progress. He surely knew that before long someone—da Gama, as it turned out, ten years later—would sail far past that pillar and be celebrated through the ages as the discoverer of the sea route to India. Seeing that last *padrão* pass behind his ships, Dias was overcome "with as much sorrow and feeling as though he were taking his last leave of a son condemned to exile forever."

*   *   *

We rounded a few more bends with Clinton, as always, out front. Would he lead us down the Lugenda in the consensus style of Bartolomeu Dias or with the iron fist of Vasco da Gama? Suddenly, the river simply ended— or so it looked. It was like coming around a corner on a forest path and instead of seeing the trunks of trees ahead, you're suddenly looking at the *tops* of trees. Known to whitewater kayakers as a "dropping horizon line," this merits extreme caution, for obvious reasons.

A swirl of mist hovered over the lip, and we heard the roar of whitewater. Putting in at the right bank, we climbed a low dome of granite. Here indeed was the waterfall that Cherri had spotted from the plane. It wasn't that high, but it was high enough—a drop of about fifteen feet in a two-step cascade into a deep swirling pool. The whole Lugenda funneled over it.

No way, I thought.

I hoped Clinton thought likewise.

"No way," he said. "We'll have to carry."

We looked for a path on the right bank. Nothing presented itself. We paddled to the left bank, and Rod, Clinton, Steve, and I, grunting mightily and pouring sweat, hauled the loaded boats down a bouldery slope and back to the river. Cherri toted the paddles again.

By now it was past midafternoon. I could sense the sun's lowering light. I was tired and hoped we'd camp soon. I'd had enough portages and rapids for one day. But Clinton kept paddling. Wordlessly, we followed.

Soon we heard the roar of a big *fifth* drop.

"I guess the fisherman was wrong," I said. "This is our fifth rapid."

"Guys," Cherri repeated. "As I've been telling you, there are still a lot more rapids after that waterfall."

We stepped out of the boats. Here granite humps squeezed the river and then sent it arcing out over a ledge like the fat stream of a giant fire hose, dropping six feet or so into turbulence below where a side wave slammed into the main torrent. It would be difficult to punch through the side wave without dumping. But it was beautiful. Backlit by the late sun, the torrent looked like a spray of roaring white-hot lava.

Clinton clambered closer, studied the drop, and looked back at us, sun reflecting off his smooth brown shoulders. His hand wavered back and forth over the roar. *Iffy.*

He hopped barefoot across the humps to scout more closely. I badly needed to relieve myself. I scrambled down the bald rocks in the other direction. The only privacy I could find was a small patch of willow bushes and sand between two of the humps, near the edge of a pool. I was now having a bout of diarrhea at every rapid. I didn't know if it was my stomach or my nerves. Squatting there, river shorts around my ankles, river knife flopping impotently in the sand, I vaguely wondered if a croc would leap from the willows or pool and nab me.

I pulled up my river shorts. Think clearly, I told myself. If Clinton decides we should run this tricky drop instead of doing the heavy work of portaging, what are your chances? Most likely Steve and I would run it without problems in our big boat. But say we do flip, what then? I'd have to deal with the chaos of flipping, the struggle of swimming through rapids holding a heavy overturned boat, and the possibility that crocs would be waiting in the smoother water below. I felt weak and drained. I didn't have the strength left to face all that.

I climbed back up onto the rocks. I'd been dreading this moment ever since I'd signed on to the Lugenda River expedition. How do you say, "I don't want to go on"? But I *did* want to go on. I just wanted to be able to say no to situations we encountered that I considered too risky. During my childhood I'd been pushed to say yes in these situations. How much more confident I would be in venturing forward down the Lugenda River if I knew that I could say no if necessary. Is this what those Portuguese sailors most feared? Not the big seas or the stone-throwing people or even sailing off the map but that once their captain, Bartolomeu Dias, had rounded the Cape and set course in the direction he thought India lay, there would be no turning him back no matter how vehement their protests? They would be trapped. This is what I most feared on the Lugenda, being trapped into going forward against my will.

Suddenly, I was defiant. They could call me what they wanted. I wouldn't give in to the fear of being humiliated, the fear of being afraid. This was a test, but it was the opposite test of those early canoe trips with my grandfather. "If you let these people push you into doing something stupid and you get killed, I'm going to be really angry," Amy had said. She didn't trust me to say no. But now I'd prove that I could say no. I wanted to be absolutely sure I could say it and that Clinton would heed it. I wanted to carry the word *no* like the knife on my waistband, hold it in my hand, know it was in my arsenal to use against whatever we might face downstream in the days ahead. I'd concede the macho aspects to Clinton and Rod. I'd strive to be anti-macho.

I clambered over the granite humps to where Cherri stood.

"At forty-eight I don't have to do this shit," I said to Cherri. "I'm going to walk it. Clinton can take my boat through."

To my relief no one seemed to mind.

Clinton paddled his single down a narrow, cascading side channel that skirted the main drop, pinballing through rocks and whitewater, and declared it too technical for the big doubles. Then he and Rod power-paddled Rod's double over the main drop, arcing out on the backlit fire-hose of spray and crashing through the powerful side wave without mishap.

Cherri and I stood on the rocks and watched.

"I want to do it if they'll let me," she remarked.

I wondered if she was trying to show me up.

"No, Cherri," Clinton said, climbing out after the run with Rod. "Those hydraulics are too powerful. We need someone stronger in the bow."

Cherri looked frustrated but held her tongue. Instead, Clinton asked Steve if he wanted to go, and, agreeable as ever, Steve took his usual seat in the bow of my boat while Clinton took my place in the stern. Saying he'd patrol "safety," Rod climbed into Clinton's single below the drop. I was lining up a camera shot of Clinton and Steve, aligning their boat above the rapids, when I heard Cherri's shout of alarm. I looked downstream. Rod had tipped in the sharp eddy lines at the rapid's foot. I shoved the camera into her hands and, sensing my own opportunity to perform heroics, ran down the steep rocks of the natural dam and hopped into Rod's empty double. I chased Rod as the current swept him quickly downstream. He tried to climb onto the swamped boat, beyond reach of possible crocs, but it kept rolling over and dumping him back in the river as it had with Clinton. Finally, the river pushed Rod and the kayak across a shallow, rocky bar in midstream. Waist-deep in strong current, he got his feet under him, tied onto my boat as I grasped some midriver willow bushes, and bailed water. No crocs appeared, so apparently they didn't like this stretch of the river, either.

Meanwhile, I could see upstream that Clinton and Steve had successfully run the drop.

Sounding chagrined about his mishap, Rod said, "I'm glad no one had a camera on me right then."

If not exactly heroic, I felt at least slightly useful.

* * *

We all shouted with pleasure when we beached an hour later. Just before entering yet another rapid we had spotted a beautiful place on river right: smooth slabs of granite with beds of sand nestled between them and a big baobob tree protruding like a centerpiece. It had been a hard, exciting day; this perfect campsite felt like a reward for our efforts.

Suddenly, Rod squatted down on his haunches and ran his finger over the sand. Clinton joined him.

"Nobody go wandering off by themselves, eh?" Rod called out to us.

It was a lion track pressed in the sand. Nearby were hyena tracks. Our perfect campsite was also their stomping grounds.

"Everyone gather two or three big logs to keep the fire going all night," Clinton said.

Soon there were two fires going on the rock slab: a big blaze stoked by Steve to keep away animals, and a smaller cookfire tended by Rod. At Clinton's instructions we had all pitched our tents in a tight clump near the baobob. Cherri, who'd run plenty of safaris in African lion country, had warned Steve and me not to walk off to relieve ourselves during the night but to do whatever one had to do right beside the tent.

Rod poured out our whiskey rations. He cut up chunks of biltong— African meat jerky—from his last few strips and added them to the sauce he stirred over the flames. Cherri sat on a slab of granite beside the cookfire and peeled sweet potatoes by headlamp to add to the sauce. Sitting next to her, I wrote notes about the day's events. Yellow sparks flew up into the black sky. The Milky Way spun a luminous array of millions of stars high overhead, and nearer the horizon shone the four bright points of the Southern Cross. The river *shush*ed over rapids. Crickets chirped.

"You know," I said to Cherri as I lay back and massaged my back against the rounded knobs of rock, "I'm sore all over, I have diarrhea, and there are lions out there, but I'm strangely content."

I wondered if this was my sense of relief that we'd negotiated the day's rapids without mishap and I'd found it in myself to say no.

Cherri laughed at my remark. I felt warmly toward her, comradely. I sat up and took another sip of whiskey, hoping it augmented the antibiotic power of the Cipro so that I wouldn't have to go out in the night. I lay back again to stare up at the remarkably intense stars. As Cherri peeled, she spoke of the reasons she loved Africa. She told me of the exhilaration she felt in being around African wildlife and mimicked for me the sounds we might hear in the night.

Lion: "A kind of huffing call to each other."

Leopard: "A sound like sawing wood."

Hyena: "A whooping. They make all sorts of weird sounds."

Cherri added, "And if you're really, really lucky, you'll hear a lion come into camp and roar. You've never heard anything like it. You think you're going to die. But whatever you do, don't panic and run out."

She described the fate of a British tourist who panicked at the lion just outside his tent and bolted out the flap straight into a pride of twelve of them.

"Bear in mind," she went on, "that if lions use this spot to drink from the river, they're probably watching us right now. The thing is to be aware but not paranoid. That's what I like about Africa. It makes you be aware."

I dutifully wrote her remarks in my notebook, but I wondered: Was this true, this sense of awareness she spoke about, or was this more of Cherri's promotional hype?

I shifted myself around on the rock slab to face the big fire. Clinton helped Steve wrestle a log into it, stirring up clouds of sparks that wafted into the black sky.

"Hey, Rod," Clinton called out. "This is a white man's fire."

"The Africans would be horrified to see this fire," Clinton explained to Steve and me, almost apologetically. "They burn just a few sticks and push them in from the end. They can't understand why we need to burn so much wood. The wood we burn tonight would probably be enough to last them two weeks."

We finished dinner and washed the dishes. Rod brought out the satellite phone again and checked messages. Steve called his home in Phoenix and left a message for his wife to tell his boss that he'd be back some days later than expected. Our progress was slow.

I didn't propose another reading from *Wild Africa.* I couldn't tell if they liked the Abyssian Bruce reading I gave the previous night. I figured I'd let it rest until someone asked. Instead, Clinton and Steve grew engaged in an animated discussion about firearms—specifically, the best caliber of rifle for Africa. I listened with one ear while trying to finish the day's notes. Clinton lovingly described a large-caliber rifle he had at home, a .478, I believe. He was sorry he couldn't bring it on this expedition, but there was too much to risk carrying it over the Mozambican border.

Gun talk, a favorite topic of Montana males back home, had always left me cold. I'd never felt the least bit covetous about guns. When I had taken up an annual deer hunt seven or eight years earlier, I'd borrowed the light-weight hunting rifle of my friend Connie, who'd tried hunting once or twice before giving it up. She had let me keep her rifle on permanent loan.

But now, for the first time ever, I felt a sudden surge of warmth toward my rifle. It was a mere peashooter compared to Clinton's big-bore rifle, but I couldn't help breaking into Clinton and Steve's conversation to boast of it.

"I have a .308," I said. "I like it, but I always think of it as a ladies' gun."

"A .308 is a very nice weapon," said Clinton authoritatively.

I was pleased he approved of it.

Everyone's exhaustion soon overtook the conversation. We said good night to one another. Clinton stoked the fire, and we crawled into our tents. I slid into my bag and felt Skyler's stuffed airplane against my bare feet. Lying there with the firelight flickering against the tent fabric, I thought of the strange affection I suddenly felt toward my rifle, toward Skyler's airplane between my feet, toward the river knife I had carefully placed beside my head. Weapons and amulets. That's what I craved—what we all seemed to crave—on the Lugenda River.

I suddenly understood their powerful attraction for people who faced the unknown—primitive people, or whatever you wanted to call them, who every day came up against forces and threats that they couldn't see coming and that they didn't understand. That's in large part what we were facing on the Lugenda. We didn't know what lay around the next bend except in the vaguest way due to Cherri's aerial reconnaissance. No one really knew, at least not anybody who could tell us—not even the fisherman we had met that morning.

It wasn't so much what these weapons and amulets—croc axes, river knives, hippo charms—could actually do for me. Rather, possessing them helped give me the confidence to go on, just as knowing I could say no had boosted my courage earlier that day. *Confianza.* I now understood why people became so attached to these objects. Through the power you imagined them to possess, they gave you confidence that you had resources in the face of danger. The red cross emblazoned on the billowing sails of the Portuguese caravels was both a weapon and an amulet.

Lying there, I realized that the satellite phone was an amulet, too. I didn't think it could actually help us much in the face of immediate danger: What were we going to do, call 911 as the lion charged? But as we left the populated region of the Lugenda and paddled into the wilds, it was nice to know it was there.

DAY FOUR

"You two especially should drink lots of water today," Clinton said to Steve and me. Under a hot morning sun, our three kayaks paddled side-by-side on a long, flat stretch of river bordered by green walls of forest. "We wouldn't want to give you a saline drip tonight. Rod and I would be fighting over who gets to put in the needle."

"And it's a big needle, too," added Rod, raising his eyebrows.

Steve and I laughed. We'd both been taking Cipro. My intestinal tract was on the mend. The previous night at the lion and hyena camp had passed without incident. I felt fresh and happy again this morning. Part of my good mood derived from managing to say no to the last rapids the previous afternoon.

But today brought another series of drops right out of camp. I remembered a saying in the newspaper business: "You're only as good as your last story." How would I do on my next story? In the rapid immediately below camp I managed to miscalculate our boat's slow swing and, at 7:30 a.m., piled Steve and myself broadside into a little grassy hummock that protruded from the rapid's head. We extracted ourselves without dumping, but I found the mistake frustrating. *What did I do wrong?*

We negotiated the next rapid well, and I felt a little better. Then the river widened and slowed. The sun shone hot by 9 a.m. That's when Clinton told us to drink plenty of water or we'd be getting the big-needle saline treatment at the evening's camp.

"Paddle close together *he-ah!*" Clinton called out on the wide, slow stretch. "Togeth-*ah* we'll look bigg-*ah* to the hippos and crocs!"

"Tupp-*ah*wa-*he!*" said Rod suddenly.

I realized he was pronouncing "Tupperware" with a South African accent.

"That's all these boats are, really. Tupp-*ahwa-he* to keep us fresh for the hippos and crocs to eat."

We laughed and paddled on.

All morning the wide, quiet stretches alternated with granite shelves that created manageable and even fun rapids. Clinton led us nimbly and surely in the fast channels between the willow islands that preceded the rapids. One big rapid he ran himself while the rest of us portaged over rock shelves. Halfway down, a powerful eddy snagged him and spun his long yellow boat like a banana spun on a table, before he extracted himself with a few sure strokes and plunged back into the main flow.

A few bends downstream we spotted a slender, deerlike creature grazing on an open bank. It raised its head, saw us, and bounded gracefully into the bush.

"Bushbuck," called out Clinton and Rod simultaneously.

A bend or two later we saw a similar but heavier animal.

"Waterbuck," they said.

A steep hillock rose from the right bank. Two or three huts stood near the top. We saw movement—two people fleeing into the forest as quickly as bushbucks.

Why should they run from us, we who had the best of intentions? *Come back! Don't you understand? We're your friends!*

As we paddled beneath the empty huts, I avoided glancing up. I didn't want anyone hidden within to think we were looking for them. I imagined the long string of Europeans who had come to Africa in the previous centuries, promising, as we did, "Don't worry. Our intentions are peaceful." And then at the first hint of tension—*kablam!*—they opened fire. Or captured them as slaves.

It wasn't just the five of us coming down the Lugenda River. In some way we carried the ghost of every white explorer, adventurer, exploiter, and, one hopes, every humanitarian also who had gone before us to Africa. We carried not only every ghost but every *rumor* of every ghost. It's no wonder they fled into the forest.

The ghost of Vasco da Gama stuck in my mind—the first European explorer anywhere near these parts. On that first voyage to India he unleashed a fusillade on the people of Mozambique—"in order to show that we were able to do them harm if we desired it," in the words of one expedition member.[11] Those words could stand as the epigram of Vasco da Gama's second voyage to East Africa and India, an expedition far more brutal than the first. Some accounts say this was because da Gama had lost the "softening" effect of his gentle brother, Paulo, who had commanded a ship on da Gama's first voyage but had died in the Azore Islands on the return to Portugal, to the great grief of Vasco.

After da Gama's first voyage, Portugal's King Manuel quickly dispatched another expedition to India, this one under the command of Pedro Álvares Cabral. Taking a long loop through the South Atlantic to make use of the favorable trade winds, Cabral landed on what would later be known as Brazil and claimed it for Portugal. Recrossing the South Atlantic, he then lost four of his thirteen ships while rounding the Cape at Africa's southern tip. One of them carried Bartolomeu Dias, who twelve years earlier had pioneered the route around the Cape and, on a headland some distance east of it, had sorrowfully left his last stone *padrão* marker there like an abandoned son.

Crossing the Indian Ocean with his reduced fleet, Cabral put a party ashore at the port of Calicut in south India. Here they built a fortified trading post but quickly quarreled with the local Muslim traders. Some accounts say the cause of the dispute was Portuguese raids on local shipping. The Muslims of Calicut and the Hindus incited by them attacked the post, killing some of the Portuguese. Cabral, his fleet still at anchor in the harbor, retaliated by bombarding the city, seizing ten boats in the harbor, and executing their crews. It was upon Cabral's return to Portugal—his few surviving ships were laden with valuable spices—that King Manuel decided to send a more powerful fleet around Africa's tip to India. His aim was to take control of the entire Indian Ocean and its trade and, as the chronicler Gaspar Correa put it, "to make war upon Calecut, and take vengeance on it, since he had more right on his side."[12]

Initially, he chose Cabral to command the fleet but then replaced him with da Gama—perhaps because of the latter's reputation for forcefulness. Da Gama warmed up to the venture by calling on various "Moorish" ports on Africa's east coast. These were actually Arab-African trading posts, usually built on islands just offshore, where the Arabic language had mixed with local Bantu languages to form Swahili. At Mozambique Island the sheikh, mindful of da Gama's first visit, sent a gift of cows, sheep, goats, and fowl to the Portuguese fleet of fifteen heavily armed ships and eight hundred men anchored off his port. On visiting the ships he offered to throw himself at da Gama's feet to ask for pardon. Da Gama accepted the sheikh's obedience "with pleasure."

Sailing up the African coast, da Gama passed the mouth of the Rovuma River (the Lugenda forms its main tributary to the south), and landed a hundred miles farther up the coast at the port of Kilwa. Da Gama summoned the local amir to his ship and requested that he pledge his friendship to the King of Portugal and, to show this friendship, give a yearly payment of gold or a rich jewel.

The Amir of Kilwa, wrote Correa in his account of the da Gama voyages, then "became very sad."

The amir replied to da Gama that being a friend was like being a brother. He would always give the Portuguese a good reception, but "to have to pay each year money or a jewel was not a mode of good friendship, because it was like tributary subjugation, and was like being a captive."

Da Gama, driving home his point to the amir, noted that within a single hour the Portuguese fleet could reduce to embers the amir's city of three- and four-story houses and burn its twelve thousand people alive. If the amir didn't believe this, he was free to go ashore immediately and da Gama would give the order.

"If I had known you intended to make me captive," replied the amir, "I would not have come, but have fled to the woods, for it is better to be a jackal at large, than a greyhound bound by a golden leash."

Becoming "very irate," da Gama then gave the order to arm the crews and burn the city. He told the amir to go hide in the woods, for da Gama had greyhounds that would find the amir and drag him by the ears to the beach. There he would lock an iron ring around the amir's neck and carry him to India in order to show the people there what happens to anybody who opposed being a "captive" of the King of Portugal.

The amir, "overcome with fear," agreed to pay pearls and bracelets worth five thousand gold *cruzados*. Da Gama also demanded that the amir build a fortress at Kilwa for the Portuguese. Then da Gama, the sails of his Portuguese fleet bearing big Christian crosses like the shields of Crusaders, sailed on to India.

In the waters near Calicut, where Cabral's fortified trading post had been attacked a few years earlier, da Gama intercepted a large Arab merchant vessel. Exacting the vengeance he had promised, he looted its cargo, locked its several hundred passengers inside—including women, children, and pilgrims who had been to Mecca—and ordered it burned. Its Muslim captain offered to ransom the ship for a rich load of spices. Da Gama's Portuguese fellow-captains asked him to accept the ransom deal, but da Gama refused.

"Gentlemen and friends," he told them, "I well see all that you say; but all those who covet the property of their enemy and not his death, err against their honour and their life; and he who spares his enemy dies at his hands (say the old women); and if you look well to reason, without bearing in mind what the Moor promises, you will go yourselves to light the fire."

The ship and its passengers burned.

Arriving at Calicut itself, da Gama was angered to see that the people had cleared the harbor of ships and boats that he might have burned. The local king offered da Gama a ransom of gold plus the delivery of the Muslims whom he alleged were responsible for the grievously mistaken attack on the Portuguese trading post. Da Gama would have none of it. Instead, he captured eight or ten trading vessels coming into Calicut that did not realize the Portuguese fleet was anchored there; ordered his men to chop off the hands, ears, and noses of their crews; and sent the body parts in a boat to the King of Calicut, telling him to make a curry of the cargo. Da Gama had the still-living handless, noseless, and earless victims bound by their feet and their teeth knocked down their throats so they couldn't untie the knots with their mouths; he had them piled in another boat, set it afire, and sent it ashore, too. When three members of one late-arriving Muslim crew pleaded that they wished to convert to Christianity before they were killed, da Gama showed them the mercy of having them baptized and strangled before they were hauled aloft and shot full of arrows like their fellow crewmen. Finally, the King of Calicut sent a large fleet against the Portuguese. Da Gama's artillery blew that to splinters, too.

Thus did a "very choleric" Vasco da Gama take control of the Indian Ocean. As he went, according to Correa, da Gama gave "to the Lord great praise and thanks for the so great favor He had shewn him."

No wonder the people we had just passed fled into the trees.

"See that shiny spot on the water?" Rod said quietly, squinting ahead on the shimmering river. "That's a hippo."

"Stay behind me," Clinton instructed, "and paddle quietly."

I nosed Steve's and my boat so close behind Clinton that our bow nearly touched his stern. We all hugged the woody left bank, trying to appear submissive. Low branches scraped over our paddles, and leaves brushed our heads. The shiny spot transformed to a thick bulge of bubbles. The hippo had submerged.

Where was it headed?

We were startled by a crashing in the bushes fifty yards across the channel on the right bank. There was a tremendous splashing sound—like a pickup truck plunging into the river. Waves rolled out from a little cove behind the bushes. Two heads surfaced about sixty or seventy feet away— *big* heads. They stared at us, eyes and nostrils and shiny wet foreheads barely above the surface.

Clinton froze. The rest of us froze.

"A mother and baby," he whispered.

They submerged again with a soft snort and a swash of water closing over their heads.

"Here they come," someone said.

We paddled quickly down the brushy bank. A moment later they resurfaced slightly downriver, eyeing us again. Their ears poked up and wiggled like giant pigs' ears. You'd say it was cute if you didn't know they could crush you and your boat instantly.

This time they kept their distance. It was our first encounter with hippos. We were as jumpy around them as the people fleeing into the forest had been around us and as the Portuguese and the Moors were with each other—everyone trying to read each other's intentions.

Relieved, we paddled on.

At the breakfast break Rod took his GPS from the orange Pelican case and locked in on those high satellites to find out how far we had paddled in the morning. I asked him also to take a reading on our elevation. I wanted to know how much in elevation the river had dropped since the put-in at the Belem bridge four days earlier. By knowing our drop in elevation I hoped to get a sense of how many rapids we'd already paddled and how many were still to come. I wanted to believe the Malawian fisherman's prediction: The rapids would end soon. So far, however, they had shown no sign of slackening.

Sitting in the sand, Rod peered at the numbers on the little screen.

"We're at 576 meters," he replied.

That meant our elevation on this sandbar was about nineteen hundred feet above sea level.

"What was the elevation of the put-in?" I asked.

Rod didn't know for sure. He hadn't taken a reading there.

"About nine hundred meters," Clinton interjected.

Rod concurred.

But I knew it was a wild guess on Clinton's part and way too high— nearly three thousand feet. No way had we dropped a thousand vertical feet in a day and a half of rapids. The crude contour lines on my big aero-nautical map showed the put-in bridge somewhere around two thousand feet and the abandoned Belem bush airstrip at twenty-one-hundred feet. The only answer I could come up with was not encouraging: In a day and a half of rapids we had barely dropped any elevation at all.

This might not be the end of the rapids at all. This day and a half might be just the beginning.

The rapids usually followed the same pattern. As we paddled along, we could viscerally feel a big underground shelf of granite rising to the earth's surface. The river quickened and braided over the shelf, following narrow channels and twisting between little granite islets, thickets of tall, willow-like grasses. It then narrowed again and tumbled in rapids over a rock ledge or down a chute of some configuration or another. Then the river would quiet and widen for a stretch until we came to another granite rise. It felt as though we were rocking over the buried ribs of a primordial African continent.

In mid-afternoon on this fourth day the channels split into rivulets that raced through a nest of willow grasses, as if working through the pores of a strainer. With a *shush*ing lurch, our boats wedged between willow grass clumps that had somehow rooted amid the rocks and grew taller than our heads. Clinton, in the lighter and shorter single kayak, disap-peared ahead in the vegetation. Rod stepped from his kayak and, wading barefoot on the jagged rock of the river bottom, biceps flexing in the hot sun, tugged his boat, which carried Cherri and her straw sun hat, through the grasses.

Steve and I both climbed from our white double. He hadn't removed his neoprene river shoes, even in sleep, since the put-in four days earlier. I was barefoot, imitating the style of Rod and Clinton, hoping my feet would toughen before they shredded. The underwater rocks were both slippery with algae and at the same time sharp-edged. We dragged our heavy boat through reeds and rivulets, stumbling, banging our shins, knees, and anklebones, and plunging to our waists in invisible holes amid the rocks.

After a few minutes I stopped. I was panting and sweating. Steve was standing waist-deep in water at the bow, tugging on it, his bare chest and back plastered with bits of grass, surrounded by thickets of tall reeds.

"Hey, Steve!" I exclaimed in wonderment. "You know that scene in *The African Queen* where Humphrey Bogart is dragging his boat with Katharine Hepburn in it through the swamp? You look exactly like him!"

"Is that supposed to make me feel better about this?" he said, giving another tug.

"Wait while I take a picture."

He patiently stood in the hole while I extracted my camera from a dry bag lashed to the deck. The moment suddenly made me self-conscious again. The photo was a reenactment of a Hollywood movie that was a reenactment of the trials of the original African explorers. Even many of the British explorers of Africa, the Mungo Parks and Hugh Clappertons who flung themselves so recklessly into the African wilds in search of the Niger, I suspect, were following a script of sorts—a script written by the Romantic era in which they lived.

On some level was it all pretend, a charade? Our expedition, the Hollywood versions, the British explorers? We shared this: We all traveled with the consciousness that somewhere there was an audience for what we were doing. Virtually every one of those British explorers kept detailed journals and frequently published them to great fanfare and considerable royalties and fame. As they slogged along, they had to be at least partly mindful of how their trials might play back home. And the Portuguese? Yes, definitely. How would their deeds play with the king? How would they play with the chroniclers, and thus with the ages? How would they play with God?

I clicked the shutter, and we waded and dragged on.

Below the *African Queen* reeds the river whisked over more shelves of granite. We sped around a bend on a fast current. There was a bridge—or kind of a bridge. It was a low strip of dilapidated concrete affixed to the granite humps that poked at intervals across the river channel by crude pilings. We'd known there was a bridge here somewhere. The maps showed a thin dotted line winding through the blank green spaces of the

Steve doing a portage.

miombo forest and crossing the river in this spot. According to Cherri's original plan, this bridge was designated our first resupply depot, which we figured to reach after four or five days. But by the time we had driven to the put-in at Belem, she realized the roads—the rutted dirt tracks, rather—of Mozambique were so poor that it would take Lance days of driving simply to reach this resupply bridge. Instead, we changed plans. Rod and Clinton jammed the kayaks with a ten-day supply of food instead of five days, in the hopes we'd have enough to reach a crude bush airstrip midway down the river that the hunting camp on the Lugenda's lower reaches sometimes used. Here, at the bush strip in the forest, we hoped we would be flown in a resupply of food. Josh the photographer would also fly in to replace Steve, who had to return to his job in Phoenix.

Now the current shoved our boats quickly toward the pilings of the bridge that was supposed to have been our original resupply point.

"If you see a ball-like thing with a button on it," Rod called out as we swept along toward it, "don't touch it!"

"Why don't you two go first!" Clinton called back to Steve and me as the bridge approached. "Just plug your ears! The only thing you have to remember is to open your mouth!"

He balanced his paddle on his front deck and demonstrated by plugging his ears with his fingers, shutting his eyes hard, and opening his mouth wide, as they do in the military to equalize the change in air pressure against the eardrums during a big artillery explosion. Steve and I laughed. This was the Clintonesque brand of humor—delivered in the face of mounting danger.

"No, after you," Steve called up to him.

Clinton picked up his paddle and cut down a fast channel between two foaming pilings, paddle blades carefully raised above the water surface to avoid any possible mines hidden around the base. It reminded me of a woman holding up her long skirt to step over a puddle. He was followed by Cherri and Rod's boat, then Steve's and mine.

Just below the bridge the river dropped over a steep ledge. We pulled over to an outcrop of rock on the left bank. We'd have to portage. A few people suddenly appeared on the bridge. Children scrambled down onto the rocks. Apparently there were villages nearby—this after we had paddled for the last day and a half through an unpopulated region of forest and rapids. Still, even at the bridge we saw no houses, no bush vehicles or trucks, nothing remotely indicating the modern world except the battered band of concrete propped on the rocks. The bridge produced an odd sense of disconnect. It was supposed to *lead* somewhere, presumably to the wider world. I had the feeling that on either end the bridge simply dispersed into a scattering of forest paths.

Below the bridge, crops protruded above the steep banks—clumps of tall green sugarcane and patches of dry, stalky corn. They had used machetes and fire to cut ragged swaths from the forest. Children ran barefoot along the banktop, screaming and waving. Bare-breasted women doing their evening washing along the shore stood up and stared. It was growing late; the light was already fading, and we had to find a camp quickly. But to camp on these shores meant being mobbed by curious villagers.

Finally, we reached a mud-and-sand islet in the middle of a wide stretch, with one hundred yards of water between us and the cleared garden patches of the shore. Spiky grass grew chest high. It wasn't much of a campsite, but it was all we had. Clinton beached his kayak, and we slid into shore beside him. We quickly laid out tents on the minuscule patch of sand, trying not to pitch them in water or mud.

"Here they come," someone said.

We looked up from our work. Gliding downriver on the glassy evening current were five bark canoes, bark-bladed paddles digging the water. They beached beside our boats. Village men and boys climbed out, dressed in the same ragged T-shirts that all the males along the Lugenda seemed to wear.

We shook hands all around.

"*Bom dia,*" we said.

"*Bom dia,*" they replied.

Rod and Clinton, apparently deciding the villagers posed no serious threat, went off to build a fire and set up the camp kitchen. The villagers stood and simply watched us. Cherri told them in Spanish that we were going to the Rovuma River.

"Rovuma," they repeated, understanding.

"How many days to the Rovuma?" I asked in Portuguese.

They didn't know.

"*Muito?*" I asked, raising my eyebrows in mock surprise to make a kind of joke out of it. *Much?*

"*Muito, muito, muito!*" said one young man, laughing.

Now Cherri and Steve moved off, too. I alone remained, once again host to our visitors. I didn't mind my role partly because it seemed rude, at least to me, simply to ignore the people whose lands we were passing through. Besides, I hoped to learn more about them.

I asked what people they were.

"*Makua,*" they replied. Makua is a large tribe in northern Mozambique that includes many subtribes.

I walked to their canoes and admired them. They were indeed works of craftsmanship—like a giant folded leaf formed of a single huge strip of bark, stitched together at bow and stern to close the ends like a drawstring bag. The makers kept the canoe's shape by jamming in carved thwarts to separate the two sides of the hull and lashing the thwarts to the gunnels. Paddles were simply a long stick with a slip of bark stitched to each end using cording made of root fibers.

The men in turn went to our kayaks, bent over, and studied the brightly colored hulls.

"*Ferro?*" one of them asked. *Iron?*

"*Plástico,*" I said.

I reached down inside the cockpit and pushed my hands on the rudder pedals. As I manipulated the pedals, the upraised rudder on the stern waved back and forth, like some strange animal tail. They pointed at its wagging and began laughing hysterically, as if they couldn't believe a boat would have anything so silly as this.

"*Curva!*" one of the older men shouted, moving his hand in a curving motion.

"*Sim, sim!*" I replied. *Yes! Yes!*

They marveled at it. I think they found it both clever and ridiculous at the same time, a frivolous and complicated way to perform a very simple task. *All the effort and good metal that went into making this thing? Why can't they just steer their canoe with a paddle like everyone else?*

Clinton showed up.

"Tell them we need more firewood," he said to me.

I told the older man in Portuguese. He stopped laughing, and as if this is what one expected from a white man, an order, he wearily and sadly, it seemed to me, picked up his machete from his canoe and set off toward the tall grass. I went to help him find wood.

"Stay here," said Clinton. "He's fine on his own."

I didn't like this feeling of ordering the African tribal people to help us out, but I got the sense that this chain of command was expected on everyone's part, black and white alike. Here in our camp the ghost of Vasco da Gama and all who followed hovered again. Exactly five hundred years earlier virtually to the day, in June 1502, and some three hundred miles to the east of our islet in the Lugenda River, da Gama claimed that first European possession in East Africa when the sheikh of Mozambique Island offered to throw himself at da Gama's feet.

"We have to stop talking to them, or they'll be here all night," Clinton said to me. "Tell them to leave."

I went to my tent to change out of my wet clothes while the man was away getting firewood. I didn't like the tone of this encounter, directed by Clinton. As I changed, I brooded over how I could diplomatically phrase the request to leave.

When I emerged from the tent a few minutes later, Clinton, obviously impatient with me, had already made the message clear to the men and boys. The older man emerged from the tall grass with a few chunks of driftwood that he'd chopped with his machete. He dropped them beside Rod's fire and got into his canoe. As they all quietly disappeared up the twilit river, I was half angry at Clinton for his attitude and half grateful to him that we once again had our camp to ourselves. The ghost of Vasco da Gama haunted me, too. I wanted to be here, but I wanted to be here on my terms.

The stars shone radiantly above our island camp. Sitting in the middle of the river, we could scan the entire expanse of sky with its thick concentration of stars. No lights shone anywhere on the earth around us but for the flickering of our fire. The sand muted our voices, rendering them soft and small. I knew I was staring lengthwise along the star-dense, platelike disk of our home galaxy. Instead of insignificant, instead of dwarfed, the Milky Way galaxy tonight made me feel at home. It was the strangeness and vastness and darkness of the African surroundings that dwarfed me.

We heard a heavy splashing and snorting.

"Hippo," said Clinton and Rod.

It plied upstream, snorting and churning like a tugboat passing in the night. We finished our dinner of tinned ham in a curry sauce spooned over rice. Cherri, Steve, and I, in return for Rod and Clinton's cooking, had taken to washing all the dinner dishes, scanning the river with headlamps for red eyes while we scrubbed with sand.

When we carried the wet dishes back to camp, Clinton had already climbed into his sleeping bag. Instead of a tent he and Rod had erected a simple makeshift shelter of their tent's rainfly propped on paddles jammed in the sand, next to the fire.

"Don't we get a bedtime story tonight?" Clinton said from inside his bag.

"Sure, if you want one," I said, pleased that he'd asked.

I went to my tent, pulled *Wild Africa* from the small green dry bag that held my blank notebooks, and sat down in the cool, powdery sand near the fire, turning my headlamp on the book. I flipped to the second entry in the volume. It was the excerpt from Mungo Park's account of his first trip to the Niger when he almost had to spend a rainy night in the tree branches, out of reach of wild animals. It moved me that Park was so moved when the kind woman took him into her house and the female spinners composed a song about the poor white man.

The others seemed to like the story, but we were all so tired. No one was ready for an in-depth discussion.

"Good night," Clinton said and turned over in his bag.

We all went off, murmuring our good nights. I was so tired I could hardly write notes in my tent except for the briefest outline of the day. I wanted to reflect on where we were, really think about Africa, about wilderness, about exploration, and have insights into why this place, this expedition, was important to me personally and important to some larger good.

Instead of thinking, I fell asleep.

DAY FIVE

A cool, gray dawn. We folded tents and jammed dry bags into cargo holds. We noticed a bark canoe swerving downriver toward us from the opposite shore. We kept packing. It beached on our little island. A family climbed out of it: a spindly thin father, two daughters around ten or twelve years old, and three sons. The father wore a battered and muddy Burberry-style raincoat that must have found its way into the African bush from some Western charity. It looked as if it served as his ceremonial garb. The middle son wore a T-shirt that hung in ragged strips as if he'd run through a giant thorn bush. The girls were stunning. Graceful and slight-featured, with large eyes and silver hoop earrings, the younger one wore a flowered sarong and the older one a brilliant white and blue shawl that glowed against her rich skin.

Standing quietly back, the family watched us pack. All of them—the father, too—possessed a kind of child's softness and attentiveness. I was glad that Clinton didn't shoo them away as he had the men in the bark canoes the previous evening.

"Here," Cherri said to the girls, "I have something for you."

From a small bag she pulled a beaded necklace and held it up to the first girl in a gesture of giving. The girl looked excitedly at her father, who quietly nodded his permission. Cherri knelt in the sand before the girl, reached both ends of the necklace around her slender neck, and clasped it gently. The girl stood with the stillness that attends a solemn ritual.

When Cherri did the same for the other girl, she, too, stood with great gravity as if undergoing a ceremony whose weighty import she could only guess. Steve dug into his clothing bag and pulled out a spare T-shirt. He handed it to the boy with the shredded T-shirt. The boy received it grate-

Cherri presenting necklaces to two girls.

fully with both hands. The father took a step forward, clasped his hands together, and gave Cherri and Steve a little bow of thanks.

I was touched—by the father's gracefulness, by the gentle solemnity of the children, and by Cherri's and Steve's thoughtfulness.

The family stood on shore and watched silently as we climbed into the boats and pushed off.

"The people here are very contained," Cherri said as we paddled out into the river. "They'll probably go home with the gifts and celebrate wildly."

We paddled downstream, leaving the patch of fields behind. Soon the forest grew thickly on both banks again.

"It's as though they don't want to show their feelings," Cherri elaborated. "It's as though they've been through a lot of war."

Could the civil war have reached this little node of villages deep in the forest? I wondered. It seemed improbable. But I was constantly surprised by how much contact even "remotest" Africa had experienced with the outside world. It was as if we in the West, we of European descent, believed that Africa was a static, self-contained continent, like some giant jar with a sealed lid, until we "discovered" it and pried it open to the larger world—as if we held a monopoly on what we call "exploration."

Arab dhows plying the Indian Ocean had "explored" Africa's east coast centuries before the Portuguese caravels. So had Chinese maritime expeditions visited East Africa decades before the Portuguese. But Western historians dismiss the Chinese navigations as not amounting to true "exploration."

For much of its twenty-five-hundred-year history, the Chinese empire focused inward. Its people knew it as the "Middle Kingdom" or "All That Is Under Heaven." In other words, not much of consequence existed beyond its borders. It regarded anything beyond the two-thousand-mile-long barrier of its Great Wall as "wild lands" inhabited by "wild people," barbarians, who had nothing but trouble to offer "superior" Chinese civilization. The old Chinese stories that speak of the great maritime expeditions don't describe them as a geographical exploration but as a gigantic sheriff's posse. This was dispatched to hunt down a deposed heir to the Ming throne who was supposedly holed up on a South Seas island disguised as a Buddhist monk.

In this Eastern version of a Western film, the sheriff is played by a Muslim eunuch by the name of Cheng Ho. Born in Yunnan Province, the last bastion of Mongol rule in the late fourteenth century before all China fell to the new Ming Dynasty, Cheng Ho was captured at age ten by the invading Ming armies. Castrated and taken into the Ming ranks, he eventually rose to become loyal head eunuch to the Prince of Wen, son of the first Ming emperor. But the first Ming emperor, nearing death in the late 1390s and needing to appoint his dynastic successor, skipped over the Prince of Wen and his other sons as too ambitious for the throne. Instead, he chose his grandson as the next emperor.

Predictably, the Prince of Wen, who was indeed ambitious, soon pushed his young nephew off the throne and seized it for himself, becoming known as the Yung Lo emperor. The deposed nephew escaped his uncle's clutches by dressing as a Buddhist monk and slipping away to what was rumored to be a succession of monasteries in the islands of Southeast Asia. The Yung Lo emperor, so the old stories tell, then dispatched his trusted eunuch, Cheng Ho, to capture the escapee in order to secure the Yung Lo emperor's hold on the throne.

The first expedition embarked in 1405 from "Treasure-Ship Yard" on the Yangtze River. Even by modern standards its size was staggering, judging by accounts of eyewitnesses. The fleet carried 27,800 men, from grand eunuchs to captains to secretaries, from helmsmen to interpreters to business agents, doctors, caulkers, iron-anchor mechanics, and many more.[13] The largest of the fleet's 317 vessels belonged to a Chinese maritime class known as treasure ships. Bearing names like *Pure Harmony* and *Peaceful Crossing,* these behemoths measured 440 feet in length, making them longer than the largest sailing ship ever built in the West.[14]

The first, second, and third expeditions touched the coasts of today's Vietnam, Indonesia, and India, places where Cheng Ho established relations, accepting tribute gifts for the Ming emperor as well as giving gifts from China. Historians say the real motive for the expeditions was less to round up the runaway nephew than to extend Ming power over the maritime states of Southeast Asia. Hostile rulers such as the King of Ceylon were captured and taken to China.

Cheng Ho's fourth expedition sailed seven thousand miles from China to the Middle East, to the great trading port of Hormuz on the Persian Gulf. The fifth, sixth, and seventh visited these earlier coasts plus trading ports on Africa's east coast. They brought back ambassadors from the foreign lands plus lions, ostriches, zebras, and giraffes as tribute for the Son of Heaven. The giraffe in particular was an animal that fascinated the Chinese, who regarded it as an incarnation of a mythical beast and an auspicious cosmic omen. These latter expeditions—the last sailed in the early 1430s—may have ventured as far south on the East African coast as Mozambique Island, which historians believe they can identify on ancient Chinese maps. Certainly, Chinese ships reached as far as Malindi, an ancient port in today's Kenya where they went to find more giraffes. This was some sixty-five years before Vasco da Gama's Portuguese caravels came scudding around Africa's southern tip and, seeking gold and a sea route to the East, planted the Portuguese flag on Mozambique Island and Malindi.

The Ming Dynasty's maritime expeditions suddenly ceased in 1433. It was as if the Chinese empire had satisfied its curiosity about what lay beyond its borders and turned inward again, secure in its conceit that it was the vastly superior civilization. Within a few years the emperor, pushed by his inward-looking mandarin bureaucrats who thought the ventures far too costly, and wanting to keep their tight control over the empire, decreed it illegal for Chinese even to travel overseas, and eventually it became a crime to build seagoing junks. Ma Ching wrote in his 1444 foreword to Ma Huan's chronicle of the Cheng Ho expeditions, *The Overall Survey of the Ocean's Shores:*

> Nothing is left unrecorded; because it was this gentleman's intention, his whole wish, to make people of the future, for a thousand years hereafter, realize that the way of our country is in harmony with nature and that we have achieved this measure of success in civilizing the barbarians of the south and east.

"Compra carne?" someone shouted to us in pidgin Portuguese from the dense trees on river right. *Buy meat?*

We couldn't see his face. We had left the villages and clearings behind and had entered forest again. He remained hidden behind leaves.

"Ha carne?" I called out toward the foliage. *Do you have meat?*

"Sim, sim, sim," said the voice from the forest.

"Que tipo?" Cherri called out. *What type?*

We paddled a few strokes toward shore. The man stepped forward. There was another man with him. They were hunters or poachers. Together they held up a long red slab of meat.

"Impala," said the first man.

Clinton and Rod looked at each other, then shook their heads to each other—whether because they didn't want the meat or didn't want to get too close to the potentially armed men, I didn't know. Rod was very security conscious. But I wished we'd bought the dripping red impala. I was hungry for something more than a mug of oatmeal and a plate of pasta each day.

The hunters silently watched us drift past. Resting from paddling, we floated in a kayak cluster.

"Why buy it?" Clinton said suddenly. "Just take it."

He was joking. Still, it sounded malicious. I brooded again whether I should speak up or hold my tongue.

Cherri read my mind as we drifted along the forested shore.

"Clinton," she said, "your generation is supposed to be so enlightened. What happened to you?"

"I don't know," Clinton replied, holding his paddle across the deck and seeming genuinely puzzled by the question. "Family history, I guess."

At first I didn't know quite what he meant, but as I thought about it, I realized how Rhodesia, where Clinton was born, had been a stable, prosperous, though white-ruled country until not long ago. Now, as Zimbabwe, under the increasingly severe dictatorship of Robert Mugabe, the economy was in a free fall, and armed gangs of blacks seized prosperous white-owned farms that were presented in turn to Mugabe's loyal cronies. Clinton had relatives caught in the mess. His remark, "Why buy it? Just take it," would have a certain resonance to a white Zimbabwean.

"Pe-*tah*," Rod said to me as we pushed side-by-side down a flat, straight stretch. "Do you know why they call the AK-47 the 'African credit card'?"

"No," I said. "Why?"

"Because it works everywhere . . . and you don't even have to sign."

I laughed, but it was one of those jokes whose humor springs from an underlying sadness. Even as we spoke, the AK-47 was being used as a credit card in Zimbabwe and in countries up and down the continent. Mozambique, after a negotiated peace a decade earlier following seventeen years of civil war, remained one of the few places in Africa where the AK-47 had lost much of its currency.

Steve and I were hitting the rapids well, working as a team—at least I thought so. I called out "paddle right!" and "paddle left!" and he responded. I could now better judge the lazy swing of our heavy boat. Drop after drop we plunged along, down small fast channels, through willows and rocks, then a big frothing S-curve in a granite chute, and then more medium-sized drops.

Clinton issued a kind of mantra whenever our little group neared a rapid. "Life jackets on, splash skirts on, rud-*dahs* loosened, follow me!"

Steve wrestled with his spray skirt, struggling to fit its elasticized hem over the cockpit cowling. Finally, he left it on almost all the time despite the fact that it tended to make the cockpit feel hot, humid, and airless on your enclosed lower body.

"Remind me to give you two a lesson tomorrow morning in how to put on a spray skirt," Clinton said to us, paddling past.

This remark wounded my pride. Putting on a spray skirt was just about the first thing you learned in kayaking. I thought I was past that. But, in truth, I'd been having some trouble putting on my spray skirt, too.

A light rain began to fall. I felt chilled and pulled out my rain jacket.

Rod and Clinton remained bare-chested. We portaged a rapid, wading chest-deep over underwater fins of rock, banging shins, scraping bare feet, and then lowered the boats over a ledge. We stopped for breakfast on a sandbar below the portage. Not the faintest signs of humans here. Rain pocked river and sand. Rod assembled his fishing gear. With ten casts of a spinner into a deep, eddying pool he hooked a fat catfishlike barbel. The rod bent deeply. The fish whiskers twitched as he dragged it onto the wet sand. It must have weighed a good five pounds; it was the same type of fish that created the soft *plashes* in the river at night, he told me. He lashed it to the rear deck of his kayak, head pointing back, like some kind of sub-aquatic gargoyle.

We stroked rhythmically down a wide stretch. The rain had stopped. Downstream, the river shone like a silvery mirror reflecting gray sky and green forest.

Four or five hippos swam out from the right bank, their grunts and heavy splashes faint and delayed by distance, their rippled wakes splitting the silvery green mirror.

"Okay," said Clinton, squinting downstream, "let's stick to the right bank *he-ah!*"

We made it past the hippos. The tension eased, and the river remained flat ahead. I brooded about exploration. Why didn't Western historians consider China's expeditions to Africa true exploration?

Wrote one British historian: "The great expeditions were not followed up but remained isolated *tours de force,* mere exploits."[15]

"Fully equipped with the technology, the intelligence, and the national resources to become discoverers," writes an American historian of exploration, "the Chinese doomed themselves to be the discovered."[16]

But if these were "mere exploits," with nearly thirty thousand men, navigators, chroniclers, mapmakers, and all the rest, what constituted exploration? What did it mean to follow up on the discoveries? Establishing trading outposts in the new lands? Planting the flag? *Colonizing* them? Colonization, it would seem, was one definition of exploration and discovery in the European mind.

"Is what we're doing exploration?" I asked Clinton as we paddled a flat stretch.

"I'd say it is," he replied. "I'm sure that no white man has ever been down this entire river before."

"How can you be sure?"

"There's no reason for it."

He had a point. The Lugenda River was a very difficult way to get from point A to point B. So then why were we doing it?

The river tumbled over another fractured hump of granite. We dragged the boats through shallow, mossy side channels fissured in the rock, toward a small beach of sand that lay at the rapid's foot. The beach looked nice, and beyond lay only dense forest and mud banks. Although it was still early—3:30 p.m. or so—Clinton and Rod announced we'd camp here. We made decent distance today, they said, and needed a chance to dry our rain-soaked gear.

Completing the final bit of portage, Clinton slid his kayak back into the swift-moving main river when the boat suddenly rolled over in his hands.

"My splash skirt!" he cried out.

He had left his spray skirt lying loosely on the deck. As the kayak rolled, the skirt tumbled into the swirling current.

He ran down the shore watching for it to reappear. Nothing.

No one had to say anything. All of us knew this was a problem. Without the skirt, rapids could swamp his cockpit. How big a problem depended on how many rapids—and how large they were—between this spot and the Lugenda's mouth five hundred river kilometers downstream.

We finished portaging, pulled up to the beach, and unloaded the kayaks. Rod strung up a line to dry our clothes and then went to work cleaning and filleting the barbel to fry for our dinner. Clinton, busy kindling the cookfire, asked me to take a quick look downstream for his lost skirt.

I walked across the little sandbar and then along the muddy shore, heading downstream. The forest enveloped the riverbank. Branches hung low, and vines draped from trees. The gray-green shadows within lay silent. It felt like no other humans had ever set foot here. As I left our little sandbar, I crossed leopard tracks. Hippo tracks lay everywhere—first in a kind of highway across our patch of sand and then, as I moved farther from camp, fresh tracks pressed deep into the riverbank mud like a dinosaur's imprint.

After a while I stopped. No spray skirt. The river swirled past the bank under the drooping branches. I was alone. I heard something in the forest. Was that a hippo in the thick trees on my left?

I looked. My eyes, never keen, seemed unable to distinguish shapes in the gray-green, vine-hung forest.

I listened. My left ear felt blocked.

I sniffed. Only my nose remained clear. I detected an organic, musky odor, as if big animals were about.

I suddenly understood Cherri's comment about how Africa "makes you be aware." I'd never been so cognizant of the power and dullness of my senses. This is how animals lived, I realized: sniffing, looking around, stopping to listen. It came home to me in a way that it never had before that I was an animal. I belonged to this animal world. I was both a member of this world of animals and yet set apart from it. My senses—my dull eyes, my blocked ear, my slow run—weren't nearly sharp enough to compete on an equal basis with the animal world. The human senses, even in their prime—which mine decidedly were not—weren't sharp enough.

The sound in the forest again. If something large suddenly charged out, say a hippo, could I climb a tree? I looked around. I could grab one of the drooping limbs, but could I pull myself high enough, fast enough?

I took another glance down the shoreline for the missing skirt. I turned back, heading upriver toward camp, listening, watching. I felt humbled, physically frail, against the immense power of the forest. I had no weapon other than my puny river knife, although in theory I possessed the ability to make a more powerful weapon. What I did have that both set me apart as well as allowed me to compete with the animal world was brain capacity—an ability to make decisions in order to outwit animal threats, an ability to *think* rather than *smell* to locate food. Plus, I was able to flee or climb, however slowly.

I was far, far past my physical prime for this animal world. I now understood that, too, in a way I never had before. If I were an African hunter-gatherer, I'd be washed up at age forty-eight—an elder relegated to a place near the fire, relying on others to bring me food, relying on youth like Rod and Clinton. Or I'd be like an old elephant—my multiple sets of teeth finally ground away, wandering off alone to an imminent death.

Was this why we were here, so that we—so that I—could learn this?

DAY SIX

The day was tense from the start. Clinton thought I tarried while we prepared to leave our sandbar camp. He paddled away while Steve and I
scrambled on the beach still stowing our gear and I finished readying the
camera for the day. Rod and Cherri paddled away right behind him. By
the time Steve and I jumped into our boat, they had nearly disappeared
down the sun-shimmered river. I put on my sunglasses and squinted
downstream directly into the rising sun to spot them. Steve paddled hard.
I still hadn't applied sunscreen and insect lotion—pre-river rituals for us
all though the insects were few. I steered with the rudder pedals while
hastily smearing my body with creams, feeling like some aging diva
shoved unwillingly into the African jungle. I accidentally splattered a few
fat white drops of sun lotion on my sunglasses. I wiped the lenses with
thumb and forefinger. It smeared. I snatched the glasses from my nose,
tossed them into my lap, and grabbed my paddle. A searing gold light
bounced from the river into my eyes.

"I can't see a goddamned thing!" I called out to Steve. "Where are
they?"

"I think they're headed into that channel," he called back, pointing his
paddle far downstream to river right.

We dug in our paddles. The river braided through willow islands—the
warning sign of rapids. Squinting into the glare, I spotted the small black
silhouettes of the two boats disappearing down the side channel. I steered
toward it. Suddenly, we were in the swift side channel, tree branches
whapping against boat and paddles. The sun blinded me again. We
lurched into a rock, then another rock. I sensed a rapid coming but
couldn't see it. I was in a frenzy of unreadiness, but I didn't want to stop

and lose the others. I grabbed my sunglasses and shoved them back on my face. I saw a panorama of SPF-30 cream.

"Can you see rapids ahead?" I shouted to Steve.

"There they are!" Steve shouted back.

He jabbed his paddle at the right bank where they had beached the two kayaks. The three of them walked along a woody isle, scouting rapids ahead.

I steered our boat to shore, and we hopped out. I was angry with Clinton for leaving us, for our having to scramble so, for our not being properly ready for the river. *If he gives me any shit about being slow,* I thought, *or hassles us about how we're "Team Daisy," I'm going to throw it right back at him and say something about losing his spray skirt.*

But he didn't say anything except "We can't get through here."

I climbed back into my cockpit, and Clinton started to climb into his, which was minus the lost spray skirt.

"Hey, Clinton," I called out, still angry. "I thought you said you were going to give us a lesson this morning in how to put on a spray skirt."

"Fuck off," he muttered, or so it sounded.

"That's a vicious joke!" Cherri said to me.

I apologized for my remark. Was it because I didn't want to sound like I was whining that I didn't simply speak up and ask them to wait for us? Clinton ignored our little contretemps. He patiently leaned over the cockpit of Steve's and my boat and showed us how to fasten the spray skirts properly. I'd forgotten that you lean back hard to pin the skirt's back while attaching the front. It was easy.

"You have a really good river instinct," I said to Clinton an hour later as we drifted alongside a grassy bank after stopping for a quick pee break. "You know how to find the best channels."

"Really?" said Clinton as if he didn't quite believe me.

"I really mean it," I said.

"It's just luck," he said modestly.

"No, it's not. It's good river instinct."

"Wait till I lead you wrong," he said.

"Then we'll blame *you*!" I laughed, aiming my finger at him. I grew serious again. "But you've led us through so much already that you have a lot of latitude for mistakes."

I was feeling apologetic for my "vicious" remark. I didn't want any bad blood between us. I wanted Clinton to understand that I wasn't questioning him, that, in fact, I trusted his judgment on the river. At least I was pretty sure I did.

He seemed pleased. I didn't know just how he viewed me. As an authority figure twenty years his senior? As a semicompetent client? As an equal teammate? As a problem? But I knew he was aware that I was also the expedition's writer—the wri-*tah*. I represented the audience, and the audience's approval, I think, counted for quite a lot with Clinton and Rod. It counted with Cherri, too, of course, although she had stepped back somewhat from direct decisions on the river—her order-giving had mercifully ended—and followed Clinton and Rod's lead, paddling gamely along in Rod's bow. Still, this issue of self-image—all of ours—seemed to float down the river with us like a phantom kayak. Except for Steve. I don't think Steve really cared much about his river image. His attitude was more "I don't know what I'm doing, so you have to tell me."

We drifted a few minutes more. The problem with dropping compliments to guides, I'd found in previous excursions, is that flattery sometimes puts on the pressure and makes them think they have a hero's role to step into.

Clinton picked up his paddle again.

"Breakfast in an hour and a half," he called out to us, deadpan.

"But that's an hour and a half away," I pleaded.

"We must carry on!" called out Clinton in the cadence of Empire-on-the-march. "We have a riv-*ah* to con-*quah*!"

The most interesting African explorers to me were not those who sought to "conquer" a river or a land or anything else in the name of Empire but those compelled by something more personal, something inner. Like Ibn Battuta—if you can call him merely an "African explorer." Famous as a traveler in the Muslim world of the 1300s, it is estimated that Ibn Battuta covered some seventy-five thousand miles in his thirty years abroad—farther than any other known medieval traveler including Marco Polo. It seems that an almost mystical urge drove him to "travel through the earth," as he wrote in his *Travels,* and "never, so far as possible, to cover a second time any road."[17]

Born in Tangier in today's Morocco to a prominent family of Muslim *qadis* (judges), Ibn Battuta first took to the road as an educated twenty-two-year-old pilgrim headed for Mecca and the great Muslim centers of learning in the Middle East such as Cairo and Damascus.

> I set out alone, having neither fellow-traveler in whose companionship I might find cheer, nor caravan whose party I might join, but swayed by an overmastering impulse within me and a desire long-cherished in my bosom to visit these illustrious sanctuaries. So I braced my resolution to quit all my dear ones, female and male, and forsook my home as birds forsake their nests.

By the time Ibn Battuta reached Tunis, a thousand miles east of his home, he was struck by a familiar traveler's lament. He had joined a caravan of merchants traveling on asses and had been taken with such a case of fever that he'd had to tie himself into the saddle with a turban as the party pushed hard, riding day and night, through bandit territory. Finally, they reached the haven of Tunis town. Townsfolk rushed out to greet the other members of the party, one of whom was the son of a famous *qadi*, but to young Ibn Battuta no one said a word.

> I felt so sad at heart on account of my loneliness that I could not restrain the tears that started to my eyes, and wept bitterly. One of the pilgrims, realizing the cause of my distress, came up to me with a greeting and friendly welcome, and continued to comfort me with friendly talk until I entered the city, where I lodged in the college of the Booksellers.

By the time he reached Tripoli, another four hundred miles or so east, Ibn Battuta had taken a wife. "I set my tent up over her," as he expressed it in the traditional Bedouin phrasing. But by Alexandria he had quarreled with her father, separated from her, and had remarried.

All this occurred within the first ten months of Ibn Battuta's life on the road as he made his way across North Africa. What turned him from an ordinary pilgrim to Mecca into a full-time traveler—one of the first professional adventurers, really—forms a tantalizing mystery that lies between the lines of his four-volume *Travels*.

I like to think that Ibn Battuta saw himself as a spiritual traveler in many senses, not simply as a pilgrim to Mecca. His physical journey along the road equated to a spiritual journey of the soul. He had a deep interest in Sufism, that offshoot of Islam which encouraged warmth and humanity among its adherents and whose ultimate goal was a merging with God. The Sufi adherent was a traveler who followed a way—*tariqa*—guided by a spiritual master. The path led away from the self: "the deliverance from self by the alchemy of divine love."

"Any *qibla* [direction] is better than self-worship," wrote the great fourteenth-century Sufi poet Hafiz.[18]

There were no more villages. The river grew rambunctious, opening into sun and sandy patches, closing into forest, braiding, twisting, dumping over riffles and rocks. It felt as if we were now truly alone. No other world existed but our boats. We spotted more bushbuck and waterbuck bounding on the banks, and new birds: a martial eagle, a huge, gray goliath heron beating downriver ahead of us with its long wingtips flapping nearly to the water's surface. A formation of slender black-and-white birds flying in perfect unison swooped over a wide stretch of smooth river, wheeling with graceful joyousness and at times slicing their beaks through the water.

"African skimmers!" called out Clinton and Rod.

"Those are some of the coolest birds I've ever seen!" I exclaimed.

They barrel-rolled downriver, reminding me of terns with their long pointed wings as they flew just over the surface, opening their long, razor-like lower beaks to furrow through the water and skim up tiny fish.

A spiky palm poked above the forest on river right. Near it stood an enormous tree with a thick whitish trunk that we guessed might be a mahogany. I wondered if this change in vegetation signaled that the river had dropped to a lower, warmer elevation. Or was this my wishful thinking? The lower we dropped, the fewer the rapids that lay between us and the Lugenda's mouth.

"My binoculars! My binoculars!" Cherri screamed at Steve as the finely crafted Swarovskis bobbed downstream in the fast riffles of a braiding channel. "Go get my binoculars!"

Rod hadn't worn his spray skirt in some small rapids, and waves had washed into his cockpit, flooding it. He had then aimed their boat at an island clump of willows midstream to beach it and bail. The bow of the kayak flew high in the air with the impact, as if they had struck an iceberg, and Cherri's binos, which she had bungeed to the foredeck for easy access when she wanted to spot wildlife this morning, popped into the river.

Under Cherri's storm of noise, Steve and I piled our boat onto the island shore just below them, hopped out, dragged the kayak into the channel where the binoculars had disappeared, hopped in, and sprinted downstream. Cherri was still yelling at us. It was as if it was *our* fault that she'd left her binoculars in a precarious place and lost them in the river.

Around the first bend of the channel we encountered Clinton, gripping a tree branch to hold himself against the swift current, quizzically watching us rushing toward him.

"What's going on?" he called out.

"Have you seen Cherri's binoculars?" I shouted breathlessly.

"Cherri's pretty upset," added Steve as we pulled beside him.

"She's saying they cost her nine hundred dollars," I said.

"That's her problem," Clinton said with a dismissive shake of the head. "Cherri has to be responsible for her own shit."

He didn't budge from the branch to look for the binos. We held on, too. Clinton and I consoled Steve that this was the lot of a younger brother to an older sister, a position I well knew and I believe Clinton may have, too. As we waited for Rod and Cherri, Clinton told of guiding a tourist canoe trip on the lower Zambezi and the Frenchwoman who had dropped $5,000 worth of camera gear into the croc-infested river. She demanded of Clinton that he dive down and recover it.

"I'm not diving down there," he'd told her, relishing the memory of this easy trump of wilderness over civilization. "If you want it, you can swim for it yourself."

The Frenchwoman's camera gear remained on the bottom of the river, and so did Cherri's binoculars.

Steve and I tipped over slowly at first, then fast.

We had all been getting casual about rapids. Clinton didn't bother to step from his boat to scout this one. He simply stood up in the kayak and peered over the low hump of granite that partially blocked the river.

"It's a long chute that makes an S," he called back to us, drifting in slack water just upstream. "Start on the left, then angle right.

"Okay, life jackets on! . . . Splash skirts on! . . . Rud-*dahs* loosened! . . . Follow close behind me!"

The first part was fun, like a summer whitewater outing. Trailing Clinton's yellow stern, Steve and I rushed between the low granite walls and pillowed over sparkling standing waves. The current accelerated; wind rushed against our faces. Clinton's boat pulled ahead. A granite tongue protruded from the left bank, and the river ricocheted off it like the banked turn of an auto racetrack. We whipped around it. Suddenly we were face-to-face with Clinton—his boat pointing *upriver* at us.

What was going on here? Was he warning us to stop? Then I realized a massive whirlpool had caught his boat. But it was too late. Steve and I were caught in the whirlpool, too.

Its powerful eddy line—the juncture between two currents running in opposite directions—snagged our hull. Before I could lay a paddle blade flat in the water to brace us upright, the eddy line flipped our careening, overweighted kayak as easily as someone sticking out a foot to trip a top-heavy runner.

Oh, shit! I thought. *Here we go! Take a breath!*

I watched from behind as Steve's bare arms and life-jacketed torso toppled over into the river like the statue of some overthrown dictator, knowing my torso was doing the same.

Splash! Blue sky and sunlight merged into bubbling green water. I hung upside down underwater from the kayak cockpit.

How hard is it to get out of this boat? Will the spray skirt release?

I pulled the loop that released it. The skirt let go from the hull. I rolled forward underwater, extracting my legs from the cockpit. Whirlpool currents grabbed my limbs and torso, buffeting me. I sensed myself being pulled down. The water deepened from frothy green to dark green, to darker still. Now it was quiet. I paused, trying to collect myself. *Where am I? Way down? I must be out of the whirlpool by now.*

I started to swim upward. The dark water slowly turned from dark green to light green. My head suddenly broke into blue sky and sunshine. I gulped the cool air that brushed my face. I looked around. I was treading water in a pool at the rapid's foot. The white hull lay beside me, overturned. I grabbed it and quickly flipped it back over.

Where's Steve?

A head plastered with wet dark hair popped up nearby. Steve's water bottle bobbed past. I started swimming the boat toward shore. The trees looked fuzzy. *I must have lost a contact lens underwater.* I blinked, treading water, looking around, testing my vision. I saw we were in a big, deep, quiet pool.

Crocs?

I kicked my legs wildly to heft my torso onto the swamped hull. It simply rolled over again, as it had with Clinton and Rod's attempts, and I spilled back into the pool.

"Don't panic, it's okay!" shouted Clinton from his kayak near the riverbank. "Swim the boat to shore."

I calmed down. I kept swimming the boat in, now trying not to kick too hard and attract underwater attention. Clinton held a throw rope ready, presumably in case a croc should seize Steve or me and drag us under in order to execute on our bodies its "kill spin."

We reached shore and clambered onto a rock shelf. Steve and I rocked the boat, each at one end, back and forth to dump cascades of water from the cockpits. We joked about our mishap, trying to make light of it.

"More sacrifices to the river gods," said Clinton of Steve's lost water bottle and my contact lens.

It was our baptism in the Lugenda. It hadn't been so bad after all. Still, I wasn't eager to do it again.

"Come here!" Clinton was screaming upstream at us as Steve and I came tearing around a bend in a fast, narrow channel through the forest. "Come right fucking *here!*"

He was standing barefoot atop a big boulder midstream and shouting and wildly jamming his finger at his feet. For some reason he wanted us to stop right there and nowhere else.

A few minutes earlier, we had traversed an odd piece of geology. The river's main channel angled swiftly left through dense forest while fast little side channels split off to the right like branch lines from a main cable, and disappeared into the woods as if the river were being drained away. It felt as if we were paddling along the brow of a wooded hill that dropped away to the right.

We followed Clinton, weaving left, left, left as he felt his way for the clearest channel. Suddenly, the largest channel swung hard right and funneled down fast and narrow. It rushed us twisting through dense forest. Cherri and Rod's boat tangled up in low-hanging branches. Steve and I bumped against them but kept going, trying to keep up with Clinton's yellow stern as it disappeared around a bend. With branches flicking against our paddle shafts, Steve and I swept around the bend after him.

That's when we found him standing atop the boulder midstream screaming at us to *stop!*

I aimed at his feet, letting the channel sweep us toward him. Then, with foot pedals and paddle, I swung our big kayak sideways and piled it broadside into the boulder. I climbed barefoot onto the rock to see what the problem might be. I poked my head over the far side.

"Holy shit!"

The channel split around the boulder and instantly dropped away into a roaring waterfall. Its thick white torrent fell a good thirty feet in a powerful S as it plunged through forest and massive chunks of rock. The air shook and a cool mist swirled. If we had missed the boulder . . . The thought made my stomach drop.

We heard shouts from upstream. The three of us swiveled around to see Rod and Cherri's overturned kayak being swept down the swift channel toward us. The two of them were swimming beside it and grabbing at bushes on the left bank.

"Waterfall!" we shouted. "Waterfall!"

They managed to stop themselves and their kayak fifty yards from the drop by clinging to the bank. Rod righted the boat, quickly dumped out the water, and they climbed back in.

Clinton shouted and gestured that they should paddle across the channel to the opposite bank, only about fifty feet away. Portaging looked easier on that side, he thought, although to me it looked like very dense forest. Rod and Cherri started paddling across the fast channel. The current suddenly spun their boat and sucked it backward toward the waterfall's lip.

"Paddle! Paddle! Paddle!" shouted Clinton.

Rod's big shoulders and biceps flexed. Cherri's arms spun like a windmill. Their kayak surged upstream, a big white porpoise lifting out of the waves. They made it to the far side, their bow touching the bank only a few dozen yards upstream from the drop. Clinton now turned to me.

"Do you think you can ferry across to them?"

This meant starting from the boulder at the waterfall's lip, aiming the boat upstream, paddling hard into the swift current, and angling across, only twenty or thirty feet above the lip, to the bank where Cherri and Rod stood.

I studied the channel. I looked at the waterfall's lip at our feet. There was zero margin for error. If the boat started swinging sideways in the channel's swift current, I knew Steve didn't know how to correct its course, and I wasn't sure I had the strength or skill to correct it alone before we went over the edge.

"I think we can make it across," I told Clinton, "but I really don't like the consequences if we don't."

"Okay, that's fine," Clinton replied. "We'll tie a rope across, and Rod and I will ferry you over. Get me the throw rope!"

He sounded like a doctor calling for instruments to start surgery. I reached down for the throw rope bungeed to the deck of his kayak. I hesitated. I was the patient here. I wanted a second opinion. Clinton's rope tactic sounded even worse than the ferrying idea. If we tipped, the rope would secure the kayak in place while Steve and I washed over the lip.

Branches suddenly shook in the trees across the channel. *A baboon family*, I thought. But it was Rod, reconnoitering.

"It's an island!" he shouted down from the branches over the waterfall's roar. "It doesn't look good for portaging over here!"

"We'll cross anyway and keep looking for a portage!" Clinton exclaimed, although now he spoke with something less than certainty.

I suddenly sensed that I had more experience than he in situations like this. I'd portaged canoes hundreds of times over all kinds of obstacles. For him the first option to come to mind was the heroic, the dramatic, and the riskier one. For me the first option was the one that could avoid all heroism—the safe one. I surely didn't want to ferry across the swift lip of the falls if I could help it.

"Why don't we look for a portage on the near side before we start screwing around over there," I said.

I proposed instead that Steve and I paddle through easier water to the nearer shore rather than Rod's island. Then I would bushwhack through the forest in search of a good portage spot. Maybe I wanted to be a hero, too—in my own cautious way.

Clinton gazed at me with those intense blue eyes. The waterfall roared behind and below him. It felt to me like subtle psychological chess was going on. Was he being usurped by an upstart? The river delineated an animal sense of hierarchy among us. I was usually near the bottom of it and he at the top. Was he feeling threatened?

"Okay," he finally said.

I felt relieved. I didn't have to fight him. Steve and I climbed carefully into the kayak while Clinton held it for us against the boulder. As I steered as straight as I could, we paddled hard upstream, away from the falls, and instead of trying to ferry across the swift channel to Rod's island, we eased to our right through slower water and beached on a steep, muddy bank.

Leaving Steve with the boat, I clawed my way up the bank with kayak paddle in hand. I struck into the forest.

For the first time on the expedition I felt I was doing something truly useful. I knew this type of exploring, this route-finding, this picking-your-way-along through mountains or rivers or forest. But I'd never before done it in Africa, never in a place so uncharted, never with so many unknowns, with so many wild animals about. It was instantly thrilling— a boyhood explorer's dream come true. It was heady, even intoxicating. The others back there, stuck at the waterfall, waited for me to find the route that would see us out of trouble. Who knew what curious things, what marvels I might discover? Surely no European had ever been here before at this waterfall. There was no reason for it. Who knew what I might find and come back and tell the others?

I imagined what it was like to be a Mungo Park or a David Livingstone, a Vasco da Gama or a Bartolomeu Dias, returning to announce to your breathlessly awaiting king and his empire your discoveries: vast swatches of continents, gold and spices and subject tribes, great rivers and enormous oceans leading to magical lands. I had just the tiniest taste of that now. It made me fearless. I ducked under low branches and thorns, and emerged on a semi-open hillside covered with tall grass. I cut across it, first probing with the paddle into the stands of grass to warn off snakes. It felt like a spear in my hand. I dropped off the hillside and bottomed into a dry, sandy channel about ten feet wide that the river used when it flooded. It ran like a path under low, thick trees. *This has to lead back to the river,* I thought.

I followed the dry bed. It soon opened into a little sandy beach over-hung by trees. The beach fronted a small covelike pool. Across it the waterfall thundered into the pool in a great white froth, its waves lapping over to the beach.

I'd found a good portage. And I'd found a perfect camping spot!

I was eager to tell the others of my discovery. I started back by a more direct route, skirting the cove and climbing up big boulders like a ladder at the side of the falls. In places the trees grew thick from the mist, and I had to climb through the branches. Near the top, amid the great chunks of rock, a slow channel of water blocked my way. I couldn't see a way around it. I slid off the rocks and into it, wading through the forest in water up to my neck, with my paddle in hand like a spear or a rifle, carrying my dis-coveries back to my waiting companions. I laughed out loud, giddily.

This is so great! This is like being Bogart himself!

Right then—for that moment at least—the romance of African exploration lived up to its reputation.

I clambered out and scrambled higher up the rocks and through branches until I stood on shore near the roaring lip. Clinton still stood atop his midstream boulder. I knew it was all in the presentation. I didn't want him to feel usurped from his top spot in the animal hierarchy.

"If I may make a suggestion," I shouted over the roar of the waterfall, taking as gingerly an approach as I could given the high-decibel circumstances, "there's a good portage in the forest and a beach down below! We can unload the boats, carry them down empty, and camp there!"

He looked thoughtful for a moment, gazing back at me.

"Okay," he finally called back.

We settled around the campfire on the sliver of beach—except Steve, who was still trying to untangle the poles of his supposedly self-erecting tent. The waterfall pounded nearby, crashing into the pool. All of us were banged up. Clinton sat on the sand and plucked huge thorns from Rod's palm with a set of pliers. Steve's shoulder was hurting him. So many portages and stumbles over submerged rocks had sliced everyone's legs into masses of cuts. I'd taken to slathering my shins, ankles, and knees with antibiotic cream as if it were suntan lotion.

Earlier I had passed Cherri on the little stamped-out portage trail we made through the forest as she was toting dry bags down toward the campsite and I was coming up for another load. It was the first I had seen her since those moments above the falls. Wet blond hair was plastered to her head. She looked grim.

"You survived!" I said, trying to lighten the moment.

"Barely!" she replied. "I'm terrified of tomorrow!"

She spoke so calmly that I couldn't tell if she meant it. She had come very close, twice, to going over the lip of the falls—first swimming, then backward in the kayak. I was amazed she was this calm about it. Steve told me that Cherri had always been like that—the more dangerous it got, the calmer she became—and that as a child she'd always been organizing and leading some kind of adventure. Was it simply her nature to be so cool in the face of danger? Or had she spent enough time with males in the outdoors that she knew not to show her fear?

That was the lesson I had learned growing up. "Don't be a sissy," my grandfather had admonished me on those early canoe trips.

I tried to earn his approval—"River rat!"—but mishaps occurred, especially with my father. In some way I think my father was still trying to show *his* fearlessness to *his* father. My father's risk-taking overflowed onto me whether I wanted it or not. Under my father's care I broke my leg at age two when for fun he hung me by my hands from the living room rafters and proudly went out of the room to fetch my mother to show her. When I was five, I fell through the lake ice with him. At seven we tipped over at high speed in an iceboat, and when I was ten, we dumped in powerful rapids in a whitewater canoe. I suppose I trusted him and at the same time was scared of the situations he might get me into. Would my father—or my grandfather, for that matter—know where to draw the line? Or did I have to draw it myself? At times it made me very anxious.

The waterfall roared just above camp. The trees, watered by the continuous mist of the falls, spread in a thick dark canopy overhead. Rod tinkered with the sat phone, trying to tie into a satellite. No reception. Our camp lay too deep amid rock and forest. No one would be calling offices or girlfriends or wives tonight. It was just us—us and the leopard whose tracks Cherri had spotted down the shore.

Instead of protection, the satellite phone now felt like a kind of joke. If we had gone over the waterfall's lip, the sat phone would have served as little more than a heavy anchor to pull us deeper, although it might have been used to call in a rescue if we'd managed to survive. The waterfall, with its dense forest cover, had entirely escaped Cherri's aerial reconnaissance. How many more could there be like it ahead? It felt as if the rapids were intensifying instead of easing. Plus, I now could see plainly the limitations of our own party. Only that morning I'd praised Clinton's river judgment, but now my trust in him—near total at first—had been shaken by the way he'd tried to get us to ferry near the lip. Even Steve, not given to criticizing or questioning, had seemed greatly relieved when I finally persuaded Clinton to let us try an alternative.

"I trust Rod completely," Steve said as he and I carefully paddled to shore above the falls, "but Clinton sometimes takes too many chances."

The evidence was plain in the scars that scored his body. Did he know where to draw the line?

Our whiskey supply was almost gone. I sipped my ration from the blue mug and stared into the flames. I felt alone. I was with companions but without them—alone with my thoughts. Ibn Battuta had felt the same way at first. He had tied himself to the saddle while weak with fever and rode hard day and night to keep up with his fellow travelers through North African bandit country. When they arrived in Tunis and no one came out to greet him, he wept. No wonder he married soon after. It was lonely and hard, this life of the road. His bride's father was an official of the city of Tunis. The family had joined a Mecca-bound pilgrim caravan. The young and educated Ibn Battuta had signed on for the same caravan. Each caravan to Mecca operated like an intact society, a kind of nomadic community, with its own leaders and judges. Ibn Battuta was appointed the caravan's *qadi,* its jurist who settled disputes among the party.

One senses from his *Travels* that at this point Ibn Battuta's life on the road changed forever. No longer was he the lonely, homesick stranger; he was now a man of position—a *qadi*—and a married man besides. But he didn't stop moving. The road became his life. He traveled with caravans and with his retinues of wives, concubines, servants, and retainers. A learned man to start, he made it his business to meet and study with famous learned men and Sufi sages throughout the Muslim world. His own fame as traveler and scholar grew, and he was greeted warmly by sultans and governors, by judges and Islamic scholars, by Sufi mystics and saints.

During that first journey to Mecca he took a side trip up the Nile—which he declared surpassed "all rivers of the earth in sweetness of taste, breadth of channel, and magnitude of utility"—and toured the Middle East. He lived a studious life for three years in Mecca and Medina before taking to the road again in 1330. On this venture he sailed in Arab trading dhows on the monsoon winds from the Red Sea down the east coast of Africa to the Muslim trading posts that the Chinese and then the Portuguese would finally "discover" a century later. "For Arabs and Persians of the arid northern rim of the sea, East Africa was a kind of medieval America," writes one historian of Ibn Battuta, "a fertile, well-watered land of economic opportunity and a place of salvation from drought, famine, overpopulation, and war at home."[19]

Ibn Battuta called at the towns of Mogadishu and Mombasa, in today's Somalia and Kenya, and as far south as the port of Kilwa, well below the equator in southern Tanzania. Kilwa lay a mere three hundred miles from where the five of us sat below the thundering waterfall on the Lugenda. Ibn Battuta described it as one of the "finest and most substantially built towns" with wooden buildings roofed with reeds. The Sultan of Kilwa waged *jihad* against the heathen black Africans of the interior, "raiding them and taking booty"—which included slaves. Nevertheless, Ibn Battuta writes admiringly of the generosity and humility of the sultan, who, following the rules of the Koran, gave one-fifth of his booty to charitable causes.[20]

One Friday when the Sultan of Kilwa was leaving the town's mosque after prayer, Ibn Battuta witnessed a poor man approach and ask the sultan for his robes. "Certainly," the sultan replied; he then went to his palace, removed his clothes, and had them given to the man. The people of Kilwa were so praiseful of this act of generosity that the sultan's son then approached the poor man and gave him ten slaves in exchange for the clothes. The people praised the son, and the sultan, hearing the praise, then topped his son's generosity by ordering that the poor man be given another "ten head of slaves and two loads of ivory," writes Ibn Battuta, "for most of their gifts consist of ivory and it is seldom that they give gold."

Ibn Battuta, always recording the wealth and generosity of the rulers he met, or their lack of it, traveled on: Constantinople, the Russian steppes, Central Asia, Afghanistan, India (where he served for several years as grand *qadi* of Delhi), and then China. Heading back to North Africa after more than twenty years on the road, Ibn Battuta still had left two Muslim countries unexplored. First, he went to Granada in today's Spain. Two years later, in 1352, the Sultan of Fez dispatched the famous traveler across the Sahara Desert to the kingdom of Mali in West Africa, the fountainhead of the stream of gold that made its way north. The sultan sought intelligence about this rich kingdom just as, nearly five centuries later, the African Association in London had when it dispatched John Ledyard, Mungo Park, and all the other eager young men to seek out the Niger River and the gold-paved streets of Timbuktu.

This, historians say, was Ibn Battuta's toughest journey. He bought camels and a four-month supply of fodder at an oasis on the Sahara's northern edge in today's Morocco, and on February 14, 1352, he and a company of merchants headed south. They rode for twenty-five days out into the desert before finally reaching the salt mines at Taghaza. The houses in this squalid, fly-blown settlement were built of salt blocks and roofed with camel skin. Black slaves worked the mines while traders, despite the squalor of the place, exchanged "qintars and qintars" of gold dust for salt slabs. Here, the caravan filled its skins with brackish water for the ten-day trek across a particularly dry section of desert that lay beyond, although en route they would find a few rocky pools of sweet water collected from winter rains.

One merchant argued with his cousin and fell behind the caravan, became lost, and was never seen again. Stragglers from other caravans were found dead curled up in bits of shade beneath bushes. After that, writes Ibn Battuta, he and others did not stray ahead as they had before to find pasturage for the animals. The caravan closely followed a desert guide who was blind in one eye and mostly blind in the other but possessed "keen intelligence." It was said by later Saharan travelers—the precise Major Denham, for instance—that these blind "Arab" desert guides could literally smell the location of water. Despite the hardships, the desert, as many later European travelers such as Paul Bowles would discover, exerted powerful attractions: "This desert is luminous, radiant," wrote Ibn Battuta, "one's chest is dilated, one is in good spirits."

The caravan, now traveling at night to avoid the day's heat, sent ahead a man customarily known as a *takshif.* He proceeded to Iwalatan, the settlement on the desert's far edge many days away. He carried letters from the caravan's merchants asking the townsfolk for houses to rent and requested them to bring water four days' travel out into the desert to meet the caravan. Writes Ibn Battuta:

> There are many demons in that desert. If the *takshif* is alone they play tricks on him and delude him until he loses his way and perishes. . . . [Then] the people of Iwalatan know nothing of the caravan, and its people or most of them perish.

I couldn't just sit there. I had to do something. I felt our vulnerability so strongly while sitting in the small flickering ring of firelight, under the thick canopy of trees, with the waterfall pounding. I'd felt it so strongly when looking for the lost spray skirt—the weaknesses of my senses, the inadequacy of my strength against the great beasts of the forest. Mulling what had happened that day, our tipping in the rapids and near disaster at the waterfall, I began to understand that my greatest asset was not strength or boldness or good eyesight. My greatest asset was my own judgment. I had to think my way through the Lugenda wilderness. From here on I would not totally rely on anyone else's judgment. I would, if necessary, make my own calls about what I could or could not do. I'd watch out for myself.

"What's our elevation?" I asked Rod.

Beside the fire, he was working his GPS and marking our latitude and longitude on my big aeronautical map. For some reason the GPS could lock in on satellites here below the falls, but the sat phone couldn't.

He punched a few buttons and shined his headbeam on the screen.

"Four hundred and eighty-six meters," he replied.

I took the map. It was contoured in feet, not meters. I bent over my notebook, doing the conversion: 486 times 39 divided by 12.

"Fifteen hundred and seventy-nine feet," I reported, reading off my calculations for our current elevation.

That was still really high. Although the map's contours were hard to read, it looked like the mouth of the Lugenda, where it emptied into the Rovuma, lay at about five hundred feet above sea level. We had hardly started to drop. Since I last figured our elevation, two days earlier, we had lost less than three hundred feet. I was hoping fervently we were near the end of the rapids, but by these calculations we'd done merely a little more than a quarter. We had over a thousand vertical feet of rapids and river fall still to go.

"It looks as if the next couple of days are going to be a real bitch," I said.

The others listened while I explained my reasoning based mostly on how the contour lines of both Cherri's maps and mine seemed to drop off steeply for the next one hundred kilometers or so, compared to what they'd been doing.

Cherri reiterated aloud what she'd told me on the path—that she was terrified about tomorrow. But again she said it so calmly and was so cool that I couldn't tell if she meant it. I was anxious, too—plenty anxious. I didn't know if I was "terrified." That was something I couldn't admit to myself, much less out loud. Males didn't say they were "terrified." It simply wasn't done. Were women that much more accustomed to being physically vulnerable that it made it easy for them to admit these things? But for a male, at least in modern times in our society, that sense of extreme physical vulnerability was novel, and in these African wilds, with the waterfalls, the carnivores, the crocs and hippos, and the unknown I was finding it extremely disconcerting.

I felt my mind speeding along, as if playing another game of chess and looking for a strategy to deal with the vulnerability that the next days might bring. I couldn't admit I was terrified, not to myself or to our bare-chested leaders, Clinton and Rod. That would make me feel even more vulnerable, by giving myself over to them completely. Nor, on the other hand, did I want to say, "No problem, I'm fearless." If I said that, I could just imagine Clinton pushing us even harder and faster. I had to choose some middle ground. I had to rely on my true strength—not physical power but my own judgment.

I looked down at the map with the falling-off contour lines and the numbers scrawled in my notebook. I looked up again, as Clinton and Rod stirred pots over the fire. Steve, having finished wrestling with his tent poles, came into the circle.

"I think we just have to proceed cautiously," I said to the group as a whole.

I tried to say it evenly—not frightened, not lightly.

I hoped Clinton was listening. I couldn't tell.

DAY SEVEN

Another tense start. More psychological chess. Cherri and Rod flipped again before we had gone three hundred yards. I might have prevented it except I was angry at Rod. He implied that because my boat had bumped into theirs the previous afternoon above the falls, I was responsible for his and Cherri's dumping.

"We need to keep a proper distance between boats," I was cautioned.

It pissed me off that Rod didn't take responsibility for his own mishaps. I felt as if a competition had sprouted between us. It may have started back at Lake Nyasa when I had suggested that if Cherri and Steve went together in a tandem on the Lugenda and he and I shared a boat, I'd be happy to paddle stern, which is where the more experienced paddler usually sits. I told him that I had a lot of canoeing experience.

"No way, no way," he said adamantly. "I'll be paddling stern in one of the boats. You wouldn't know what to do if we ran into problems with animals."

I let it drop. Then, in our first couple of days on the river, both he and Clinton greeted whatever suggestion I might offer—about river distance, map navigation, whatever—with a cool silence. Despite my own experience on rivers, I felt as if they were two close chums of river and wilderness experience. I was the odd man out.

I finally stopped offering my advice, but now I sensed that Rod was keeping track of who piloted his tandem better through the rapids. He had been really chagrined when he tipped while paddling Clinton's boat as "safety" below the last rapid on day three. He blamed that mishap on the lack of a spray skirt while it seemed to me a sharp eddy line had caught him unawares. "I'm glad no one had a camera on me right then," he'd said.

When Steve and I tipped in the whirlpool three days later while he and Cherri aced past the trouble spot, I sensed a certain satisfaction on his part. *I* felt chagrined by tipping instead. It seemed that we both possessed a prickly, silent river pride—angered by our own mistakes and each trying to show Clinton, by far the expert whitewater paddler among us, how well each of us could do.

Then again, maybe I was projecting this on Rod. Maybe Rod wasn't keeping track at all.

But I know I was.

So the seventh paddling day started soon after dawn in a set of rapids just below the waterfall pool. Following Clinton's lead, Steve and I banged our kayak's bottom hard over a big rock hidden within a pillow of white-water. We lurched, almost tipped, recovered, and kept going.

Should I yell back to warn Rod and Cherri of the hidden rock? Could they hear me?

I twisted around and saw them heading right for the pillow.

Okay, I thought. *Let Rod figure it out for himself. Let's see how he does. Clunk!*

They hit the rock hard. The kayak lurched and then spilled them out. I watched the white overturned hull and Cherri's wet blond head bobbing down the river again, now in the chilly dawn. I felt sorry for her, the victim of some stupid male competitiveness. Surely it wasn't the first time.

With grim determination—what else could they do?—they wrestled the boat to shore and emptied out, and we carried on downstream. Not five minutes later it was Steve's and my turn again, as if the wheel of karma or justice or whatever had turned against us due to my mean-spiritedness about Rod and the hidden rock. We were wending through beautiful channels that reminded me of the classic "green mansions" from the title of W. H. Hudson's novel about the jungles of South America. Or, better, "green cathedrals." Pillars formed of stilt-palm roots lined the banks and rose to a vaulted ceiling of palm fronds and hanging vines. The clear green water danced between rocks down the "aisle." I couldn't make a turn quickly enough and broadsided a boulder. Water flooded the cockpits, and the kayak flipped upstream, dumping us out.

The current bowed the swamped boat around the rock—"wrapped it," in river lingo. The force bent the metal stiffening tube inside the hull. We waded the boat the few feet to the palm pillar–lined shore—surely there would be no crocs here in shallow fast water—and emptied out. Rod beached his boat, assessed the bent bar, and pressed his bare heel against it. Using his powerful leg like a hydraulic jack, he wrenched it straight.

"You're paddling way too fast in these narrow channels," Clinton advised me.

I had sped up the pace because I was under the impression from Clinton that I'd been paddling too slowly. I now began to sense that whatever speed we paddled, I didn't have the strength nor Steve the skill to turn our heavy boat quickly together. Or maybe, though I didn't want to admit it, I just didn't have the skill.

We climbed back into the boats and headed down more green cathedrals.

"We've taken a wrong turn," Clinton called out, "and we're paddling a South American river."

Repeatedly, our heavy boat got hung up on rocks. I hopped out into the shallow rocky water and shoved Steve, still sitting in the bow, and the boat over the shallow spots and into the next little pool. Then I quickly jumped back into the cockpit to steer again. Once the boat got ahead of me. It spilled into a little pool, turned sideways to the current, and headed crossways into the next little chute, ready to wrap again. Steve didn't know how to begin to straighten it out or what to do. There was no time for me to explain.

I hope there aren't crocs in here, I thought, leaping off a boulder and plunging into the pool to grab Steve and the boat.

Finally, a hummock of granite blocked our cathedral channel. The water poured through fractures like fountains into a vine-hung emerald pool ten feet below. We heaved our boats over the hummock and handed them down.

"Pe-*tah!*" Rod called up from below. "Let's see your knife for a moment."

I pulled my shiny river knife from its sheath and handed it down to Rod. He pried a thorn from Clinton's foot as he sat on a boulder at pool's edge, then handed it back up to me. I accidentally let the knife slip from my hand. It fell, disappearing into one of the foaming cracks.

I felt a wave of devastation—a child who has lost a favorite toy. The shiny knife was my protection, my totem. How else could I stab out the croc's eyes? From atop the granite hummock I stared down into the surging whitewater in the narrow slot, nearly nauseous at the loss. I was doomed.

Wordlessly, Rod waded from the pool up into the foaming channel. He spread his arms wide to grip the rock walls on each side. Whitewater surged against his thighs. With bare feet he carefully probed the bottom, then raised his right foot, and there was my river knife gripped in his toes.

He handed it up to me. I felt like giving him a hug. I mentally forgave him for whatever he had said the night before.

"Rodney," I called out, "you're a wonder!"

He looked pleased.

Beyond the green cathedrals we hit rapid after rapid. They were easy to spot from the way the treetops suddenly dropped lower on the riverbank ahead.

"Life jackets on! Splash skirts on! Rud-*dahs* loosened! Follow me!" called out Clinton.

When we finally paddled a flat section, Steve and I cheered to celebrate a break from whitewater. But the flat stretches in truth were long natural pools dammed up by the low granite ridges over which the rapids spilled, over those ancient rib bones of the African earth.

In one easy rapid, my foot slipped from the rudder pedal and couldn't find the pedal again. Steve couldn't straighten us. Our boat veered, rudderless, broadsided a rock, and flipped again. I was glad the others were ahead and didn't see us. We righted, emptied out, and caught up. Steve seemed unperturbed by our two flips before breakfast, but I was frustrated, angry at myself and my stupid mistakes, and wishing Steve didn't seem so helpless without me there.

"I need to give you a lesson in hydrodynamics," Clinton said to me after we had run one rapid.

The remark really pissed me off. I thought Steve and I had done particularly well on that rapid and had more or less followed Clinton's line. I'd even cheered to Steve when we made it through. But Clinton claimed I hadn't set up well enough, hadn't positioned our boat properly before the rapid began. Setting up was easy for him, however, in his light, maneuverable single, but it was much more difficult for Steve and me to position the big, heavy tandem. As a result I'd had to drop below a certain rock at the rapid's head instead of paddle above it as Clinton had.

"I know a lot about hydrodynamics, too—though I admit you know more—and I thought we did it really well," I argued back.

Lake Nyasa, near the Lugenda River's source.

The lower reaches of the Lugenda River, from the air.

Unloading the kayaks at Belem Bridge.

The first strokes, with villagers watching from the bridge.

Approaching the first rapid.

Clinton capsized, after a big rapid.

The quiet, leafy upper reaches of the Lugenda.

Clinton running a big rapid.

The waterfall gorge.

Rod belaying kayaks to
Steve and Clinton and into
the waterfall gorge.

Dawn in camp on the middle river.

The broad lower Lugenda.

An elephant in the Niassa Reserve.

Loading up to return home.

Mbemba village women dancing with Peter.

Baobab tree, a symbol of Africa.

I wanted some credit, goddamn it, for guiding a heavy boat through tricky water with a total neophyte in the bow.

"Okay," Clinton finally said.

He didn't sound convinced.

I was tired and cranky. We had been paddling hard and fast for three hours. Steve and I had flipped twice, Rod and Cherri once, and we still hadn't had breakfast. We had smashed and scraped our shins dozens of times while portaging and stumbling over the hidden underwater ribs of granite. Clinton and Rod seemed to be determined to keep up the pace. What were they trying to prove, pushing on like this? What was the big fucking hurry? I brooded.

We paddled more rapids, dragged boats over more rocks, muscled down more flat stretches. I didn't want to say anything, didn't want to sound as if I was complaining. They were so much younger than I. Had I been like that at their age? Pushing, pushing, pushing? And for what? Or did it only seem as if they were pushing so hard because I wanted to go slower?

"Daring youths"—that's the phrase the Greek historian Herodotus used. He was describing five young Nasamonians—inhabitants of Africa's Mediterranean coast in today's Libya—who, several centuries before the birth of Christ, crossed the Sahara and reached the Niger River. The adventure that Herodotus describes could easily have been hatched in modern times. A group of youths, sons of powerful men, came of age and cast about for ways to make themselves known. Among their many "daring plans," wrote Herodotus, was a scheme to explore the African desert and "see if they could make any further discovery than those who had penetrated the furthest."[21]

They drew lots to choose five of their number. Well supplied with food and water, they traveled south for many days, first across inhabited country, then the territory of wild beasts, and then far across the sands. Finally, they came to a fertile plain where fruit trees grew. The hungry Nasamonian adventurers were plucking fruit when small men whose language they could not understand came upon the five, seized them, and carried them off across vast swamps to a city of black men of the same stature. "[B]y the city flowed a great river, running from the west to the east," wrote Herodotus, "and . . . crocodiles were seen in it."

This may well have been the Niger. Herodotus heard the story third-hand, but all the facts add up. The five young Nasamonians had "discovered" the Niger fifteen hundred years before Ibn Battuta and two millennia before Joseph Banks and the African Association dispatched a succession of other "daring youths"—John Ledyard, Mungo Park, and the rest—to discover it yet again.

Is that what Clinton and Rod and all explorers were? *Daring youths.* We use that phrase, as did Herodotus, so lightly, a catchall term to capture a whole parcel of qualities that no doubt have existed as long as there have been humans. Why do youths dare? Is it genetic, some basic animal instinct, or do we as a society or do all societies train our youths to dare? Was it a necessary component for the survival of human society? Without some individuals who dared, would a group simply withdraw into itself and vanish?

I was struck forcefully that whatever this mysterious power was that drove "daring youths," Clinton and Rod had it in abundance. As we paddled and portaged and ran rapids far into the day with no food in our bellies, I realized I might once have had it. But I now knew I'd lost it years ago.

The river braided. We swept down a swift channel thirty or forty feet wide. Rounding a tight bend, we saw that a fallen tree blocked the way. I tensed, well aware that on the rivers of Montana where I'd spent years, getting entangled in the branches of a "sweeper" or "strainer" is how most drownings occur. Clinton neatly avoided the sweeper, scooting into a smaller side channel that opened on the right bank. Steve and I wrenched our boat right and followed him. But Rod and Cherri didn't make the turn. Their kayak piled sideways into the sweeper's branches. They stayed there, holding on to the branches against the current.

"Backpaddle!" Clinton called out to Steve and me so we could all rejoin Rod and Cherri where they were stuck.

Backing out of the side channel, Steve's and my boat caught the current. It pushed us into the sweeper's branches, too, near the right bank where the current was swift.

I envisioned the next moments—the current tipping us, spilling us from the kayak, pulling us under the sweeper. I leaped from the boat to prevent it, to hold it in place. Still, our kayak tilted and the cockpit filled partly with water. I was up to my neck in the river, barely touching the bottom with my feet, and getting pushed toward the branches. Steve was still sitting in the bow, not knowing what to do. I struggled with my arms around the half-swamped kayak to keep it upright and shove both Steve and our boat forward toward the safety of the steep, thorny bank.

"You have to bail, Peter!" Cherri shouted.

"Just shut up, Cherri. Okay?" I yelled back in frustration.

I managed to shove Steve, who was still sitting in our boat. Maybe he was asking me what he could do to help, but I was too busy trying to save us from tipping under the strainer to think about it. Now Steve yelled at me from the bow.

"You're pushing me into the thorns!"

I jerked back on the boat, thoroughly entangling it in the sweeper's branches.

I wanted to scream at both Briggs siblings: "What the fuck were you doing coming on this trip without knowing how to paddle a kayak?"

We slowly began to untangle from the sweeper.

"Watch your paddle, Peter," said Cherri.

I gritted my teeth and kept going.

Not three minutes past the sweeper, around the very next bend, the river literally poured down a hillside. It was bizarre—the river spreading out and cascading down among scattered bushes and over mossy-looking stones, as if the Lugenda, bored with its usual route, had jumped its bed to take a jaunt into the bush.

It was too late to stop. Clinton and his yellow kayak tilted over the brow and began to rush down the hill. We were close behind, and Rod and Cherri were behind us. Clinton's light boat passed easily over the mossy stones, but Steve and I went *thump-thump-thump*ing down the hill like a toboggan over moguls. While focusing hard on Clinton to see if he ran into trouble, I dragged my paddle blade over the rocks as hard as I could, like a brace, to keep us from flipping as we careened over stones. The wind whistled in my ears. It might have been fun if only I knew what lay around the sharp right bend at the hill's bottom. Another strainer? The Lugenda's next waterfall?

Wham! My paddle blade smashed into a submerged boulder. It jerked the paddle shaft upward while I was muscling down with my right hand. My own left fist, wrapped around the upper shaft, struck me hard, a punch to the jaw. My head snapped back, my vision dimmed. *Don't pass out here!* I saw Clinton whip around the blind bend. *Hang on!*

The current funneled off the bottom of the hill and torqued us around the bend. There was Clinton, serenely floating in a calm eddy on river right. With a few easy strokes and pedal pushes of the rudder, I steered us beside him. Our noses touched the mud and sand riverbank, pocked with washbasin-sized dried footprints from elephants. Rod and Cherri pulled up beside us.

"We'll have breakfast here," said Clinton.

I felt like getting on my knees and kissing the beach.

"Do you think anyone has ever stood on this spot?" asked Cherri as we spooned up our mugs of oatmeal in the shade of a tree.

I was so hungry, I was stuffing fistful after fistful of nuts into my mouth, at least half a pound, between spoonfuls of oatmeal.

"This place didn't see a lot of action during the war," Clinton commented dryly.

We had seen no one since yesterday—or was it the day before?—and then only a fisherman in a bark canoe. To me the question was academic. Had anyone stood here before? Who knows? How far back did you want to count? This mud-and-sand riverbank itself probably didn't exist a mere two decades ago, given the constantly shifting course of rivers. In my reading I'd found again and again that the farther back you went, the more "explorers" you encountered who had "discovered" any given region. It was like peeling the layers of human curiosity, like the layers of an onion, to find still earlier layers beneath. Where was the core?

In 425 B.C., Hanno, King of Carthage, led an expedition that sailed out of the Mediterranean into the Atlantic and far down West Africa. This was nineteen centuries before Prince Henry the Navigator sent his caravels from Portugal to discover the same region of West Africa. Hanno's stone carvers engraved an account of the journey on a temple stele, the text of which survives:

> I. The Carthaginians decided that Hanno should sail beyond the Pillars of Heracles and found cities of Libyphoenicians. He set sail with sixty penteconters and about thirty thousand men and women, and provisions and other necessities.

> II. After sailing beyond the Pillars for two days we founded the first city which we called Thymiaterion. Below it was a large plain.

III. Sailing thence westward we came to Soloeis, a Libyan promontory covered with trees. There we founded a temple to Poseiden.

IV. Journeying eastward for half a day we reached a lake not far from the sea, covered with a great growth of tall reeds, where elephants and many other wild animals fed.

By the ninth entry of this engraved itinerary, the explorers were encountering "savages clad in skins of wild beasts" who threw stones to repel the Carthaginians. By the tenth entry they had found a big river "teeming with crocodiles and hippopotamuses." Another three weeks of sailing brought them to the waters off a forested island where mysterious fires burned at night and they heard flutes, cymbals, drums, "and a great din of voices." The Carthaginians grew frightened; their soothsayers commanded they leave the island.

Finally, by the eighteenth and last entry, the ships had reached a great gulf they called the Horn of the South and an island full of what they thought were savages.

XVIII. . . . By far the greater number were women with shaggy bodies, whom our interpreters called Gorillas. Chasing them we were unable to catch any of the men, all of whom, being used to climbing precipices, got away, defending themselves by throwing stones. But we caught three women, who bit and mangled those who carried them off, being unwilling to follow them. We killed them, however, and flayed them and brought their skins back to Carthage. For we did not sail farther as our supplies gave out.[22]

"Shhh!" Clinton whispered, turning back to us.

We were back in the boats. He pointed to a forested island we were gliding by in the afternoon sunlight on river left. Rod put his finger to his lips. We all stopped paddling. I smelled a musky odor and saw that the bank had been trampled. I heard the cracking of sticks and then a sound as if a wrecking ball was smashing through the forest. Here was an island as mysterious as those found by the Carthaginians that were inhabited by strange beasts.

"Elephants!" Clinton whispered. "Don't move!"

Hoping to catch a glimpse, we drifted silently as sunlit drips of water from our upheld paddles pocked the smooth greenish current.

"Hey!" Clinton suddenly shouted with alarm. "Hey, get out of here!"

Ahead, I saw sprays of water fly from his paddle and heard a *whump! whump!* as the blade struck down on hull and water and I didn't know what else. I couldn't see what it was that he struck at. In an instant it was gone.

"Croc!" he called back to us.

The croc had bitten at his kayak just in front of the cockpit as he drifted silently along listening for elephants, its jaws snapping at the yellow plastic. Of course it would go for Clinton, the lead boat and bite magnet. We watched for it to come back, but the croc had disappeared.

"Yay, Clinton!" we cheered.

Rod paddled up and slapped him victoriously with a high five. "Nice work, bru!"

"It was just a testing bite," Clinton said modestly.

Past the island, by popular demand he called a "toonda break"—the South African slang we used for a pee stop. Paddling toward the left bank, we spotted what looked like an abandoned fishing camp. I was curious, as always, about the ways of the people in this forest. I suggested we beach there for our toonda break and have a look.

Four big bark canoes lay neatly stowed on the sloping sandy bank, and a dilapidated child-sized canoe lay cockeyed near the shore like a discarded toy. At the top of the bank, just where the forest began, stood three low thatched roofs supported by poles without walls. The roofs sheltered soot-covered racks and grids of stakes planted in the earth over beds of cold ashes—clearly racks to smoke fish.

There was something both pristine and mysterious about the camp. I was fascinated. I couldn't find a single scrap of evidence of the modern world—not a piece of paper, not a shred of plastic, not a bit of wire, only bits of twisted vine, sharpened stakes, and woven thatch. It wasn't "primitive," at least to me. It reminded me of visiting the tribes of the highlands of Irian Jaya, usually described by more urbanized visitors as "recently emerged from the Stone Age." True, those tribes didn't possess metal tools until the mid-twentieth century and still make stone axes today. But when you see one of their stone axes, you realize that you—as a modern, Western-educated *Homo sapien*—could spend the rest of your life trying to perfect a "Stone Age" axe and not make one half so ingenious and superbly crafted as theirs.

The abandoned fishing camp on the Lugenda showed the same kind of human ingenuity: nets woven of vines, canoes shaped of bark, racks crafted of sticks. What was "primitive"? I knew that alone I'd be lost and helpless in this forest where they were at home. Likewise, without an Inuit guide or desert nomad—local expertise—I would probably be dead within a few hours on the Arctic ice or on the Sahara's sands. This forest was neither "uncharted" nor "undiscovered" terrain to the people who had built this fishing camp. They surely had names for many of the places— the rapids, waterfalls, certain bends of the Lugenda—that looked like raw, uncharted wilderness to us.

In my reading I had encountered so many arrogances about this concept of "exploration" and "discovery." It started with the first written accounts I could find, accounts that glaringly showed the Carthaginians' inability—or indifference—to distinguish between people and "Gorillas." The arrogance carried on through the Chinese "discovery" of Africa and then its discovery by Portuguese, Dutch, Spanish, French, German, British, Americans, and on and on.

I was guilty, too. Just what was I—what were we—trying to prove? As the stone axe had taught me in the highlands of Irian Jaya, the abandoned fishing camp reminded me that right here in this particular spot on the sand and forest bank of the Lugenda River it was really I who was ignorant.

We now encountered many baboons. Running fast and gracefully along the sandy bank on river right, they oddly didn't seem frightened of us, unlike earlier baboons.

Steve and I studied them while drifting along in the calm water of a big pool. Clinton was far out front, and Rod and Cherri were somewhere well behind us, having paused for something. The baboons stopped their graceful run. They turned and watched us drift past, inquisitively. There was something undeniably humanlike about them, maybe less the way they moved than their curious gazes and the quick, chaotic communications among the group. I wondered if this was how a bunch of human toddlers would behave if they had the ability to run and swing from trees.

A huge bubble of water suddenly welled up in the calm close behind Steve's and my stern, maybe fifty feet back.

"Whooaa!" I said.

I thought it was a croc swimming just beneath the surface. Curious like the baboons, I looked back to see what it would do. Then another big bubble erupted just next to the first.

Clinton, alerted by my exclamation, saw this bubble, too.

"Paddle! *Paddle!*" he screamed at us. *"Hippo!"*

Steve and I paddled like hell, downstream and toward shore, as fast as we possibly could, the boat nearly surging out of the water. Clinton took refuge behind a cluster of big boulders. Putting our boat into a turn, we dove after him into this little safe-harbor refuge.

He now shouted instructions to Rod and Cherri, still well upstream, to cross over to the opposite bank of the pool, as far as possible from the hippo. Clinton, fearless in whitewater, really, really didn't want to risk a tangle with a hippo. Oddly, for me it was the opposite: I was much more concerned about big rapids, hidden waterfalls, and strainers lying in fast current than hippos, perhaps because I'd never seen firsthand the damage the hippos could inflict, whereas I knew of many deaths from the former.

But the hippo remained submerged in the deep pool. Whether it was because it planned to charge but we'd moved quickly out of the way, or because it, too, was scared and hid from *us* was impossible to tell. No one wanted to bet on the latter.

"I'm too burned out to paddle this one," I said to Cherri. "I'm happy to portage or let Clinton and Rod paddle my boat through, or whatever."

We were standing on a granite rib watching Clinton scout a passage through a foaming slot. Cherri appeared as tired as I. She lifted up her wristwatch in agreement.

"Do you realize we've been paddling for eight solid hours, nine if you count the breakfast break?"

"I don't really want to paddle it, either," Steve said, and he moved away down the rocks.

"There's a good spot," I said to Cherri. "We could camp right there."

I pointed downriver where the slot emptied into a beautiful little cove rimmed by sandy beach and granite shelves. Just then Clinton joined us. He began describing how we should set up for paddling the slot.

"What about camping?" Cherri blurted out.

"We can still make more distance today," he said.

"It's four o'clock," Cherri and I replied in unison.

"How late do you plan on going, Clinton?" she added.

He paused.

"I vote to stay here at that nice beach," I said, nodding to the cove.

He looked at me with those steady, intense blue eyes. It was as if he hadn't heard anything Cherri had said, as if she wasn't there, as if I was the only one having the conversation with him.

"That's fine," he said, talking only to me. "I didn't know it was so late."

Steve was standing nearby. Clinton asked him if he wanted to paddle the rapids in the bow of our boat while Clinton took stern in my place.

"Sure," said Steve.

I felt slightly wounded because Steve had just said he didn't want to paddle it. I didn't know if his refusal and then agreement to run the rapid had to do with suggestibility on Steve's part or because he trusted Clinton in the stern more than me, or what.

They climbed in the kayak, paddled upstream, and set up for the slot. I could see that Clinton had to pull hard to get the stern around at the last minute to make the setup, as if the lack of maneuverability of my boat, especially with heavy Steve in the bow, surprised him. I was watching him closely to see the technique he used to handle it. He got a bead on it, and they shot through the slot without mishap. They beached at the little cove on river left, and Clinton walked back up over the granite shelves and climbed into the bow of Rod's boat. Steve and I watched, standing beside Cherri who was aiming her video camera at the two.

"I'm really glad you guys are grown-up," Cherri said while tinkering with the camera. "You don't feel you have to do something when you're not up to it."

She looked through the viewfinder again. Clinton and Rod were setting up. They began paddling toward the slot.

"Watch," said Cherri. "When Clinton and Rod see I have the video on them, they'll go wild."

The two shot through the whitewater slot below us. Exactly as she had predicted, Clinton raised his paddle triumphantly overhead in one hand and twirled it like a rodeo rider while smiling and waving at the camera with the other. But halfway down the slot his propellering blade banged into Rod's, who had continued to paddle normally, and Clinton's paddle flew from his hands into the water. Rod steered the boat through and paddled them into the pool to fetch the dropped paddle.

"These guys, these South Africans, are so macho," Cherri said, obviously feeling miffed by the way Clinton had shut her out a few minutes before. I had felt shut out by them, too, on earlier occasions and had a sense of how frustrating it could be. Her instinct was to strike back verbally.

"They're even more sexist than they are racist," she went on. "They're nicer to their 'mates' than they are to their girlfriends. Do you see how nice Rod and Clinton are to each other? In America people would think they're gay. And did you notice how Clinton didn't listen to my suggestion to camp but agreed only when you said it? I've been dealing with this for twelve years in my business. They have a hard time that a woman is the tour leader. The whole game is a matter of massaging egos."

I made sounds of empathy. Although her reaction was often heavy-handed, I was finding Cherri perceptive when it came to matters of human insight. But I knew that somehow my ego was being massaged, too.

Is that kind of machismo what it took to push forward on these explorations? Why else would you keep going forward if it was possible to go back? Because it was unseemly to turn back, unseemly even to quit the day early? It would be cowardly to give up when the going got tough? What did it take to keep going? If not greed for gold, if not religious fervor, if not simple wanderlust and curiosity, how about pure *macho*? Check this out! I'm going to *conquer* the *wilderness*! I'm such a badass, I'll go where no one else has gone before!

Here lay one motive of those Nasamonian "daring youths" out to make a name for themselves. But how far could pure daring—machismo, testosterone, whatever you want to call it—get you finally? How many years into the unknown would it be before you finally asked yourself, "Why am I doing this?" Or maybe the secret was never to ask that, only to fixate on your goal. Although then, like James Bruce at the source of the Blue Nile, when you finally did reach your goal—a swampy hillside riven with a few springs—you might undergo a sudden and potentially fatal crisis of faith.

Maybe, in some way, the exploration is itself a test of faith. Not necessarily religious faith or even faith in a king or a leader but more than anything faith in yourself. Faith in an idea. Faith in a destiny. By having faith—I *will* succeed—you will become a person of destiny. Exploration created a self-fulfilling prophecy for greatness.

One of the most remarkable explorations the world has known occurred some two hundred years before Hanno's voyage when around

600 B.C., the Egyptian king Necho dispatched Phoenician ships with orders to sail around the whole of Africa. How had he heard that it was a continent surrounded by sea?

Herodotus reports the stories he heard of how the Phoenician ships embarked from the Red Sea and set sail down the Indian Ocean. As autumn came on that first year, they beached their boats and planted crops. When spring arrived, they harvested their crops and sailed on. For two years they did this, and in the third year they reached the Pillars of Hercules, the entrance to the Mediterranean at Gibraltar. Back in Egypt they reported that the sun had shone *north* of them when they were far to the south. This voyage, wrote Herodotus, let the Carthaginians claim thereafter *that Libya is surrounded by water.*

How much faith that took! Gone over two years on a voyage to the unknown, with the sun passing to the north instead of the south. Herodotus doubts this business with the sun actually happened and leaves the reader to judge the veracity of it all, but it would in fact be the case sailing south of the equator. Christopher Columbus was a lightweight by comparison, sailing a mere nine weeks to the west across the Atlantic on the easy trade winds. Where did the Phoenicians place their faith? In their gods? In Baal, the Phoenician storm god, the "cloud rider." In the Egyptian king, Necho? Or did they place faith in their own abilities? They were, after all, Phoenicians. Long-distance sea voyages were their stock-in-trade. *Around Libya? Sure, we can handle it. When do we leave?*

Whatever this mysterious quality was—confidence, faith, daring, machismo—it was revealed to me through Herodotus that not all the ancient seafarers possessed it. Herodotus went on to tell the story of Sataspes, a Persian royal youth who deflowered a Persian royal virgin. King Xerxes was going to punish Sataspes by having him impaled, but Sataspes's mother intervened and convinced Xerxes that she would inflict an even greater punishment on her son—making him undertake an exploratory voyage around the whole of Africa.

Sataspes, wrote Herodotus, took ships from Egypt and sailed out the Pillars of Hercules and down the west coast of Africa. But after many months of voyaging there was still land to his left, and he turned back the way he had come. Although Herodotus provides no such phrasing, I picture Sataspes as a kind of coddled wastrel; after all, his mother bailed him out of trouble for his sexual indiscretions. He lacked the true explorer's spirit or, as Herodotus put it, he was "dreading the length of the voyage and the desolation." Sataspes, clearly and simply, was putting in his time at exploration in order to save his skin.

"This is far enough," I imagine him saying to his sailors who may well have been Phoenician seafarers. "This ought to satisfy Xerxes."

He was wrong. Returning to the Mediterranean, Sataspes reported to King Xerxes that he had reached a land of little men dressed in palm leaves who fled into the mountains at the Phoenician approach, and for this reason Sataspes turned back.

"Xerxes, however," wrote Herodotus, "being persuaded that he did not speak the truth, as he had not accomplished the task imposed upon him, impaled him, inflicting the original sentence."

Setting up camp along the sandy little cove, I felt a deep spasm of homesickness for Amy and Molly and Skyler. I, too, was beginning to feel the "length and desolation" of our voyage, minuscule as it was compared to the ancient Phoenicians. So far each of our campsites had displayed a different set of animal tracks. Now I pitched my tent beside croc tracks that squiggled across the flat sand. I wished I could show them to Skyler and Molly. Nearby grew a jasmine tree. I plucked three of the perfumey white blossoms, one for each of my little family, and placed the yellow-centered flowers in my tent beside the dry bag that I used as a pillow.

I went to the fire and began writing up the day's notes. So much had happened, I had to ask the others for the exact order of events. I think everyone was both exhilarated and exhausted by them.

"Sat phone's working!" Rod called out, holding up the phone in firelight. "Anyone want to make a call?"

Cherri did. She got on the phone to Heather in the Steamboat Springs office. Cherri tried to give businesslike instructions to order up a new spray skirt for Clinton, but with the excitement of a schoolgirl, she kept interrupting herself to tell Heather of our adventures.

"It's very intense!" Cherri exclaimed to Heather. "There are a lot more rapids than we anticipated. A croc attacked a boat today. It's quite dangerous!"

"Jesus Christ, Cherri!" I exclaimed, sitting near her beside the campfire. "Don't say that! We're going to have a lot of people flipping out—including my family!"

Cherri ignored me. She kept talking excitedly to Heather. Clinton rose to put more wood on our big fire. Bite magnet that he was, he discovered two scorpions hiding on the log he picked up from the pile. Holding it out from his body, he tossed the log, with scorpions on it, into the fire, no doubt remembering the scorpion sting he had received at Lake Nyasa.

As Cherri jabbered on the phone and the fire blazed, it occurred to me that I wanted to downplay the dangers of this expedition in order to convince both myself and my family that this was a reasonable undertaking. Cherri's tendency, on the other hand, was to play up the dangers, as if to accentuate her—and our—boldness and heroism. I'd come to think of her as a combination of "Cherri Danger," putting the most dramatic face on things, and "Mother Hen," looking out for her hatchlings.

Certainly there were plenty of dangers. Certainly one could make the case that the expedition was bold and even heroic, and maybe this is one of the things that propelled Cherri: a kind of female explorer's machismo, a desire for recognition. I, however, wanted to think of the expedition as bold in *retrospect*. I didn't want to be a hero now. At the moment I didn't even care if I was a hero *later*. All I wanted to do—and do very much— was simply get ourselves safely down the Lugenda River, one paddle stroke at a time.

But now Cherri was off the sat phone and consulting her laminated sheet.

"Tomorrow," she said, looking up in the firelight, "is going to be a real bitch."

DAY EIGHT

I woke at 4:00 a.m. I lay in my tent pitched on sand, sore, exhausted, and badly wanting to sleep until Rod's bird whistle at 5:30 a.m. But my mind was spinning. I listened to the *shush*ing/*thump*ing of the rapids that I had opted to walk around late the afternoon before and where Cherri had discoursed on South African machismo.

I didn't want to face another day like yesterday: two capsizes before breakfast and one swimming encounter with a strainer, followed by that punch to the jaw on the downhill run; then another long series of rapids after breakfast, the croc biting Clinton's kayak, the sprint away from the hippo, plus the tension with Clinton about whether I was paddling poorly or well and the sheer exhaustion of the long day's paddle.

Each day seemed to get worse: bigger rapids, closer calls. That's what scared me. We were skirting the edge. Maybe it was just me, Steve and me in that heavy boat. I didn't have enough control—of the boat, of our pace, of anything about this expedition.

Would I crack? It was one of those dark 4 a.m. thoughts. Would the pressure get to be too much? I could walk around the rapids and waterfalls if I saw them coming, but cracking usually came out of nowhere, unseen, unbidden. Now that could get *really* messy. I'd seen it happen in my father. I'd had something almost like that happen to me. Under extreme pressure about writing—or what I imagined was extreme pressure—a kind of craziness set in, a sense of utter, inescapable failure. Maybe this was the dark underside of the family propensity for risk, for adventurousness, for putting oneself out on the line. All the self-confidence that you counted on to carry you through suddenly collapses in a bottomless black hole of doubt. Twice I saw it happen to my father. Twice he thought he was going broke as head of the family candy-manufacturing business. Twice he tried to kill himself—once with sleeping pills and once by lying down in front of a freight train.

I tossed in my sleeping bag on the sand. It was quiet outside except for the rapids. No animals in the night. None of the dramatic lion roars or hyena shrills that Cherri had described. Only the vision of silent crocodile tracks squiggling past my tent. Where do they go at night? Already I had been for four involuntary swims in the Lugenda. Where in the river do the crocs hang out during the day?

Stand back from this, I told myself. *When you get that panicky feeling, stand back and observe what's happening to you.*

It had taken me years to learn this strategy to deal with my fears. Ask what is frightening me and ask what I can do to counter it.

It was out of my control. I felt I was on this juggernaut with no way to get off, and no one knew where it was headed. I felt panicky because I was afraid that I couldn't say "Stop!" and have any reassurance that it would stop. I was afraid I couldn't say "This is too much for me!"

I'd managed to say "Stop!" twice at rapids I thought were too big for me. Could I do it again?

But it was out of their control, too, even if I yelled "Stop!" for all I was worth. No one really knew what lay around the next bend, and the river got so crazy sometimes, there was nothing anyone could do to stop. Like flying down that hillside yesterday on a toboggan ride over the mossy rocks. If a strainer had been waiting at the bottom, hidden just around the bend, it could have been utter disaster for us. Or when we were ripping around the narrow, fast bend in the forest the day before. We were all stopping as hard as we could, and even then we barely escaped going over the waterfall's edge.

I just wanted to sleep. I needed to sleep so I wouldn't get too crazy thinking. But I'd already wasted fifteen minutes letting my mind whir. *Goddamn it!* I clicked on my headlamp, unzipped my little nylon mesh Dopp kit, and unscrewed the cap from my bottle of sleeping pills. With my thumbnail I shaved off half a tablet. *I hope this isn't going to make me feel groggy all morning,* I thought. *I don't care. I just want to sleep.* I swallowed it with a gulp of water from my canteen. I noticed the three jasmine blossoms where I had placed them beside my pillow.

I clicked off the headlamp and put my head back on my clothes-bag pillow. I already felt more relaxed.

What am I fighting? I asked myself.

For one thing, I was fighting Clinton, however subtly.

Why fight him? I asked myself. Put away your pride, your ego. Especially don't put your ego up against his. He'll resist you every time, and so will Rod. Clinton's here, you're here. Accept that. He knows a lot more about whitewater paddling than you do. Accept that, too. Yes, that's it. Try to learn from him. Do the Taoist thing. You've read the *Tao Te Ching*. It constantly invokes the image of flowing water. Instead of resisting where the current is taking you—instead of fighting Clinton—it tells you to flow *with* it.

Water yields and overcomes.

I remembered the green cathedral pools and the sun-sparkled rivulets flowing between pillars of stilt-palm roots. Then I fell asleep.

I heard Rod's cheery whistle. I checked my watch. It was 5:40 a.m. Dawnish light pressed on blue tent fabric. I resisted the thought of leaving my warm sleeping bag and dug myself deeper into its soft folds. I counted to thirty—a little break. *Okay, here we go,* I thought. *Use your lessons.*

It took me a long time to get ready. Contact lenses to insert. This was always unpleasant. No matter how hard I tried to keep them clean, a fine sandy grit coated the lenses. I removed them from the case, clenched my teeth, and pushed them onto my corneas, blinking and cursing, eyes watering. Then camera film to load and sorting out the previous day's rolls of film. Camera lens to clean. A few stray notes to write that I'd forgotten the night before. I'd stayed awake in my tent writing notes, as usual, an hour or two after everyone else had gone to sleep. Climb from the bag. Change from warm, silk long underwear shirt to damp, chilled river shorts and shirt. Deflate the sleeping pad, roll it, and stuff it in its sack. Stuff the sleeping bag back in its sack. Move faster now, get warm in the chill dawn.

"Your tent should be down by now," Clinton said, walking past my door, trying to make me move faster.

Pack the *Wild Africa* anthology (the previous night around the campfire I'd read aloud from Nile explorer John Speke's 1858 account of how a fluttering beetle had lodged against his eardrum while asleep in his tent, and how he finally dispatched it with several stabs of a penknife, thereby inflicting a wound to his ear canal that leaked pus and sprouted tumors for months). Carefully, very carefully, pack my medicine kit. Pack my Portuguese pocket dictionary, my notebooks and pens, my headlamp, my

Dawn on Day Eight; Clinton and Rod at their shelter.

spare clothes. Toss stuff sacks and dry bags out the tent door into a heap on the sandbar. Climb from tent.

It was a beautiful dawn. A golden band of sky radiated in the northeast, and its reflection heaved gently on the sand-rimmed cove around which we'd beached the boats. Near the rock rib that sheltered the upper end of the cove Rod and Clinton tended the fire on which a pot of water simmered. Nearby stood their tarp sleeping shelter, propped by paddles stuck in the sand. Steve and Cherri were climbing from their tents, too, assembling their own piles of stuff sacks before their doors.

"Good morning, Pe-*tah*!" Rod said.

"Great sky!" I replied. "I'd better take some photos while we have such good light."

I snagged the camera from my gear pile, clambered onto the low rib of rock, and took a few shots overlooking our pretty sandbar camp. Early in the morning the Lugenda River always looked so serene and inviting, but as the day wore on, it—or I—inevitably grew nastier.

Back at the fire I poured a mug of tea, then stirred in sugar from a packet that lay on the unrolled canvas cloth that served as our kitchen table. It had pockets containing utensils and condiments—salt, sugar, coffee, tea, wheatso and oatmeal packets, energy bars—and the whole of it could be rolled up and stowed neatly in a kayak hull. African safari gear. *I should remember the roll-up kitchen,* I thought, *for future adventures.* I choose an energy bar. The chocolate chip ones were already gone, everyone's favorite and the first to go. I tore off the wrapper and burned it in the fire, then sank my incisors into the sticky mass more with duty than pleasure. Here was the early twenty-first-century edition of hardtack. I laid it down after a couple of bites along with my mug of tea to do a little more packing.

Everyone was focused on the intricacies of their packing chores. We first sealed our gear in the heavy, waterproof sacks known as "dry bags," rolling their ends closed and fastening them with straps. We stuffed the dry bags through hatches in the deck into watertight compartments in the hull's bow and stern. Then we fitted plastic covers over the hatches and neoprene covers over the plastic covers, tightly sealing the hull compartments against the smashing of waves. Any extra gear that wouldn't fit into the hulls we lashed to the decks under a web of bungee cords.

"Clinton," I said as we leaned over the kayaks. "Sometime when you have a free moment, could you give me some instruction on how to move the kayak sideways more easily?"

He stood up from packing his boat. He seemed pleased to be asked.

"Come with me," he said.

He led me to the rock rib, we scrambled up it barefoot, and I followed him along the top to where it projected into the river like a natural dam of granite. We stopped where it broke to create the foaming slot through which he had paddled the boats the previous afternoon while Cherri and I watched.

"Ninety percent of running rapids," Clinton began, gesturing to the slot like a professor to a chalkboard, "is setup."

He delivered a concise lecture on what "line" to follow through this particular rapid. The central lesson was that if you're set up properly, the rest falls into place.

I knew that—of course I knew that, I told myself. *Learn from him, don't fight him.*

I asked some questions, which he answered informatively, and I thanked him for the lesson. We climbed down off the rock rib into camp. I felt a surge of warmth toward Clinton. *He's eager to help me.* I didn't have to compete. We could be a team.

* * *

We broke camp at 7:15. Around the first bend a sharp, churning drop blocked the river midstream. We pulled over to the left bank. I thought: *Here begins the day's hazards and choices.* Clinton said we could run it, but none of the rest of us showed much enthusiasm and he agreed to portage. Because Clinton always scouted ahead in the lead boat and would be the one to first encounter any unexpected hazards, Rod had lent his spray skirt to Clinton to replace the one that Clinton had lost. But now that left Rod's boat vulnerable to swamping, and this drop looked as if it could do the job neatly.

Instead, we dragged the boats down the left bank through rocky rivulets. Beyond lay a broad stretch of shallow rapids that Clinton's light boat passed over easily. Steve and I hit them well, dodging boulders and angling right, while Rod and Cherri got hung up on the shallow rocks. They dislodged themselves and we regrouped, paddling quietly in the calm stretch below. I felt good. I'd run the rapids well. I wasn't resisting Clinton. And Cherri was helping me out, too. As I was toting my gear that morning to pack our boat, she had intercepted me out of earshot of the others.

"I told Clinton and Rod that they need to slow down," she confided. "I told them we need to take more breaks. We need to go at a pace that you guys—you and Steve—can handle. We have a long way to go, and we don't want to get burned out. I don't want anyone getting hurt."

I thanked her for speaking up for us. I told her I agreed. Now, paddling along after a set of rapids done well, I felt warmly toward Cherri, too. She was very good about watching out for those in her care, very big-sisterly— too much so at times. In other instances I wished she hadn't intervened on my behalf, but this time I was glad. She nudged us this way and that as individuals and as a group, always with the idea of going determinedly forward. Years ago I'd heard stories from a Sudanese man that Amy and I had met in Cairo about the women of his warrior tribe. It was the women who really sent the men into battle, he told us, with their songs about the men's courage and ferocity. It was the women who kept the men in battle, because the women's songs would mock and shame anyone who turned and ran. Now Cherri reminded me of those warrior-tribe women, keeping all the men in her little tribe on track.

We stopped paddling to drift for a few minutes in the warm sun. It was pleasant just to sit.

"Look there," someone whispered.

Ahead on the right bank a waterbuck mother and fawn lifted their heads. We sat motionless in the kayaks, drifting past as they watched us with their big eyes. They didn't spook. Had we reached a region of the Lugenda basin with so little human presence that the animals had no fear of hunters?

Clinton picked up his paddle again. Wordlessly, we picked up ours. Everyone began to stroke at almost the same moment. A certain bonding among us had even grown from that, from the unison of our paddling motions.

Hypnotized by the repetitive paddle strokes in the warm sun, my mind drifted. A little band pushing along an unknown African river. Little bands like ours had been pushing along the rivers of Africa for tens of thousands—hundreds of thousands . . . even millions—of years.

Before the Phoenician circumnavigation of Africa in 600 B.C. there were Egyptian expeditions to the sacred land of Punt—probably the Horn of Africa—such as one in 1492 B.C. to bring back myrrh trees to decorate the mausoleum of Queen Hatshepsut. In the earliest written references to African exploration that I could find, Pharaoh Sahure dispatched expeditions to Punt ten centuries earlier, around 2500 B.C.

That makes nearly five thousand years of documented African exploration, not to mention all that came before the invention of writing. Whether you called them explorers or traders or nomadic wanderers, the sheer human endeavor devoted to exploring Africa is staggering in its scope. Waves of humans and protohumans had moved out of Africa, by some estimates, nearly two million years before Pharoah Sahure's expedition. These were the beings who peopled the world.

Evolving around two million years ago, *Homo erectus* traveled all the way from its African birthplace to Southeast Asia, where *H. erectus* fossils have been found along the Solo River on the island of Java. This great, mysterious migration may have taken a mere one hundred thousand years or less, the blink of an eye on an evolutionary scale. One theory about this exodus compares the Sahara Desert to a giant pump. During the wetter phases of the world glacial cycles, the Sahara grasslands, then offering abundant food, would draw early humans from their original territory farther south in Africa. During the drier phases, when the Sahara reverted to desert, it pushed the humans northward into Europe and Asia, where large mammals migrated, too. The Nile Valley was almost certainly a major—or *the* major—corridor. On the basis of one-million-year-old campsites excavated in Ethiopia, our ancestors preferred, as we did on the Lugenda, camping beneath the "forest galleries" along riverbanks.[23]

Paddling in the morning sun, I imagined a small band of *Homo erectus* moving along beneath the waterberry trees. What were they looking for? Was it a desultory search for food, relatively aimless in its way? Here some berries, there a lizard, there an insect nest or the chance of larger game? Or was it more purposeful? Were they hurrying because another band was chasing them? Or was a forest fire burning behind them or was the savannah ablaze? Or did something much slower push them on, such as the long slow droughts that had set in to the south? Were they pushed toward those moist bluish hills on the far north horizon, toward more food, more water, a better view to spot game? Or were they following a huge, swinging cycle of life that took the shape of ritual? The big animals with each wet season traveled a little farther north than the year before, and did the band of *Homo erectus,* waiting for certain weather, a certain moon, a certain smell in the air, move after them?

There were a thousand reasons to move on.

Toward the end of the morning Cherri consulted the GPS coordinates on her laminated sheets from the reconnaissance flight. We were nearing the spot where she had marked a "bad gorge," or at least so it had appeared from the plane. We looked ahead expectantly as we rounded every bend, both wary and eager. About noon the river's flow slackened under the warm sun. We heard thundering. We paddled cautiously forward around a broad bend. The forest on each bank simply disappeared into brushy rock shelves and airiness.

We followed Clinton to the left bank and beached among a scattering of granite humps and grasses. I removed my camera from its dry bag and, barefoot, scrambled after Clinton and Rod over the rocks.

"Wow!"

It was big—far bigger than the last waterfall. Clinton and Rod stood there, coolly assessing how we'd get past it but clearly impressed. The Lugenda broadened out onto a great granite shelf, but this shelf was broken, lacking a pie-wedge fragment that pointed upstream. This created a gorge into which the river rolled over and tumbled down in crashing white. Along the gorge's mossy rock sides, slender, silvery threads of smaller waterfalls bounced down to join the tumult below.

Rod estimated the total drop at around fifteen meters, about fifty feet. Fleecy white clouds drifted in the blue sky to the north of us downstream, almost at eye level, it seemed. It felt as if we stood atop a cliff partway up a mountainside, and the mountain eventually eased out into plains far below. Here, it appeared, is where the Lugenda cascaded off the back slope of the Great Rift Valley.

It was unthinkable even to approach the apex by kayak. We'd have to maneuver around it to the side somehow. Whatever route we chose, it was plain that we were in for a lot of heavy portaging.

I returned to the boats. Clinton and Rod went ahead again, leaping barefoot across the boulders, following a side channel. They traced it along the gorge's left rim, through tangles of forest, and discovered a possible portage route to the gorge's bottom. The side channel didn't drop as fearsomely or powerfully as the main drop, but it tumbled over the rim and dropped the whole distance to the bottom nevertheless—first by ricocheting down steeply between big boulders and foaming pools, then plunging in a slender waterfall the remaining thirty feet to the gorge's bottom. It was going to be difficult enough to get down the boulders and waterfall on foot, and unthinkable in our kayaks.

Returning to the boats, we waded them along the side channel toward the lip, dragging the kayaks over mossy plates of rock and small pools, through thickets and forest. There was something inherently heart-quickening about portaging a major waterfall marked on no map. We had seen absolutely zero evidence of human habitation. I felt a sense of surprise and wonder, like a small child who has discovered a beautiful shiny rock and, marveling, turns it over in his or her fingers. As we waded along, I noticed that the water swirling around my feet was tinted a distinct bluish color. Cherri had mentioned that from the reconnaissance flight it looked as if a major tributary entered the Lugenda here on the left. Was this tributary a blue river? Where did it come from? What made it blue?

I didn't know the answers to the questions, but it left me with a sense of wonder just to ask them and to feel the thundering presence of this uncharted waterfall. This was an indefinable feeling that I'd read in no explorer's account—this feeling of wonder and of gratitude, too. Gazing down at my rock-cut white ankles wading through blue water and blackish boulders as I tugged the boat, I felt grateful that I'd had the experience and maybe also that I'd never have to have it again. I'd always wanted to

Rod belays a double kayak down into the waterfall gorge while Steve and Clinton help.

be in a place like this, someplace marvelous and undiscovered, and now I was here. It might be enough to last a lifetime. Part of me wanted to stop and absorb this moment, but—the bane of so many expeditions about which I'd read—we were too busy going forward to stop and marvel. Whatever greater philosophical or emotional reflections our journey inspired were jammed between the cracks, into the spare moments, subsumed to the all-consuming task of moving on. My fleeting thoughts were interrupted by effortful grunts and shin-banging yelps as we all stumbled along.

We reached the jumping-off point: the place where the side channel tumbled over the rim, bouncing down among boulders and pools and then into the slender falls. Rod quickly went to work with all his wilderness survival skill. He produced a climbing rope and rock-climbing hardware. I had no idea that he had stowed this equipment. *This is going to be cool,* I thought. He rigged a figure-eight belay device around his waist, propped his feet against a huge boulder, and payed out rope in order to lower the heavy kayaks one at a time down the steep bouldery slope where the side channel ran. A distance below him, where the bouldery slope and side channel plunged over the clifflike brink and formed the slender falls, Steve—who always did heavy, yeoman's work on the portages, regardless of his performance in tricky paddling—waded up to his neck in a churning little pool, manhandling the belayed kayak over the lip. He passed the boat down to Clinton, who, clinging to ledges and granite nubs, monkeyed his way up and down the waterfall's rock face to slide the boat to the gorge's bottom.

"You looked as if you were swimming and rock-climbing at the same time," I later said to my boatmate Steve.

I had no physical hand in the operation. I chased over the rocks with my Nikon trying to get good angles.

"I feel guilty not helping," I said to Cherri.

"Your job is to record it," she said, readying her own video camera.

She was right. That was my greatest contribution to the team effort, the way Clinton's contribution was his whitewater expertise, and Rod's his wilderness skills. And so record it I did, as best as I could.

We had "breakfast" under shade trees in the early afternoon. The river *shush*ed swiftly out of the gorge. Back in the boats, it felt as if the Lugenda eased right afterward, broadening and mellowing. Far to the north of us, afternoon thunderheads billowed puffy and white, as if to mark the Tanzanian plains. I felt my own tension ease. Had we now passed the worst of the rapids? Every night when Rod took our GPS reading for latitude and longitude, marking the day's progress on my big aeronautical map, I asked for our elevation and worked the numbers. Each night I found us substantially lower. Still, a long drop remained before we descended to five hundred feet above sea level, the approximate elevation of the Lugenda's confluence with the Rovuma, judging from my map. We had now paddled slightly less than half the Lugenda's length. I hoped that the river had completed its run off the rocky Great Rift escarpment and in the 350 kilometers still to go it would fall in steady, gentle riffles rather than the pool-and-drop rapids we'd encountered so far.

The vegetation suddenly seemed more inviting. A jasmine tree with its fragrant white flowers bloomed on the shore and near it was a huge pillar of a tree whose thick outstretched arms supported a crown like a shiny green globe on its shoulders. Clinton tentatively identified it as an African star chestnut. A flock of green pigeons winged past while the "hadeda" birds called their own name, the lonely cries echoing up and down the mirror of the river's surface.

Maybe because I had relaxed slightly and a tentative sense of relief had set in, each sight, each sound had a richness; each one was like collecting a small treasure. I allowed my mind to wander in the hypnotic succession of strokes, thoughts spinning quietly on the horseshoe-shaped swirls left behind in the river's surface by our paddle blades. I thought of Molly, Skyler, and Amy. I had tried to avoid dwelling on them. I'd been reluctant to use the sat phone to call them even though I knew I could at almost any time. I had told myself at the beginning of the trip that I would call them once—when we were about halfway down the river.

We had nearly reached the halfway point. I decided to call them when we made camp that night. I tried to remember their schedule. They had embarked on their own trip, driving and camping down the Oregon and California coast to visit Amy's sister in Los Angeles. I had her phone number with me. What would I tell them? I'd tell them it had been hard but that we were past the worst.

Tears began pouring down my cheeks. I missed them so much. It had been hard and frightening, and I loved them so much and wanted to be with them. I choked off a sob. It was gratitude and relief and a flood of love for them. I had a flash of self-consciousness: Were these histrionics? I didn't care. What would Steve do if he heard me? I looked at the back of his head, now shaggy instead of close-cropped as when I first met him. He didn't turn around. The others were ahead by several boat lengths. Without breaking my double-bladed paddle stroke, I wiped my eyes against my forearms—one forearm, then the other. A fast tongue of current swept us close past a willow island. *A willow island,* I thought. *Rapids ahead?*

But rapids didn't appear. I tried to shift my thoughts to the reasons I was here. We kept paddling rhythmically down the calm river accompanied by the echoing, lonely hadeda cries—Clinton in front, then Cherri and Rod, then Steve and me. I was the last person in our little flotilla. My reasons for being here seemed vague to me. I had to recite them in my head like some litany. I wanted to understand the wilderness. It was important to understand the wilderness and the human reasons for venturing into it, in order to save it. I wanted to save the wilderness. I had joined this expedition with a nobler purpose than that it was something I wanted to do. I was doing this for the good of the planet and not just for myself.

I was no different, I realized, from all the explorers who came before. It was much too hard to do something like this only for yourself, much too easy to ask when the going got truly terrible, "Why am I doing this?" Every explorer had to come up with his or her own answer, to come up with some greater reason, because ego alone can take you only so far.

I envisioned a broad plain stretching to a distant blue horizon. Scattered about were the carcasses of various causes that explorers through the millennia had employed to carry them across. Some of the causes lay abandoned in the middle of the plain like camel skeletons bleaching in the desert sun. Others had reached the lush meadows on the far side. The explorers had done it for King and Queen and Country. They'd done it to spread the True Word of God. They'd done it to reach the City of Gold that would reward them and their descendants with riches for all time. They'd done it to build an Empire, an empire of trade or an empire for their people. They'd done it for Science, and they'd done it for War.

But, finally, were all these merely excuses? Was it really that beneath it all the explorer simply felt compelled to explore by some insatiable curiosity and hunger for adventure? Was it, in fact, an *instinct*?

Would that explain why waves of early humans set north out of Africa—not once but probably many times? A million and a half years after *Homo erectus* migrated from Africa to populate the world, so did modern *Homo sapiens*. Our species evolved around one hundred thousand years ago in tropical eastern and southern Africa (a region that includes the Great Rift as well as the Lugenda River) and spread north into Europe and Asia—a migration scenario that is now bolstered by both the fossil record and DNA evidence from humans the world over.

What compelled them to leave Africa? Drought or fire or hostile bands seem only the half of it.

For one answer I just had to look to the boats ahead of me where Clinton and Rod—bare-chested, strong-armed—paddled purposefully down the Lugenda. What does a young man do? Or what do many of them do? They roam. I had years of personal experience in the roaming phase. If my experience was any indication, a young man often is not even sure what he's looking for. It could be he's looking for bigger game or for flecks of gold or for a mate more desirable and farther off than those he finds in his own little band. I knew all that personally. I knew that a young man is out looking for *possibility.*

But now I had a wife and children. I had a house and a career. So what was I doing here?

We camped at dusk on a sand island shaped like a whale's hump where a side channel met the main Lugenda. Our campsite was backed by "forest galleries" like those *Homo erectus* preferred a million years ago. I wanted to place my tent a bit apart from the others, but the island didn't offer much room and there was also the animal threat. Before unrolling my tent I had to clear dried elephant turds off the little flat spot of sand I'd chosen. I studied them for a moment, wanting to remember just how big they were. I decided that each of the five or six pellets was roughly the size of a half-gallon milk carton. Leaves and twigs and entire small branches flecked the dung, making it look as if someone had shoved a treetop down a garbage disposal.

Earlier that afternoon we had drifted quietly past a group of four elephants, two females and two infants, that reached up with their trunks into the tops of small trees, and some not so small, and stripped them bare of vegetation, jamming the green bundles into their mouths. These were the first elephants we'd seen instead of heard on the river. They fed only a few boat lengths away but didn't seem to fear us, as if they, too, had not been molested by humans.

We had carefully paddled past several pods of hippos, too, including one of about seven animals that were playfully plunging out of the water like dolphins, with grunts and tremendous splashes.

We were all tired as we pitched tents, gathered wood, and started the fire. Everyone knew without saying aloud that the pace was beginning to wear on us. But with the rope-belayed portage into the waterfall gorge it had been an exciting day, a day to recount around the fire. This we did without our usual whiskey ration because our supply had given out the previous evening. Our food was almost gone, too, Rod had reported then. If we ran out, we'd fish.

As the black pot of rice simmered on the fire and the quick tropical night fell around us, I wrote a few of the day's notes, but I kept thinking of my family. I worked the time difference in my head between our sandbar and California. I hoped to catch them about breakfast time. I had figured out that this was the day they were planning to head to the southern California desert.

"If you want water," Rod suddenly announced, "get it now!"

With halogen headlamp gripped in hand, he had been doing some reconnoitering—scanning the darkened channel just in front of our sandbeach camp. A red glaring eye shone back, not fifty feet away. I had been down there a few minutes earlier to fill my canteen. Had the croc been assessing me as I obliviously squatted at the water's edge?

I asked Rod if I could use his satellite phone. He obligingly took it from the Pelican case and, in the beam of his headlamp, showed me how to dial. As everyone else in the group usually did when speaking on the sat phone, I moved a little ways off from the fire circle. It was odd, this bit of etiquette for phoning in the wilderness—partly for privacy, surely, but partly because it was difficult to reconcile the two wildly different worlds: the dark, earthy African one in which your feet were planted and the sunlit, chromium one to which you addressed your words.

The phone rang on the far end. I heard the answering machine of Amy's sister, Noel. I'd missed them, I thought. They'd already left. I started to leave a message.

"This is Peter/Daddy calling from Africa . . ."

Noel picked up the phone. We both skipped the pleasantries. This electronic bond seemed so tenuous, it was as if neither of us wanted to overburden it. She said Amy was in the shower and put on Molly while she went to get her.

"Hi, Daddy," Molly said in her small, sweet telephone voice.

There was a long delay while our words bounced up to satellites and down again, as if we spoke in short verbal telegrams, delivering them and waiting patiently for a reply. I asked her if she had been having fun on her camping trip. She enthusiastically launched into an account of the Oregon coast, of jumping off sand dunes, of motels and swimming pools, of her friends they'd visited on the way. I heard less of the details than of the pleasure in her voice, which pleased me.

"That sounds like fun," I said.

"Where are you?" she asked.

"We're along the river in Africa. It's dark, and I'm standing near the campfire. Can you believe that?"

"Really, it's dark?" Molly said.

I could picture her pretty, roundish face and her blue eyes and blond hair. She was smiling, maybe a little indulgently to humor me.

"When I set up my tent a little while ago, I had to move a big pile of elephant poop."

"Really?" Molly said, laughing. "Are there lots of animals where you are?"

"I saw elephants today and hippos—nice hippos, not mean ones—and yesterday a crocodile tried to bite Clinton's kayak. The crocodile probably thought the boat was a big fish."

Molly laughed again. I loved to hear her laugh.

"Is Mom there?"

Amy got on the phone and asked how it was. I replied that everything was fine, that it had been a lot of hard work but fun. I could have told her a lot more, but I was careful to say nothing that might alarm her.

"How are the people?" she asked, then caught herself, guessing I was standing near them. "You probably can't say."

"I can't really," I said. "It's been fine for the most part."

She asked about the hippos and crocs, the subject of all that speculation before I'd left home. I told her the hippos had been mellow and so had the crocs, mostly, except the one that had nipped Clinton's boat yesterday.

"Right now just across the channel from our camp I can see the firelight reflecting off the red eye of a croc," I said.

"Is that something you have to worry about?" she asked.

"No," I replied. "It's scared of the fire."

I hoped I was right. Nobody had told me that. But most of all I wanted Amy to know I was fine and not to worry. Like Cherri effusing to Heather about the Lugenda's dangers, however, I couldn't help telling her a bit of the drama we had encountered. It felt as if I was speaking to her and she to me in dense, intimate code, each sentence freighted with much more emotional information than it literally said.

"It's really been the rapids that are more than anyone expected," I told her. "We've portaged the big ones and paddled the rest. Just this afternoon we had to lower the boats down a waterfall on climbing ropes. But I think we're past the worst of it.

"How has your road trip been?" I asked her.

"Really, it's been just wonderful," Amy replied. "It's been walks through redwood forests, and collecting rocks and shells on the beach, and camping—cold camping. . . . We should have brought our winter sleeping bags—but it's really been wonderful."

I felt flooded with warmth. I wanted to cry again—out of relief, out of gratitude that my family was well, and out of gratitude toward her for managing so well.

"I miss you all," I said. "I love you. I love you all so very much . . . and I miss you all so very much."

I stopped. I was choking up. In some ways it had been so hard—the constant uncertainty of the river, with this precious family at home that I somehow had to protect as I went through every unknown rapid. The others were sitting nearby, in the circle of firelight with the red crocodile eye glaring in the darkness beyond, like the emblem of watchful uncertainty itself. I could only offer Amy my trembling silence that bounced to her around the rim of space. I tried to speak again. My mouth moved, but no words came out. Instead I gave a teary muffled intake of breath.

"I understand," she said, and I knew that she understood exactly. "I love you very much, too, and miss you and think of you every day."

"I have to go," I finally managed to say. "We're trying to save the batteries, and it's very expensive."

"Before you go, Skyler wants to say hello."

"Hi, Dad!"

"Did you have a good time on your camping trip?"

"Yes," he said. Then he launched into a long rapid-fire account of what he got—something about a squirt gun and a lot of details about it that I couldn't understand. Finally, I had to stop him and tell him that I'd see him soon, and then one at a time they all said good-bye and in the darkness I punched the glowing yellow "off" button. Before I rejoined the group, I stood there for a moment, beyond the circle of firelight, and wiped away the tears.

DAY NINE (PART 1)

I slept poorly, waking in the night with aches and twinges emerging from what seemed like my body's every square inch—from the rock cuts on my toes, feet, ankles, and shins, up to a developing set of hemorrhoids from sitting so long and lifting so much, up to an aching back and shoulders and forearms from long days of paddling, and out to the nicks and scrapes and gashes on hands and fingers from hauling boats over portages. I almost laughed aloud ruefully, I felt so thoroughly battered by the river. Every night climbing into my sleeping bag, I chanted a kind of mantra of soreness as I squirmed and tried to settle in: "Fucking shit . . . fucking shit . . . fucking shit . . ."

"Good morning, Pe-*tah*!" Rod greeted me with his Empire-on-the-march morning cheerfulness as I emerged from the tent at, according to my digital watch, 6:08 a.m.

But where were the Empire's boiled eggs and buttered toast points? I picked up yet another peanut butter energy bar from the kitchen canvas.

Steve admitted that he, too, was sore all over.

"I feel as if I slept on an anvil," Cherri said with customary under-statement.

I laughed. A certain crazy spirit had infected our undertaking. We were pushing hard to make kilometers, driven on by Clinton and Rod, and it felt as if the river was pushing back against us equally hard.

The river let up slightly, however, for early morning. Under gray skies we made good time paddling down broad, calm stretches of silvery water, each bank bordered by a dark band of forest. We lifted our paddles across our decks a few minutes to rest. It felt so very wild and African, drifting there with just the quiet drip off the paddles and the lonely, echoing bird sounds:

Cooo . . . cooo . . . cooo of the loerie.

Waaa . . . waaa . . . waa, like babies crying up in the trees—the trumpeter hornbill.

Hadeda . . . hadeda . . . hadeda, the crowlike call from the forest edges of the bird who says its name.

After two hours we spotted a bark canoe poling upstream, pushing out a silvery V-wake over the mercury-shimmering water. Here was only the second person we'd encountered in the last four days. The previous afternoon a man with a deep voice had called out to us from the forest but kept himself hidden as we paddled past, although I had explained in Portuguese we were paddling to the Rovuma. Now this fisherman stopped poling, propped his boat against the current, and stared at us as we approached.

"Bom dia!" we said cheerily.

He appeared to relax slightly. He warned us in Portuguese that a hippo lay just downstream on the right bank and that we should cross to the left. We thanked him and took his advice but saw no hippo, which must have submerged.

We ran a nice rapids—a wide chute dotted with boulders. Following Clinton, Steve and I cut S-turns around the boulders, but Rod and Cherri, behind us, got hung up on one, piling into it sideways. With his incredible arm strength, Rod managed to pry hard on his paddle and pop the boat right over the boulder. He had lent his spray skirt to Clinton; his cockpit swamped with water during the course of the rapids.

"Were you *trying* to bounce off the rocks?" Clinton teased Rod when he and Cherri lurched out of the bottom of the rapids and joined us in the pool below, his boat riding low.

"What were you two trying to do up there?" added Steve.

I kept my silence. I could see what was coming. Rod was proud of his abilities and didn't like to make mistakes.

"It's very difficult to steer a boat half-full of water!" Rod fired back angrily. "You all should count yourselves fucking lucky to have splash skirts!"

That abruptly ended the discussion. We paddled on in silence. The day had suddenly shifted in tension that would only build.

*   *   *

The maze of boulders, morning of Day Nine.

Soon the river spread wider than we had ever seen it—maybe a third of a mile wide—blocked by another granite barrier across its breadth. We climbed out and poked our heads over the edge. A boulder field gently sloped away below, an enormous one, acres upon acres of granite chunks and tiny, twisted channels, most of them too small to fit a boat through. Here was a giant sieve made of rocks.

"Wait until you see the braided section," Cherri had warned us, having spotted it from the air. Judging by the sight of it and the GPS bearing, this was the area that she had seen.

Clinton set off, deftly slaloming his single through the tiny channels and down rocky ramps. Rod and Cherri followed, picking their own course where their big double couldn't follow his smaller, lighter craft. Steve and I went last. He climbed into the bow seat while, holding the stern, I waded the boat around in the shallow water until I'd aimed it properly into the first little chute. I clambered in. The boat immediately thunked to a stop on protruding rocks. I climbed out and straightened it again between the rocks. But this time when I tried to climb back in, I slipped on the algae-covered rocks of the river bottom and fell.

The kayak took off down the chute with only Steve in the bow. Half sliding on my rear, half swimming down the rocky chute, I clutched at the stern of the kayak, trying to slow it, trying to crawl back in. I got a grip on it and managed to stand up in waist-deep fast water. I was about to boost myself in when my feet slipped. I fell again. The current swept me, banging me along, legs, knees, shins, over rocks. I was lurching and trying to swim after the loose boat.

Steve couldn't steer it. He couldn't stop it. He looked back to me for help as the boat ricocheted between rocks.

"What should I do?"

There was nothing I could think to tell him while bouncing down the chute. There were so many obstacles, and things were happening so fast. Or maybe I thought I could handle it alone—the hero.

The chute mellowed. I caught up to the boat and grabbed the stern. When I tried to climb in, I fell again. Steve and the boat lurched down another small, fast chute, a crevasse between big chunks of granite, while I battered along the bottom.

The kayak wallowed in a pool. I quickly heaved myself in. We caught up to the others, waiting just ahead in a little pool in the labyrinth. Clinton tilted in his yellow single down another little chute. Rod chose a different route and dragged his and Cherri's boat over a shallow bed of rocks. I decided to follow Rod, preferring the effort of dragging the boat over shallow rocks to the chance of swimming and banging down another chute. Across the shallows, Rod climbed back into his cockpit and paddled into a small fast channel. I aimed our boat after his and hopped in.

I had lost my confidence. The little channel swept us toward a phalanx of boulders that sat in its midst. It wasn't dangerous or scary or even difficult. But I really didn't want to go swimming and banging through the rocks again. I hesitated as to which way to steer around them—I didn't want to make the wrong choice—but with that moment's hesitation it was too late to turn either way. We plowed straight into them. We dumped, both spilling out into the Lugenda.

I silently seethed with frustration, too angry even to swear. We stood in swift thigh-deep water, grabbed the swamped boat, and waded it, stumbling over the slippery bottom, to a dry patch of rocks. Steve diligently pulled without a word. We emptied out and quickly climbed back in.

Smash! Into another boulder I couldn't avoid.

"I can't turn this fucking boat!" I screamed in frustration.

We bounced off and careened toward another boulder.

"Right! Right! Paddle to the right!" I screamed at Steve.

Clinton paddles the big drop, Day Nine.

This was the first time I'd yelled at him. It didn't feel good.

"If I paddle right, we'll hit that rock!" he shouted back.

Smash! Into another boulder.

And on it went. We bumped. We bounced. We dragged over rocks. And finally we emerged at the bottom of the boulder field.

The boulder field was only the beginning. Pouring out of the granite sieve, the Lugenda slid left. Within a few hundred yards another granite dam blocked it. We heard water roaring and noted the trees drop away ahead. We climbed out where the river cut through a big granite hump and disappeared. Depending on how you defined it, you could call it a major whitewater chute or a decent-sized waterfall. The drop looked about twenty feet. It was possible to portage in fairly straightfoward fashion over the granite hump and down a series of ledges to a beautiful pool below.

Except that Clinton wasn't looking at the portage.

"I think I'll run this," he said.

I could only marvel. Here was the difference between Clinton and me: He thought running this big drop in a loaded sea kayak looked like fun. At some point in my life I might have thought that, but I surely didn't now.

Clinton scouted the rapid and then readied his kayak by removing spare equipment lashed to the deck. I prepared my Nikon, then swam a

Clinton's overturned hull at the bottom of the big drop.

narrow channel with my camera held overhead to keep it dry and climbed onto a rock promontory that overlooked the drop. Cherri set up her video camera. Meanwhile, Rod and Steve, bent and sweating in the warm sun, now shining after the clouds had cleared, laboriously dragged the double kayaks over the granite hump and down the ledges to the edge of the pool below the falls.

Clinton slowly completed his preparations, climbed into his yellow single, carefully fastened the spray skirt he had borrowed again from Rod, leaned over, and scooped up a double handful of water, which he splashed on his face and into his mouth, as if giving himself a baptismal taste of the river. He and Rod usually drank water straight from the river without boiling it if we weren't near villages. Clinton shoved off. Making a few strokes above the granite dam, he swiveled his boat, lined it up, and came paddling downstream straight at the middle of the falls.

I clicked photos as he entered. Through the camera lens I watched him slide over the brink; then he and the kayak entirely disappeared, swallowed by a huge pillow of whitewater just past the lip. The boat's yellow nose speared out the other side, coming toward me where I crouched on the promontory; then Clinton and the yellow boat plunged down, down, down the steep, tumultuous chute, smashed into another big pillow, and disappeared.

A moment later, well below my promontory, I spotted his overturned

Steve and Cherri in the beautiful pool below the big drop, Day Nine.

hull twisted crossways in the thundering froth, rushing toward the bottom. Then the waggle of a paddle blade protruded above the surface, and suddenly Clinton popped upright again, completing an Eskimo roll just as the chute spit him out into calmer water below. He drifted there in the spinning froth, boat swamped, and spray skirt stripped off the cowling. The fierce whitewater had torn it off and flooded his cockpit, capsizing him. He regained his bearings and slowly paddled into shore.

It was a great performance, but the vibes back on shore weren't good. Neither Rod nor Steve seemed too happy about having portaged the boats alone.

Cherri went for a swim in the pool, and Steve and I joined her. It looked the picture of a tropical pool, with threads of a small waterfall splashing down a ledge into the shallow sandy pool. The water felt cool and soothing after the warm sun. We lolled. It was now well past mid-morning. I hoped to stop here and have breakfast.

Rod seemed sullen and wanted us to move on. Clinton was in a hurry, too—we could still make more distance before breakfast. By early afternoon Rod also hoped to get into radio range of the hunting camp on the lower river.

We reluctantly left the pool and climbed into the boats. I was irri-

Peter in the idyllic pool.

tated with their impatience to be moving all the time. Why couldn't we *experience* this place instead of rushing through it? I felt I was always behind, behind even in my notes. I wanted to understand this place. I had started to blame it on that goddamned satellite phone. They now were checking their email messages by sat phone at least twice a day—at breakfast and in the evening, and sometimes in the morning, too. Clinton and Rod had safari dates coming up later in the month. I hated the twin feelings: the vulnerability of being in the wilderness while at the same time being subjected to the rigid time pressures of schedules from the modern world. I wanted to follow the natural rhythms of the wilds, to stop and listen and look and sniff the wind before proceeding. The satellite phone—reminding people of the outside world, of appointments to keep—was short-circuiting our collective animal senses.

I felt we were too hasty and not careful enough in scouting the rapids. Besides, according to Cherri's reconnaissance, we were supposed to have been out of the biggest section of rapids days ago, but each day they got worse. I felt we were skirting the edge of disaster. Only that morning Steve and I had come within a hairsbreadth of dumping in a powerful trough of whitewater along a rock wall that would have been a real mess. Clinton had advised me how to enter it, letting the current turn the boat, and I had followed his instructions, but it was clear he didn't appreciate the heavy, slow swing of our tandem. The current took a long time to swing us; we entered late, which caused the roaring trough to flip us up on our side. It was only the snap of my hips and the brace of my paddle blade at the last instant—finally successful—that saved us.

All this was weighing on me as they hustled us out of the beautiful pool below the falls. I knew we would end up squatting on some slimy mud bank to eat our mugs of oatmeal.

"What's the hurry?" I said to Rod as we pushed off from the pool's edge.

"This is an expedition, Pe-*tah*. We have distance to make."

"I'm willing to spend as much time as it takes."

"People are counting on us," Rod said.

We did, in fact, end up squatting on a slimy mud bank for breakfast. Under the hot sun I perched on a mud-caked boulder and wrote notes, begrudging the very spot. No one else seemed too cheery, either. Halfway through this desultory oatmeal stop—our "gruel," Steve had taken to calling the oatmeal—we heard the faint, distant buzz of an airplane engine. Instantly, we were all on our feet and squinting downriver, over the ragged forest edge, toward the northern horizon. Whatever tensions hung over our mud bank vanished, at least for the moment. This was the first engine we'd heard since Lance had left us in the Land Rover nine days before. Not even high-altitude jets flew over the Lugenda, as if it existed in a separate pocket of time.

"There it is!" someone called out.

We spotted a faint gleam far off, banking here, banking there over the forest.

"It's Jamie's plane!"

"He might not even be coming here!"

"Get the radio!"

"He's coming this way!"

"Maybe he's dropping the spray skirt!"

Jamie Wilson was the safari hunter who ran the camp on the Lugenda River's lower reaches, called Luwire Camp. He had flown Cherri on her reconnaissance scout, and Clinton happened to know him, too, having worked briefly at the Luwire Camp a year or two earlier. Jamie had cleared a landing strip in the bush both at his camp and farther upriver at a village marked on the map called Mussoma. It was at the Mussoma bush strip that we hoped to get our resupply flight; Jamie would fly Steve out, fly Josh the photographer in, and resupply our food. But we hadn't expected to meet Jamie's plane flying here, still many kilometers upriver from the Mussoma bush strip.

We now heard the engine's buzz clearly. Suddenly, it seemed so much of our hope and energy was staked on the unpredictable behavior of that little bit of metal buzzing insectlike over the forest. This piece of metal represented our only physical connection, except for the ephemeral voices through the satellite phone, with the world from which we came.

The plane made a long, lazy circle over forest and river a mile or two downstream. Then it straightened out and flew upriver, passing over the forest behind us, obviously not seeing us.

"Shit!"

Clinton scrambled to his yellow kayak and paddled into the river, raising his paddle in the air like a staff. From the mud bank we could hear but not see the plane buzzing over the forest upriver.

"What's he doing?"

We could hear the sound growing louder again.

"Here he comes!" Clinton called to us. "Coming down low!"

The plane buzzed down the center of the river about five hundred feet over Clinton and our mud bar. Rod was on the handheld radio trying to find a common channel. Surely he saw us now. The airplane circled back, circled patiently overhead, until Rod made radio contact. He handed the radio to Cherri.

"You know those rapids that look so small from the air?" Cherri said into the radio to Jamie circling overhead. *"Not!"*

It was hard to hear Jamie's response through the static. In the cockpit with him was his hunting partner, Derek Littleton. Cherri told them that we'd be at the Mussoma strip in two days' time and arranged for Jamie to make the supply run then. But Jamie expressed skepticism that we'd make Mussoma that quickly.

"We're moving fast now," Cherri insisted into the radio.

So we left it at that: We'd meet at the Mussoma bush strip in two days. They signed off.

"Maybe he sees something we don't," someone on our mud bar remarked presciently.

* * *

I wanted to get out of my boat and scout the rapid myself, but Clinton discouraged me.

"It's just some good-sized waves in a straight chute," he reported, hopping barefoot back into his kayak.

We weren't even out of sight of the mud bar oatmeal stop. Another big shield of granite blocked the river, slanting away in a long, half-mile hill down to the forest edge. The Lugenda funneled into a split in the granite, creating a very fast chute about five hundred yards long. Near the bottom it slammed into a house-sized boulder on the left, ricocheted off in a tumult of whitewater, and disappeared around a bend.

"You won't have a problem," Clinton reassured us as we lined up our boats in the calm water at the top. "Just eddy out left at the bottom of the chute."

"And if we *do* have a problem, what's down below the eddy?" I asked.

"I don't know," Clinton said. "The river turns, and I can't see around the corner. Just eddy out, and then I'll have another look. If you swim, swim left."

I could feel the anxiety coalesce in my stomach. We were about to enter a major chute almost totally blind. I didn't know what lay beyond it. I knew Clinton didn't know, either. But I also knew that beyond the bottom of the chute the river continued to drop steeply because I could see how far away and how far down the forest edge lay. It could easily be another major rapid around the bend or another major waterfall.

You're frightening too easily, part of me said. But then another part of me spoke up. *You* should *be scared!*

I heard the reverberating echoes of a hundred other uncertain situations in the outdoors, some with my father: falling from the rafters, tipping over in the ice boat, breaking through the lake ice, clambering out of the capsizing canoe. My instinct for survival argued with itself. Yes, I could simply walk around the rapid. But that carried a risk, too: that I might lose whatever respect I had from Clinton and Rod. How might that play out in the days ahead? No one would want to wait for all the inconvenience of my walking it and having Clinton come upriver and paddling my boat. They'd try to convince me. I'd have to argue back. I could hear the echoes of my grandfather.

You don't want to be a sissy, do you?

I felt trapped between danger and shame. A sense of doom rose up in me like a cork released at the bottom of the pool. There was no way out, only two unhappy options.

Okay, I'll risk it. I shoved the cork down and held it there.

"Life jackets on! Splash skirts on!" Clinton called out.

We pried the elasticized edges of the skirts over the cockpit cowlings. The white plastic hull felt warm in the sun. The water spread calm and glassy upriver, bordered by the dark green forest. The sky looked very blue. *Focus.* That's what the survival instinct told me now. *Don't think about your fears. Simply focus on what's at hand!*

Clinton went first, sliding over the glassy bulging water of the lip, accelerating down the chute, suddenly bouncing far ahead and below us, like a sled gone down a hill. Rod and Cherri followed, shooting ahead. Then Steve and I made the strokes to commit us over the lip.

Almost instantly, I knew we were in trouble. Maybe if my confidence hadn't been so damaged in the morning, banging my body through the rock sieve; maybe if I wasn't angry at the pace we were keeping, the lack of more thorough scouting, the fear of paddling straight into trouble; maybe if I'd had more presence of mind to yell instructions to Steve; maybe if I simply *went for it* instead of trying to be conservative. These were all things that might have helped us through.

The first wave rose far bigger than any we had encountered on the Lugenda before—an enormous green roller crested with white that sparkled in the sun.

Jesus Christ! How are we going to get over this? I thought.

The kayak felt like a half-sunken log caught in the current, so heavily weighted was it and the river so powerful. I remembered an emergency move for situations like this, taught to me by an expert whitewater canoeist only a few weeks before I came to Africa. Intentionally going sideways through rapids to demonstrate the maneuver's stability, he had planted his paddle blade straight down into the water and used it to hold his boat upright through big turbulence. I now did the same with my paddle, using it like a steel girder planted straight down into the river.

Was it the right move? I still don't know. Should I have yelled to Steve, "Paddle, paddle, paddle," so we could blast through the waves? I may have yelled that. Probably I didn't.

I remember going up, up, *up* over the wave, the kayak's white bow shooting out into the blue African sky, Steve hovering far overhead in his cockpit, paddle blades extended like wings, then plunging down, down, *down* in the big green trough that followed. The kayak dove underwater and sluggishly heaved itself to the surface again. But we didn't tip.

Then I saw the next wave right after it, even bigger than the first—an ocean-sized wave. I planted my paddle more firmly into the river. We rose up and over, the bow shooting out into the air again and plunging down into the deep green trough.

The boat felt just barely stable enough with my paddle planted like a girder. I didn't want to take it out of the river, but on the third huge wave the current started to spin the boat sideways to the left. Two hundred yards ahead the torrent bounced off the house-sized boulder and dropped into the churning fallaway bend to the right.

Oh, shit! How are we going to make the turn with the boat cocked sideways! No way . . . no way!

We'd do a backflip into the huge whitewater hole that surely lay on its downstream side. I clung to my girder-paddle for security. Then I spotted an eddy on the left, just above the big rock. *When in doubt, eddy-out.*

"Let's grab that eddy on the left!" I shouted to Steve. "We'll regroup for the last drop. Paddle hard on the right!"

Steve paddled. I stroked and then steered. The kayak spun counterclockwise across the current, bow headed toward the eddy. I could hear the roaring of water crashing down and around the big rock.

We each gave a few hard strokes. We were going to make it! But we now carried all our momentum from the ripping chute into the swirling calm of the eddy just above the big rock. I wasn't ready for the transition, and Steve was utterly clueless.

I should have yelled "Lean left!" so we could both have tilted the boat like a bicyclist leaning to the inside of a turn. But I didn't yell, and neither of us leaned.

The kayak's right edge dug sideways into the slow water, wallowed deep, and came to a stop. Steve's and my torsos kept their downstream momentum. With all our weight, plus the gear strapped to the boat deck, it was like a tree toppling: Beyond a certain point, there was no stopping it. I tried to react, but it was too late. Steve's torso dropped into the water like an anchor thrown overboard, pulling us over the rest of the way.

We're really screwed now, I thought, remembering the yawning turbulence just downstream.

It was always a surprise, the sudden acoustical shifts when tipping—

Splash!
Burble.
Burble.

—so peaceful underwater after the roar of the rapids that shook the air overhead. But even underwater in the calm I heard a distant thundering.

I surfaced instantly. I was surprised to find myself not plunging into rapids but surrounded by flat, swirling water. I was still in the eddy. So was Steve and so was our kayak.

I spun my body around, eyes scanning the river in quick bursts. *How do I get out of this?* I saw I had a moment's reprieve. Just downstream loomed the bulk of the huge boulder, with the swirl of the eddy piling up against it before cascading down and to the right like an enormous gushing spigot discharging into the rushing chute.

If I can just climb up on that boulder—

The eddy shoved me toward the rock. I kicked my legs hard and lunged up at its steep face. I managed to cling with my fingers to a few nubbins of rock. I scrabbled with toes to gain purchase underwater and managed to get an algae-covered hold on the rock face with one big toe. I felt a kayak paddle brush against my arms and back. I looked down to my right to see it plunge down the spigot of water and disappear into an enormous whitewater hole created by the boulder shoving the spigot's flow out into the chute's rush.

I now felt the boat brush against my arms and back as I clung tenaciously to the boulder's face. It, too, slid away and tumbled down into the hole, disappearing. Then I felt Steve's soft skin brushing against me. I could do nothing to help him. I looked down to the right and watched his dark, wet head of hair shoot down the spigot and disappear into the hole.

My toe slipped on the underwater algae. My fingers slowly began to slip off the tiny nubbins of rock.

I tried to heft myself a little higher. Instead, I lost what little grip I had. Slowly—very slowly at first—I slid inch by inch down the boulder's face like the cartoon cat with extended claws sliding down the wall.

I looked down to my right into the quivering, roaring maw of the hole below. Either I cling to the boulder, slowly peel away, and finally fall straight into its center, or I spring off the boulder like a frog and leap as much of it as I could.

I leaped.

Whoossh!

A flurry of thundering white engulfed my body. Then long muscular tongues of white-and-green water lashed and buffeted my limbs, spinning me sideways, flipping me upside down. No sense of up or down, top or bottom. No sense of buoyancy from the life jacket. Only swirling bubbles.

Then I saw green water. I saw light. I swam for it . . . up . . . up.

My head broke through the surface. There was sky and air and more water—big waves—another wave train. I was facing upriver. My head and body bobbed up, plunged under, and bobbed up again.

I spun around in the water, combing the river ahead, seeing how it churned into whitewater again and rushed around the bend to the right between low granite walls, out of sight, dropping away. To what? A big chute? Another waterfall?

I sensed motion and color along a cove or eddy on the rocky right bank.

"Swim!" I heard voices scream.

I was already swimming toward them—hard.

I broke my pace for a moment and quickly glanced downstream again, assessing my position and direction. The powerful sweep of the current was pulling me around the bend. Backlit by glints of sunlight off the water, I spotted a small dark head of hair bobbing through big waves—rising and submerging, heading around the bend.

That must be Steve, swept downstream!

"Swim!" I heard Cherri scream from shore. "Swim harder!"

I kicked and stroked, angling across the powerful current toward the cove. It didn't matter if the shouts were for me or for him or for both of us. He was being swept around the bend. I was just barely keeping even in my struggle to prevent a similar fate. I was frightened, but I tried not to panic and thrash, tried to extend my body long and muscular in the water. *Keep your form!*

Head swiveling as I breathed, I glimpsed something like an orange sky-rocket streak across the blue sky. Rod crouched at the streak's base. With his tremendous strength he had hurled a throw rope across the entire river toward Steve.

I raised my head above the cascading current to see if I'd make the eddy.

"Swim!" screamed Cherri from shore.

I dug in again with all my strength. It was going to be close. I pulled and pulled, gasping for air, harder than I'd ever swum in my life. I refused to go around that bend without giving it everything I had, without giving everything for Molly and Skyler and Amy. *You're in really good condition. You can do this!* Then suddenly I popped across the eddy line into calm water. I had made it.

Clinton appeared immediately before me in his bright yellow boat, shoving our overturned kayak along with his bow. He knew that if we saved ourselves but lost the kayak, we'd be in deep trouble anyway out in this Lugenda wilderness.

"Take this!" he shouted. I grabbed it. "Swim it in!"

"Get Steve!" Cherri was now screaming at Clinton from shore. "Leave the kayak and get Steve!"

The throw rope had just missed Steve, or he had missed it. His black bobbing head disappeared around the bend. Clinton was already sprint-paddling after him. I kicked across the eddy to shore, pushing the kayak. I dragged it and my body, panting, onto granite slabs about a hundred feet downstream from Rod and Cherri.

"Are you okay?" they called out.

Hunched over at the waist, panting, I nodded and raised my hand.

They jumped in their kayak and took off around the bend in pursuit of Clinton and Steve.

For five minutes I could do nothing but hunch over with the swamped white tandem kayak on granite slabs in the midst of the African wilds and hyperventilate. It was everything I could do simply to catch my breath. Slowly, I was able to think of the consequences of what had just happened. The last I'd seen of Steve was that black head plunging on waves around the bend into the unknown. A chute? A waterfall? Had he made it to shore?

Had he drowned?

Panting, I tried to straighten up.

How would I feel? Guilty? Because I might have prevented it? That was too much to think about right now. But if he had drowned, what would we do next? Keep paddling? And if he hadn't drowned, what then?

This was ridiculous, to go so blindly into a rapid that big. I knew one thing absolutely: That was the last time Steve and I were going to paddle a rapid like that, largely unscouted, at least unscouted by me. "If you let them push you into doing something stupid," Amy had warned, "and you get killed, I'm going to be really angry."

That had been really stupid. We were going to slow down; that was all there was to it. I was pissed. I didn't give a flying fuck about Clinton's or Rod's safari schedules or making distance or whatever the fuck the hurry was. This gung-ho expedition business. This first descent of the Lugenda. This so-called exploration. Fuck that! I was going to slow down and get home safely to my family, to Molly and Skyler and Amy, and I didn't care what it took. We'd been going too fast. We'd been taking too many risks. This was exactly the situation I'd been worried about when I signed on— that I'd be the one balking at the dangers, I'd be the one urging caution.

I partially caught my breath. I managed to straighten up, my anger subsiding momentarily, and halfheartedly tilted the tandem on edge and dumped water from the flooded cockpits. And what if Clinton and Rod refused to slow down? What would I do? I could quit. I didn't mind doing that. But what then? I contemplated the prospect of walking out on my own. We would soon near the boundaries of the Niassa Reserve, recently designated along the Lugenda's lower reaches. Would I find a road some-where in there? Even if I could find a road, however, it might be days before anyone came along it. Would I survive in the bush alone? I pictured myself stumbling along in the forest for days, huddled at night around a big log fire, yellow eyes blinking out at me from the darkness.

I had wondered exactly what wilderness is. This, I suddenly knew as I stood hunched and panting on the empty shore, was wilderness. This sense of utter animal *nakedness*. Absolute vulnerability. I was in the midst of wilderness, and I didn't like it at all.

DAY NINE (PART 2)

I could only wait on the riverbank. I had no idea what was going on downstream, no idea what had happened to Steve.

I tilted the boat further on its edge, and water gushed from flooded cockpits onto the granite slabs and drained into the Lugenda. The bow cockpit looked deserted and spooky without Steve there to fill it. I noticed half a kayak paddle clunking about inside the hull. It was all that remained of the spare paddle that had been wedged under Steve's seat. This was going to be a problem. I'd lost my paddle in the rapids, Steve's surely was gone, too, and now we had only half a spare.

Looking up, I spotted Clinton and Rod across the river picking their way over the big sunlit humps of granite from somewhere downstream. Clinton held a paddle in his hand like a spear, and, like Rod, still wore his life vest. Their presence was a good sign. If Steve was missing or seriously hurt, they wouldn't be here.

Working over the rocks until they were well upstream of me and the boat but still on the opposite bank, Clinton climbed out onto a narrow neck of rock that cantilevered over the river just below the big hole into which we had fallen. He shot his kayak paddle like a spear across the river. Standing at the brink, he rocked his torso back and forth in rhythm to the powerful pulses of current, like a snake about to strike. Timing the arrival of a weak pulse, he suddenly launched himself in a long dive off the rock into the river, resurfaced in the middle of the current, and stroked powerfully across it.

A minute later he reached my shore, a hundred yards upstream. He fetched his kayak paddle where it had washed up in the eddy and came walking over the granite slabs toward me.

"Is Steve all right?" I called out as he neared.

"He's okay, a little shaken," Clinton said.

"What happened to him?"

"He went through some more rapids and got to the riverbank a ways down."

I sensed Clinton was minimizing it. I was relieved anyway. Now I was going to face the situation straight-on. There was no way I would go on as we had been.

"These rapids are too big for Steve and me in this boat!" I exclaimed. "I wish you'd given me the chance to scout it! This is what happens when we hurry and I don't have time to check it out! If I had seen it was that big, I would have deferred to you and Rod! I would have let you two run it in our boat!"

He glared back at me with those intense blue eyes, two distilled beams of the pure African sky overhead, a child of this continent. His muscled shoulders with the wild dog tracks were dark tan against the bright sunlit rapids crashing behind him.

"It was bigger than I thought," he retorted, "but if you had stayed in the center, you would have been fine!"

Now all the tension and anger I'd been holding in came flooding up.

"I stayed in the center! We were right in the center! We started spinning to the left; you said eddy out on the left, and I saw an eddy on the left and so I thought I'd eddy out!"

"I meant to eddy left at the *foot* of the rapids!" he shot back. "That's still in the *middle* of the rapids!"

And so it went like that, half shouting at each other in the African sunlight, the Lugenda River roaring beside us. After a few of these exchanges, it was clear we were going nowhere. We both let it drop. We climbed into the tandem, with me in front gripping the short half of a paddle and Clinton taking my usual place in the stern cockpit.

"Don't bother paddling with that thing. Just hang on," he said. "Lean when I tell you to."

He shoved us off and paddled us out of the eddy and into the current sweeping around the bend. I felt how powerful and sure his every stroke was. It made me feel lame and inert, impotent, especially when just sitting there idly. The river shoved us through a big set of waves and then an S-curving set of rapids that fell away between low walls of granite. Sitting in the bow, the boat actually felt quite stable and seemed to ride much higher. I was used to the stern deck behind me being nearly submerged. Was it that Clinton and I together were a lighter pair than Steve and me? Or was it Clinton's superior paddling or simply the difference between bow and stern?

"Lean right!" Clinton called out, steering confidently. "Lean left!"

Why couldn't I steer like that?

I took up the half paddle and started stroking along with Clinton, not very effectively. I had to be doing something. We ran more rapids and rounded a bend. Standing amid the rocky slabs of the left bank were Cherri, Rod, and Steve, with the other white tandem and Clinton's yellow single pulled up at their feet. Clinton steered us into the eddy where Steve had finally managed to drag himself to shore after his swim through all those rapids.

Steve's eyes remained downcast as our bow bumped up onto the rocks. He looked grim. He looked waterlogged. He looked shaken. I climbed out of the boat and moved toward him.

"How are you doing?" I asked.

He mumbled something noncommittal that I didn't quite catch.

Neither Cherri nor Rod said much, either. A sullen pall seemed to hang over the sunlit, baked-rock shore. Were they blaming me? Were they thinking I had really screwed up? Steve had almost drowned. "That's as close as I ever came to dying," he said later. "Every time I tried to come up for air, I went back down again." Plus we were missing our two paddles, essential equipment out here in the wilds. Were they accusing me of this mess?

Well, fuck them!

I had no desire to climb back into the same boat with Steve. I'm sure he had no desire to climb back into the same boat with me. We all stood there, trying to work out the next move. There was a spare paddle, an intact one, stashed in one of the other boats, so that left us half a paddle down. Someone would use the half paddle until camp that night, and then we could carve or improvise a new one.

And what about the boat pairings? Should we change them? Clinton said he really didn't see any alternative to the arrangement we now had. Then I noticed him say something quietly to Cherri. She shook her head, her blond hair swinging no.

I didn't know what had transpired between them, but I had a pretty good guess. I suspected Clinton had quietly asked her if she'd be willing to paddle in the bow of my boat with me in the stern and put Steve in Rod's bow. She nixed the idea instantly. I didn't blame her. Rod's boat was safer than paddling with me. I may have had a good deal more paddling experience, but he was far stronger and bolder than I. This was his element. I would have stuck with him, too.

In that moment I acutely felt my place in the animal hierarchy of our little group plummet. The only female in the band had chosen a male protector. It decidedly wasn't me, the old man at age forty-eight. I may have had a chance in a different setting—in a city, for instance, where all my years of education and writing carried some weight (although Cherri, for one, certainly didn't need any male help making her way in that world) or maybe even in a village along the Lugenda, where I knew how to communicate better than the others and my age would give me status. But out here in the wilds it was abundantly clear: In terms of pure physical survival on the river I was one of the group's weaker members.

Out here Rod had won. I had lost.

Or maybe none of this had really transpired while we were standing there on the shore. Maybe this animal hierarchy and the meaning of Cherri's shake of the head was all in my paranoid imagination. But I don't think so. I think something was surfacing from far deeper inside me, inside all of us, that happens every day everywhere in the world but was simply illuminated in bold relief out here. She was so right about Africa: It makes you be aware.

There wasn't anything to do but go on. We could all only go on.

I had to hand it to Steve. He actually was willing—not only willing but totally uncomplaining—to get into the boat with me. As he was about to step into the bow cockpit, I noticed something odd about his big sunburned arms and shoulders. His life jacket was askew. I looked closer. Both shoulder straps lay on his left shoulder. Somehow he had managed to get his head out the life jacket's *arm*hole.

No wonder he had been sinking so much in the rapids. His life jacket must have been strapped on so loosely that it managed to float up over his head. Or maybe he had just accidentally put his head through the armhole to begin with.

"Here, let's fix this," I said.

I helped him unstrap it and secure it tightly the right way. I felt as if I were taking care of a small child. I could be angry at his older sister, at Clinton, at Rod, at myself for this situation I found myself in, but it was hard to be angry at Steve for not knowing what he was doing in a kayak. He was very willing, uncomplaining, loyal, physically strong, and able to endure a lot. I felt we were teammates, boatmates. He could have made it miserable to be with him through all these travails, but he helped me the best way he could—by forbearing. And for that I owed him thanks.

As I finished with Steve's life jacket and we were about to depart, Clinton chastised Cherri for screaming at him in the midst of the whitewater rescue.

"When we're in a situation like that, don't tell me what to do. I know what to do. That's my job. That's what I signed on for."

Cherri listened silently, acknowledging what he said. Finished with Cherri, he turned to the rest of us.

"Everyone has all their fingers and toes? Okay, let's go."

Just downstream the river slackened into a big pool surrounded by rocky little coves and humpy granite islands. Rod, always vigilant, circumnavigated one shore with Cherri and spotted one of the lost kayak paddles bobbing there.

"Yes, Rodney!" we cried out.

We stroked across the pool as shafts of sunlight disappeared into its dark green depths. I felt an almost overpowering sense of foreboding. We were still within the big slanting shield of rock. The forest edge remained far ahead and well below. Deep, still water like this pool dammed by these humpy barriers of rock almost surely meant more big rapids just ahead.

We hadn't paddled two hundred yards before we could hear the roaring. I was almost physically nauseous with anxiety.

If you let them push you into doing something stupid . . .

There was an opening between humps of granite. Here the river spilled away downhill with a rush and a roar. Clinton pulled his kayak up to one of the humps, hopped up, and poked his head over. More waves in a chute, he reported.

"How do you feel about this one?" he asked me, climbing back into his cockpit as we bobbed above the chute.

"Maybe I'll walk it," I said. "I'll go take a look on my own."

I didn't trust him anymore. But, worse, I didn't trust myself anymore, either. I was consumed by anxiety, by my second-guessing myself, by fear. And I felt ashamed of it, too. They were all waiting at the top of the rapids for me to screw up my courage.

"Would you feel better if I gave you the single," Clinton asked, "and I paddled the tandem with Steve?"

He gazed at me with those penetrating blue eyes. His voice was kind. He seemed genuinely concerned. Now my mind spun the way my eyes had earlier as I swam through the rapids, scoping out trouble, searching madly for an exit. Questions beset me, suspicious at his offer. Would this rapid be even harder in his boat? Would I be even worse off, make even more mistakes? *What was the hitch?*

"Do you think I'll be able to handle it okay?" I asked him, badly needing reassurance.

"I think you'll be fine," he replied, sensing my need.

"How will your boat handle compared to this big one?"

"You'll be a lot more maneuverable but maybe knocked around a little more," he said.

I tried to think. I felt utterly paralyzed. There were so many conflicting urges pushing against each other inside me—fear versus shame, caution versus the desire to appear bold—and somewhere under it all floated the image of my children looking back at me. I could hardly speak. We floated on the calm, deep pond with the roar of the rapids just past the rocks.

"Do you think I'm being a crybaby?" I blurted out suddenly.

Where did *that* come from? I never use that word. It was as if it had risen unbidden from my childhood. This was the term my grandfather used on those first wilderness canoe trips so many years ago. Maybe deep down this was my biggest fear of all: being thought a coward.

"I think you've done just fine," Clinton replied. "I don't think any less of you than I did before."

A reprieve. I felt a surge of gratitude and affection toward Clinton. I hadn't performed shamefully after all. I had struggled and struggled to meet some standard of conduct in the wilds that I'd internalized from long ago. I was terrified I couldn't meet it. Now Clinton was telling me I'd done just fine. I could feel tears of thankfulness coming to my eyes.

"Okay," I said, nodding toward his kayak. "I'll take it."

We switched places. Clinton climbed into my stern cockpit. I took his yellow single. He let me keep my spray skirt, and he went without. His single felt sprightly, instantly comfortable, so buoyant and high in the water compared to my whale-heavy, low-riding double. Rod and Cherri had already gone down the chute. Now Clinton pushed off, paddled a few strokes with Steve in the bow, and tilted into the chute. I followed behind them. Water roared in the sunlight. As they dropped over the first big rolling wave, a sharp side wave slammed into their boat from the left. They overturned instantly. Their heads bobbed beside the swamped hull as the current carried them down the chute.

I could see they weren't in any serious danger. I was secretly pleased that they had tipped. Now maybe Clinton understood how difficult it was to handle that heavy boat. He'd hardly paddled ten feet into the first rapid before he flipped it. But poor Steve! Swimming again!

I caught up to them.

"Do you want help?" I called out as they bobbed along with Clinton gripping his paddle in one hand and the upturned hull in the other.

Clinton waved me on. I could see he planned to swim the rapid and empty out the boat at the bottom of the chute. As I paddled past them, Clinton was hooting and hollering and singing as the swamped boat and the two of them bounced through the waves.

"Oh, this is fun! This is great! We're going for a swim! Whoop! Whoop!"

He was clearly trying to put Steve at ease, swimming yet another set of rapids, and maybe me, too, and maybe cover his chagrin for having flipped so quickly. I paddled near, ready to assist them, but Steve seemed to be managing.

Rod and Cherri waited at the bottom. Clinton and Steve swam the boat to shore in calm water and emptied out.

"What was it?" Rod asked Clinton. "Was it not having the splash skirt?"

I had the sense he didn't want Clinton to have flipped as easily as I did. But Clinton's response was no consolation except to me.

"No," said Clinton. "It wasn't the splash skirt. A hydraulic hit us from the side, and we didn't have a chance."

The river fell steadily through rapids and pools and more big shields of rock. All afternoon I remained in Clinton's kayak. Suddenly it was fun to paddle in the rapids. I had control. I could easily handle much bigger whitewater than before. I could lean, paddle effortlessly over waves, avoid holes and rocks, and eddy out at will. In short, I could *maneuver.*

I didn't feel so lame. Plus, Clinton had said I'd done fine. He had to at least partly mean it. I felt almost buoyant, like the boat itself.

I rounded a bend and saw my tandem boat wedged sideways in a fast, narrow, vine-hung channel. Steve was out of the boat, bouncing on his rear down the rocks, and Clinton, wading in the rushing current while trying to pry the boat free, was yelling to him to keep his feet forward to protect himself from rocks. Buoyant they were not.

We shot down another fast channel that spilled into quiet water draped by forest along the edges. Trailing the others a short ways, I heard an eruption of water behind me and another to my right.

"Hippos!" they yelled from ahead.

"Paddle! Paddle! Paddle!" Clinton shouted to me.

I sprinted toward them. I heard the bubble and swoosh as the hippos submerged again. There was a long, suspended moment as I paddled hard and the hippos swam beneath the surface. Where would they go? But I didn't feel the terror I had experienced facing the rapids. Rather, this was like an adrenaline rush, a thrill. I was somehow conscious of the romance of moment: *exploring in Africa, running from hippos.*

I caught up to the others along the left bank. We paddled sneakily along under overhanging vines. Suddenly, there was another eruption. Through thick vines ahead I spotted two more hippos charging off the forested bank into the water.

"Look ahead!" I shouted.

The others now saw the waves emanating from the hippos' crashing entry.

"Backpaddle!" Clinton ordered.

We all backpaddled wildly upriver through the hanging vines. We stopped, clinging to branches and vines along the bank, and silently waited to see what the hippos would do. They didn't reappear. We paddled on under the vines very carefully.

The river opened up again. The sun dropped low. It cast the tanned, muscled arms stroking steadily ahead of me in a rich, tawny light. The sky to the north, downstream, took on a hue of deep blue. I fell behind again in the yellow single, feeling spent after the big, hard, emotional day. The others paused and waited for me. When I caught up, they solicitously asked how I was feeling, whether I could keep paddling for a while.

"I'll paddle all night," I replied, "but I'm not up for any more major wave trains this late in the day."

It was agreed that we'd paddle a while longer, but if we came to a major rapid, we'd camp. The river spread serenely in front of us, catching the deep blue northern sky. Sensuous, purple ripples marked the faster water.

The low forested banks receded, meandering off to the sides. Flat sand-bars, golden in the late sun, eased out into the river.

The river's serenity put me in a reflective mood. Tired as I was, I thought about the day. I had been so frightened and so angry. I had struggled so. It didn't have to be that way. We could have avoided it. Except we were in such a goddamn hurry.

I stopped myself. *Don't blame anyone else for your difficulties,* I told myself. *Nothing good is going to come out of that.*

Rather than being sour and angry about what happened, try to be grateful for what they did, for their solicitousness when they saw you struggling. Yes, go the other way.

I was pleased. This felt like a much more productive response. It felt like a much better approach for my—for our—well-being, for making it down this river intact. We *needed* one another.

About 4:45, as the sun was nearly setting, Clinton and Rod called a halt on a big, flat, golden sandbar. We waded the boats through sandy shallows and beached them. It was a pleasure to feel the rippled sand under bare feet, to simply wander around the big open expanse, a vacation from the press of the forest. We collected driftwood lying on the sand and piled it near the fire spot. Soon there was a pot of boiling water and mugs of soup, and then, as darkness fell, dinner simmering over the fire.

I took a break from writing up the many pages of the day's notes around the fire.

I turned to Clinton and Rod.

"I just want to thank you guys for saving the day when Steve and I flipped. And I want to thank you for being so considerate when I reached my limits."

I didn't have to feign gratitude. I meant it. They accepted my thanks with modesty, but I could tell they appreciated it.

DAY TEN

It was a beautiful morning. A luminous cloud of pinkish mist floated up the placid river toward our sandbar camp, streaming through the lush green treetops, hanging its tendrils on branches as it crept past, propelled by the warmth of the sun climbing to the north. Just before the mist touched our sandbar, the pinkish cloud dissolved into blue sky.

Three of us shared the one last tea bag for our wake-up mugs. We were running out of everything now and needed a resupply very soon, or we would have to fish and scavenge for food. The hope was to reach the village of Mussoma late today or early tomorrow, where we'd rendezvous with Jamie and his plane at the bush strip. But it was going to be a long paddle to get there.

Clinton didn't offer me his yellow single despite my hopes, and I didn't ask. I don't think either Steve or I was eager to get back in our tandem together, but we managed to laugh about it, fatalistically.

"Maybe if we just keep our life vests and splash skirts on the whole time, they'll work like a good luck charm and keep the rapids away," I joked.

"We may as well try that," he said. "We've tried everything else."

We strapped all the gear on, although the water was dead flat as far as we could see downriver and usually everyone donned them only for rapids.

We started paddling. It was hard to get going at first. I felt creaky and chilled, like a lizard on the cold rocks of dawn waiting for the sun to hit. I had to think through again why I was on this expedition. I had found it irresistible when Cherri had dangled the words *wilderness* and *explore* before me. Both words had been freighted with romance for me ever since I was a small boy.

Was it from my father, I wondered while paddling between the sunlit bands of forest, that I inherited this romantic concept? He had been fascinated by the Woodland Indians and the pioneer Swedish settlers who migrated to the Wisconsin wilderness in the mid-nineteenth century. As newlyweds he and my mother had located the dilapidated remains of a Swedish pioneer's log cabin and reconstructed it with the help of friends on a piece of forest they purchased in an area of Wisconsin lakes and rolling dairylands.

This log cabin was where I grew up. Far from the nearest friend, I had to find ways to amuse myself. I loved to nose around the niches of that oak forest. Sometimes I set off to watch the spring melt fill a certain small valley with a pond of water; to hike a knob and check out where the wind had blown a snowdrift in a certain shape; to climb a certain favorite red oak at a field's edge and look around; to spy on things. What did I expect to find? I didn't know. That's exactly why I was looking. *Wilderness* to me meant *possibility*, the promise of the unexpected, and in the hundreds of acres around me where literally no human regularly roamed but me, I always found something unexpected.

"Where are you going?" my mother would ask.

"Out in the woods," I'd say

The woods was my wilderness, my equivalent of a secret garden—a place of refuge and discovery where I felt most at home. But now, along the Lugenda River, I was deep, deep, deep in the woods—far deeper than I'd ever been in my life—and "at home" was far from the emotion I felt. I recalled that moment of utter animal nakedness when I'd stood hunched and hyperventilating on the shore, wondering if I'd have to walk out alone through the forest.

I'd read how the word *wilderness* contains all the ambivalence I felt about being in it. Its Indo-European root word *welt* or *uelt* can be documented as far back as six thousand years, referring to a forest or wildwood.[24] But what we call wilderness, a wild place, has meant many different things to many different cultures. It has a strong history in northern Europe, where part of me is deeply grounded through Germanic family ancestry. It apparently derives from the root word *will* of Norse and early Teutonic languages: self-willed, willful, and uncontrollable,[25] while a similar word in Old Swedish refers to the "out-of-controllness" of boiling water. In Old English (or Anglo-Saxon, considered a Germanic language) the term *wild-dē or* means wild beast or wild deer, that is, uncontrollable animals. Thus *wild-dē or-ness* identifies a place of wild, uncontrolled beasts or self-willed beasts.

That depicted the Lugenda River as far as I was concerned. The day before, panting on the granite slabs, I had been *wildered*. In Modern English we say *bewildered*—a confused, disordered, wild state. Both actually and metaphorically I had lost my way in the place of wild beasts.

But today I had found it again. In the morning sun and flat water Steve and I established a smooth, steady rhythm. I let myself be pleasantly hypnotized by the metronome of the strokes and the sun off the water and the birds.

Oooo . . . oooo . . . oooo! called a bird from the forest on river left.

Clinton turned back to us and identified it as a ground hornbill, which is like a wild turkey that eats rodents and snakes. A croc slithered off a sandbank ahead and disappeared into the river. We kept paddling without breaking rhythm. It was odd how crocs didn't seem quite so menacing now but rather something that lived in the river with the fish. Still, you didn't really want to be swimming with them.

About midmorning, well before our breakfast stop, Clinton suddenly pointed to the forest on river left where a tributary river discharged from a small channel between sandbanks and entered the Lugenda.

"I recognize this place," he said. "I think that river marks the boundary of the Niassa Reserve. Somewhere back there is a road."

It amazed me that he could distinguish that tributary and anonymous strip of forest from hundreds of kilometers of similar forest and tributaries we'd seen. But it had surprised me at times, too, how I had an almost unconscious memory for certain points in a landscape that I'd only glanced at years before, as if this was part of a genetic ability necessary to negotiate the world long ago.

When Clinton said "road," what he meant was at best two dirt tracks through the forest, probably little more than a wide forest path. You could wait here for days, I well knew, and not see any traffic come along this so-called road. He had been here in a four-wheel drive with one of the reserve's "anti-poaching units": villagers armed with guns and deputized to go after illegal hunters in the reserve.

The river broadened again, and big, low sandbanks shelfed in from each side. We carefully skirted a pod of three hippos, snorting about in a patch of deeper water midstream, and then another pod of seven. We came to a fisherman who stood in his canoe and held up a string of fish for us to buy. Clinton and Rod waved it off and kept paddling, although I was hungry for the protein. Around the bend on a sunny sandbank stood a small thatched roof propped on poles and two more fishermen beneath it, smoking their catch over a smoldering fire.

I felt we were reemerging from the deep wilderness. After several days traversing a virtually uninhabited land, we seemed to have entered an area where people lived and villages existed somewhere back in the bush, although we couldn't see them. We apparently had dropped to a lower elevation and a hotter and drier climate. Spiny-looking acacia trees stood alone on the sandy, stony banks like trees in the desert. Tall palms sprouted along the moister stretches of shore. Waves of heat shimmered up from the sunbaked sand.

Clinton and Rod called our breakfast halt on a gravel bar where an acacia tree threw some shade. The fire's flames looked pale and weak surrounded by the sharp sunlight. We had paddled hard all morning, and the river had been fairly straight. Everyone was eager to know how far we had come since dawn. While the pot for oatmeal water came to a boil, Rod checked his GPS for our distance and then consulted quietly with Clinton.

"Sixteen kilometers!" announced Rod.

"That's all?" I said. "I thought we were making good time this morning. Jesus, we're going to have to paddle really hard to make that rendezvous with the resupply plane by tomorrow."

I unfolded my big aeronautical map and studied how far it looked to Mussoma village. Rod replaced his GPS in the orange Pelican case and removed the satellite phone. I left the map spread out on the river-smoothed gravel, went to the pot of boiling water, mixed up a mug of oatmeal, and stirred a pack of instant soup into it. I was constantly hungry for meat or fat or something more than oatmeal and energy bars and rice.

"Pe-*tah*!" Rod remarked, noticing my breakfast choices. "It has taken you ten days on the river to lose your mind!"

He punched the buttons on the satellite phone, put it to his ear, and waited for a moment.

"Hi, I'm looking for Lance, please."

There was a pause. A few seconds later Lance was on the line. Rod greeted him effusively and handed the phone to Clinton. It was a teleconference reunion of old buddies. Rod had reached him in Pemba, a small port town on Mozambique's Indian Ocean coast. Pemba was the nearest access point by either bush plane or road to the Niassa Reserve, and Lance had driven there to wait for us after a long jolting journey over bush roads. It also happened to have great beaches where he could kick back and relax while waiting for us to contact him for the pickup at the confluence.

Most of the phone arrangements had to do with supplies to be put on Jamie's bush plane by Lance in Pemba and flown to the Mussoma bush strip.

"I don't know if you have the kite," Clinton said, completing the arrangements, "but if you do, send in a bottle of Southern Comfort."

Clinton laughed at whatever Lance said in return. Then he listened attentively for a long time to something clearly very interesting that Lance was telling him. He signed off and handed the phone back to Rod.

"Paul Connolly is on the river—solo," Clinton announced to the four of us under the acacia tree. "Lance ran into his backup driver in Pemba. He started a week ago."

The news electrified our little camp. Paul Connolly was the expert whitewater kayaker from the former Rhodesia whom Cherri had initially contacted to lead our expedition down the Lugenda. He had agreed at first but then, according to Cherri, had ultimately backed out. There was good reason she had gone to him. Connolly had made many first descents of rivers in Africa as well as in the Himalayas, in addition to owning a whitewater-rafting company that took tourists down the rapids on the Zambezi below Victoria Falls. In short, he was one of the pioneering whitewater paddlers of Africa. And now he was coming down the river after us!

Was he trying to pass us by and claim the Lugenda's "first descent"? We all wondered. He was clearly a very accomplished and competitive person—a lawyer, a marathoner, a businessman, a first-descent kayaker. Clinton knew him personally from working for his rafting company on the Zambezi.

"Paul on the river is right in keeping with Paul's character," said Clinton. "He might claim first descent solo or first descent unsupported. There are a lot of different ways of doing this. But who knows? We'll see what happens."

"Do you think he can catch us?" Rod asked.

"No way," Clinton replied. "There's no way. He'd have to do sixty kilometers a day. And he still has all those rapids to scout."

"Maybe he's going fast and light," I said. "Maybe he's hardly scouting."

"He's very conservative," Cherri said to me. "If we were with Paul

Connolly, we'd still be up there scouting rapids." Then she turned to where Clinton and Rod were sitting in our circle in the acacia's shade. "I'd much rather have Clinton. I like his reckless style—well, not reckless, but you know what I mean. You guys are much more fun!"

Clinton warmed to Cherri's praise and sprawled his browned sinewy torso, crisscrossed with scars, on the gravel.

"I don't believe in sitting there and mulling things over," he said. "If you think about it too hard, you make mistakes. I believe in *going*!"

Jesus Christ! I thought. *So this in a nutshell is the river philosophy I've been dealing with! No wonder I've been struggling against it!*

But later, when I thought it over, I concluded that Cherri was at least partly right. Given the option, I would have chosen Paul Connolly for my personal safety, but I would have chosen Clinton for style. The writer in me appreciated that he had an unconscious knack for infusing whatever he did with, to put it mildly, drama and flair.

Paul Connolly on the river behind us, though! What a surprise! Only Cherri apparently had some inkling that he might make a descent of his own. We packed up our breakfast things and climbed back in the boats. There was a new urgency to our expedition. I realized I hated the notion that we now might be in a race against Paul Connolly to reach the Rovuma confluence first; it was still a good 250 kilometers away. I wanted to take my time and truly experience the river itself, the animals, the villages, the people. But I didn't like the notion of losing a race to the confluence, either. None of us—and most certainly not Cherri—would stand for that. I began to wonder if competition was part of this concept of wilderness, part of my motivation for being here.

We paddled hard all afternoon under a warm sun and over sparkling blue water. The river gave us all its variety: braided, broad, fast, narrow, rapids, broad again. At one churning chute Clinton asked if I wanted to paddle his yellow single, and I accepted. I had a total sense of freedom and lightheartedness to be out of the heavy double with Steve and simply enjoyed paddling through the rapids. A hundred yards behind the others, I shot out of one long, wavy chute and into a run of fast blue water. Just in front of my bow a greenish, snaggly crocodile snout suddenly thrust up from down deep and snapped the air.

That was really cool! I thought, flying past the spot.

Paddling along easily at the rear by myself, I had another chance to reflect. The Lugenda suddenly felt less threatening than it had. It felt positively cheerful. I felt almost at home here, even with crocs snapping at me. Was it because of the beautiful day? Or because I was in Clinton's maneuverable yellow single? Or because the rapids had lessened? Or because the river had opened up from deep, closed-in forest? Or because we had left the uninhabited region and had returned to the land of people?

It was still a *wild-dē or-ness* by that Anglo-Saxon definition—a land of wild, uncontrollable beasts, as that crocodile attested. The term *wilderness* contained so many concepts, both frightening and compelling. Wilderness, I thought, was something that I wanted both to explore and to avoid. I recalled how heart-poundingly excited and at the same time frightened I had been walking home at night as a child, silently moving on the long road up the big hill through the dark woods while hoping to spot the distant yellow lights of our log cabin above me, but instead seeing only the low shadows of the forest shifting around me.

One time my father jumped out from the woods with a scream: *Aaaaarrgghh!*

I literally flew off the road.

Back, back, back . . . "Wilderness" didn't exist until "civilization," urbanized and agricultural people, arose to form its counterpoint, by some thinking. Before then, humans didn't draw so sharp a distinction between themselves and "wild nature." They hadn't yet, as some have put it, "built a fence."[26]

Where do you look for a place where this fence doesn't exist? One place is in the great cave paintings that appeared during the Paleolithic era. Those chambers deep beneath Europe's surface vividly portray Ice Age mammals: bison, ibexes, lions, horses, mammoths, woolly rhinoceroses. Hunting darts fly, some animals are wounded. In some chambers, a half-human, half-animal "sorcerer" figure hovers above the animals. The pristine Grotte de Chauvet in southeast France, where the world's oldest known paintings have recently been discovered and dated to 32,400 years old, also contains a circular shrine formed of thirty bear skulls. Southern German caves have recently revealed, among other prehistoric figurines, a thirty-thousand-year-old statuette of a half-human, half-lion figure sculpted from a mammoth tusk.

Is this what the human mind saw before the fence existed, the interchangeability of human and animal forms? Or, rather, the *closeness* of human and animal that now feels so distant to us? Animals and human spirits may have been interchangeable to these early humans, overseen by a kind of spirit god. Hunter-gatherer tribes, such as the northern Plains Indians and the Inuit of the Arctic, never really lost that sense of closeness to the animal world, at least not until very recently. They have countless stories of the interchangeability of animal and human. Unlike the agricultural peoples of the earth, *wilderness* was not *wild-dē or-ness,* a place where the wild beasts lived. It was the place where they lived, too. It was home.

"We did not think of the great open plains, the beautiful rolling hills, and winding streams with tangled growth as 'wild,' " said Chief Luther Standing Bear, chief of the Ogala Lakota, in the first decades of the twentieth century. "Only to the white men was nature a 'wilderness' and only to him was the land 'infested' with 'wild' animals and 'savage' people. To us it was tame. Earth was bountiful and we were surrounded with the blessing of the Great Mystery."

"We don't have a word in our language for 'wilderness,' " a native Mozambican villager would later tell me. "What you might call 'wilderness' we call 'the place where no one lives and you are free to gather things.' "

"Peter!" Clinton called out. "Ask the zots the best way to go!"

He was using an African pejorative for blacks. He referred to three or four fishermen standing on the Lugenda's right bank watching us paddle down. Just ahead the river braided in a wide maze of channels, and it was not at all clear which looked like the easiest passage.

I steered my kayak nearer to the bank, and I haltingly put the question to them in Portuguese. They pointed to one of the channels. Rod or Clinton dug out a pack of cigarettes they carried beneath their decks for just such occasions and tossed them to the men on shore.

"Those are to share," Clinton said to the man who caught the pack, swirling his finger around in a circle.

The men seemed appreciative. We paddled down the channel, following easily through the other side of the braids.

A short while later we spotted another group of men on river right. They waved their arms at us. We paddled over. Some of them wore uniforms. They explained in Portuguese that they worked for the Niassa Reserve, in some capacity I couldn't understand. They knew Jamie and knew Jamie's camp.

"Where is Jamie's camp?" I asked.

"That way," they said, pointing downriver.

"How far?"

"Forty-five kilometers."

"Where is the airstrip?" I asked. "Is it here?"

They said something I couldn't quite make out about a bridge and a road.

"It's not here," Clinton said, breaking in authoritatively. "It's farther along. I've been to the airstrip."

The men had heard that we were coming down the river and that some of us were Americans and some Africans.

"Who are the Africans?" they asked.

Clinton and Rod raised their hands. The men cheered the two of them.

I was getting concerned about finding the airstrip. I had looked at Cherri's maps early in the day and had seen where she marked the bush strip. Near it, set back from the river, rose a large hill—actually an upthrusting tower of granite known as an *inselberg*—that appeared on both her and my maps. Earlier, not long after our breakfast break, I had spotted what appeared to be this particular hill, but then we had paddled past it.

Leaving the men behind, we started paddling again.

"I'm concerned we might miss the airstrip," I said and explained my reasoning.

"This is not the place," Clinton reassured me. "I can promise you. I've been there. I'll recognize it when I see it."

I hated the thought of missing the comforts of a camp and a few days' rest, not to speak of the food and resupply.

The river swished through more fast braids. Cherri, consulting her laminated GPS landmarks, warned us that a "bad gorge" should be appearing soon. The river opened up again, though it still moved fast through granite humps. A long, slender dugout canoe with two young men in it pulled out from the bank and started to follow us downstream. They told us there were rapids ahead. One of the young men stood on the gunnels near the stern poling. I was amazed at his agility. The canoe had only about three inches of freeboard—the amount of hull projecting above the surface of the water—but he guided it easily down fast, wavy chutes after us, telling us again there were rapids ahead.

The river suddenly broadened and slowed. The forest disappeared from its banks. We could see stalks of corn and sugarcane planted alongside, the first fields we had seen for days. Heads of villagers appeared over the bank, staring at us. They started waving. They starting shouting. They started running down the riverbank after us, and more canoes launched from shore.

At first it looked like a greeting. Then it looked like alarm.

Around the bend stood the answer: a great hump of granite blocked the Lugenda. But we could see a narrow opening in that hump and that the riverbanks fell far below it. Here was Cherri's "bad gorge."

Clinton pulled over to the left bank and beached. We followed. There was a huge collective sense of relief coming from the villagers that had chased us along the bank. We climbed over the rocks. It was a narrow, lethal, crashing drop—another full-on waterfall. The villagers pointed us across the river to the traditional portage spot.

We crossed easily in the broad, still water. On the far side a group of men and boys waited for us. We beached our boats. They offered to carry them in portage. With me translating as best I could, we negotiated. They said they needed ten men to carry the boats—four for each white tandem and two for the yellow single. They wanted something like forty thousand meticais each, about $2 each.

"That's too much," Cherri said.

"That's what it costs for a cappuccino at Starbuck's," Clinton protested to her, "and it's too much?"

"A full day's wage here is one dollar," said Cherri. "That's twenty thousand."

Clinton backed off. So it was agreed, twenty thousand meticais each.

The men hefted the boats on their shoulders. Some of them wore head cloths that looked vaguely Muslim. We had noted the sudden transition from bark canoes to dugout canoes, as if we'd entered a different cultural region. Rod and Cherri's double went up the little path beaten through the tall grasses first, two porters on each end, but when it came time to heft Steve's and my tandem, four of them couldn't manage it and they brought in a fifth porter to help. This confirmed something of what I'd been feeling in my struggle with steering.

"Pe-*tah*, this is what it's like to be a white boy in Africa," Rod said as the two of us walked together empty-handed up the grassy trail, through a patch of open forest, and down to the river again below the falls.

I felt I were almost floating up the trail, it was so physically liberating not to have to haul those heavy boats over a portage for once. But could I actually live like this? From my northern background the act of being served by blacks, even if they considered themselves well compensated for their labors, was heavily loaded with implications. It wasn't something I was going to work out during the portage. I knew that when walking on the portage trail among African villages I was a very wealthy man in a way that I wasn't on the river or in the forest—in the "wilderness"—or, for that matter, at home.

Clinton climbed into his yellow single at the base of the portage, so I was back with Steve in the tandem. We pushed off, and villagers lined the banks below, shouting and waving in both greeting and farewell. I felt as if the circus was passing through town, and we were it. The river braided a few times in swift water and then opened up. A half mile ahead of us stood a skinny concrete bridge on pilings a good forty feet above the water. It was several hundred feet long, spanning bank to bank. It would hardly have qualified as a bridge on a backroad in the States, but out here it looked like a major piece of engineering. This was the bridge marked on the map at Mussoma village.

A man was shouting and waving to us from the left bank. We waved back. He kept shouting and then running down the shore after us. What was going on here? Clinton ignored him and kept paddling. Was he a crazy man? I wondered. I couldn't understand what he was saying. Was he saying, "Stop"? He chased us to the bridge, got up on the bridge, and still yelled and waved to us as we passed under. We took care again not to touch the pilings due to possible mines.

The river broadened again. The pre-evening light was beautiful, a purplish blue sky and dark blue water between tawny banks of tall grass. Inselbergs, high hummocky hills, could be seen in the distance, their rock faces lit by the low sun. I caught up to Clinton's boat.

"I'm worried we missed the camp," I said. "If we missed it, I'll sacrifice all your toes. Or you can paddle me back to it personally."

"We'll fly you," said Clinton, paddling on.

Of course, we missed the little camp and the bush strip. We discovered that when we pitched our tents on a nice sandbar and Rod took out his GPS and took our bearings in the dusky light. The little hunting camp was back where we had spoken with the uniformed men. The airstrip was somewhere back near the bridge where the man had been yelling to us. It was surprising how far we'd come so quickly. We had made good time that morning, too, but as a joke Rod and Clinton had told us we'd paddled only sixteen kilometers by the breakfast break when in fact we'd made twenty-four.

Now everyone looked toward Clinton.

"I don't speak Portuguese," he replied defensively. "How am I supposed to know that was the camp?"

"Goddamn it!" I said.

The others acknowledged that I'd been right in my suspicions. This was little consolation to me because we missed it anyway, and, besides, I knew that if my Portuguese had been better, I would have known we'd reached it. On the other hand, I was the only one who had even bothered to think about learning Portuguese for just this sort of eventuality.

"It's fine," Cherri said, consoling me. At the same time a Heuglins robin—"the happiest bird in the world," she called it—chirped merrily with the setting sun.

She and Rod had been looking at the map while I'd been cursing and stewing. They had realized we'd paddled so far today on these broad straight stretches that we came within striking distance of the main hunting camp.

"This is even better," she said. "This means we can paddle to Luwire tomorrow where there's a *real* camp."

They got on the sat phone again to Lance to make new arrangements for a resupply—now at Luwire Camp's bush strip, our third attempt at a resupply.

"And make sure there's beer on that fucking airplane!" Clinton exclaimed to Lance before signing off. "We've all lost our drinking stomachs! It's embarrassing!"

DAY ELEVEN

We could almost smell Luwire Camp ahead. If we paddled very hard, we'd make it sometime in the afternoon—fifty kilometers as the crow flies, more than we had done on any single day except the previous one. The river had straightened and broadened greatly since those early days, however, and the rapids had lessened. We had hopes as we crawled from our bags at dawn, quickly packed, and hopped into our boats.

Another beautiful morning. I loved these mornings in the African wilds, the freshness and clarity and possibility of them, in contrast with the sadness and anxiety that could settle in at dusk. We paddled along cheerily and vigorously on the broad, smooth river. Inselbergs protruded like steep tropical islands from the sea of forest. I studied them with fascination as we paddled past—their sheer rock faces, over a thousand feet high, richly textured by the morning sun and their tops capped with clinging green vines and forest. I savored the way they appeared to have heaved so powerfully and smoothly from deep in the earth, and the delicate, even magical way the forest nested on the rounded top. Plants clung to tiny cracks in sheer rock—evidence of the sheer persistence and innovation of life on Earth.

Not far into our morning a granite rib projected into the Lugenda from an inselberg on the right bank, kicking up a froth of rapids. We ran them easily, even gracefully, and then shot down a chute whose banks were lined by what looked like date palms—a whitewater river charging through a desert oasis.

The Lugenda broadened again, and the forest thinned almost to savannah. It felt drier, with tawny grasses beneath the blue sky, acacia trees spreading along the banks, and inselbergs rising in the distance. I felt

almost carefree here, out of the forest, past the rapids, and knowing Luwire Camp lay not far ahead.

One theory of our relation to nature maintains that humans feel most at home on a savannah landscape like this. This is the landscape where we evolved. It offers everything we need: trees to hide among, long views out of the groves to spot enemies or game, plus firewood, shelter, and water. Our modern aesthetic, accordingly, favors home landscaping that features broad, open lawns patched with trees or forest. We don't like to be choked by dense thickets and endless woods. We like our homes to be tucked in a grove from which we can look out into the open.

Here survives the vestiges of our earliest relations with the wilds when we felt at home within certain "wild" landscapes. But forest and mountain and desert and ice—did we ever feel at home there? I suspect those Paleolithic hunters would have felt at ease wherever there was good game to hunt, whether forest or mountains or desert or ice. But how did that "wall" appear, to separate us and make those landscapes feel hostile to us, make us think of them as wilderness, as places where we didn't feel at ease? It might have been the Agricultural Revolution that built the wall, as some believe, or, later, the Judeo-Christian religious tradition that saw a need to subdue the wild earth and its wild creatures instead of live among them.

The Agricultural Revolution started about twelve thousand years ago when hunter-gatherers in the Middle East, in order to obtain a more predictable food supply, began to plant the seeds from cereal grasses they usually harvested from the wild. At the same time the big game mammals of the Ice Age were dying out. Slowly the hunting-gathering bands of humans settled and farmed the land, while others roamed short distances to herd domesticated goats and sheep. The surplus harvests that resulted meant that some individuals were freed from the burden of farming or herding directly for their food. They became specialists—craftsmen, priests, and, finally, in ancient Sumer, scholars who invented the world's first-known system of writing, using cuneiform characters pressed into clay tablets. Cities grew, books came to be written, and "civilization," as we define it, came into being.

It is no coincidence that the "world's first book," as it is known—the five thousand-year-old *Epic of Gilgamesh*—opens with the description of an enormous wall. The crowning glory of Gilgamesh, king of the Sumerian city of Uruk, this wall is intimately and lovingly portrayed—its kiln-fired brick, its enameled facing that gleams like copper, and its layout by the Seven Sages. It encompasses three and a half square miles of the city's buildings, its palm gardens, and the Ishtar temple. But beyond the great wall of Uruk lies what we would call wilderness: the wild steppe and, still farther off, the giant cedar forest.

Five thousand years ago that barrier between human and wild was already massive and glorified, and it protected within its confines an expanse of rich, cultivated gardens. Much of the poem's movement consists of various efforts to subdue the wilds. A wild man named Enkidu lives on the steppe with the wild beasts and is tamed only after sleeping with a harlot sent out from Uruk by Gilgamesh. The youthful king and tamed Enkidu befriend each other and embark together on a great quest into the unknown—to travel to the wilderness of the cedar forest, subdue its guardian monster, and, wielding axes whose blades weigh 180 pounds each, chop down a giant cedar tree. From its fragrant wood they would craft a giant door—another barrier between humans and the wilds—and float the door down the Euphrates River like a raft and offer it to Enlil, who happens to be the Sumerian god of agriculture and inventor of the hoe.

Felling a giant cedar, say the anthropologists, represented a kind of trophy and a display of power for the ancient kings of Mesopotamia. The forest wilderness had to be subdued in order to spread their agriculture and city-states (not unlike the American western settlers "conquering" the forests, prairies, and mountains for "civilization").

Says Enkidu to Gilgamesh:

> *You killed the guardian by your strength,*
> *Who else could cut through this forest of trees?*
> *My friend, we have felled the lofty cedar,*
> *Whose crown once pierced the sky.*[27]

By the breakfast stop that morning we had done twenty-nine kilometers, the equivalent of an entire day's paddle at the beginning of the trip. The river had straightened considerably in this section and the current flowed quickly, without major rapids and portages to slow our progress. We huddled in the shade of a small tree on a hot sandbar, mixing up our oatmeal and what I called my "haggis," my blend of dried soup and oatmeal, after the Scottish dish and in acknowledgment of Rod's Scottish family background. When Rod and Clinton announced the morning's twenty-nine-kilometer distance, reading it off Rod's GPS screen, everyone gave happy exclamations. Steve happened to be standing next to Rod. Rod seized Steve in a bear hug and started doing a little jig with him, spinning around and around on the hot sand.

"Beer, beer, beer, beer!" Rod sang delightedly as they danced.

We all laughed with giddy pleasure. Luwire Camp waited just over the horizon. It beckoned with not only beer but food and company and the chance to stop paddling for at least a few days. Luwire represented a tiny oasis of civilization—the word *civilization* derives from "city," the life we knew, anyway—surrounded by African wilderness. I had longed for wilderness, but now I was more than ready for a taste of the city.

Clinton squinted downriver at a hazy blue inselberg.

"It's near that mountain," he said.

Cherri, who had visited Luwire Camp during her aerial reconnaissance, confirmed this.

It didn't look that far—ten or fifteen kilometers maybe. We packed up our breakfast things and stepped quickly over the hot sand into the boats. With each paddle stroke I watched the bluish mountain move infinitesimally closer. Finally, I had to tell myself to stop looking at it. The river remained broad and pleasant, the channels braiding between big flat sandbars. We skirted a pod or two of hippos in deeper water midriver. We passed a few fishermen in their dugout canoes, poling along.

After an hour and a half of paddling, the mountain still lay a good way off. We stopped for a floating rest break. Cherri extracted a few small bags of dried fruit and nuts and passed them around, as she had done occasionally on our rest breaks. But now they seemed more abundant, as if she had been holding them in reserve for an emergency but could afford to break them out because Luwire and more supplies lay just ahead. From his boat Rod handed me a bag of sundried pears. I plucked out a few and gave it back, noticing the French labeling on the package. I chewed the pears— sweet, firm, delicious. I thought how far they had come to enter my mouth. Grown in a French orchard, they had probably been flown down to Johannesburg, where Cherri had purchased them, then flown north with us to Malawi, crossed into Mozambique in the Land Rover, and came down the Lugenda River in our boats.

As I chewed them, thinking about the pears' long journey, we drifted past a Makua fishing family on a big flat sandbar to our left. They had built a shelter roof from grasses and wooden poles and a fish-drying rack from sticks. Fish lay smoking in the plume from a smoldering fire on the sand. Dressed in shredded T-shirts and simple sarongs, the family stood at the water's edge near their dugout canoes and stared at us floating past.

I looked at the dried French pear in my hand.

What a chunk of the world's resources I'm using!

I saw in my mind's eye the millions and millions of calories of energy it required to provide these few calories of a tasty snack for my body: tractor fuel for the farm in France, chemical pesticides and fertilizers, gasoline that powered the farm workers' cars to bring them to the fields, trucking of the pears to processing, their plastic packaging, their advertising and marketing, and the enormous quantities of jet fuel to fly them from Europe to South Africa and then again to Malawi.

The Makua fishing family used only the sunshine on the river that grew the plant food for the fish; felled a single tree to hollow out a log for their canoe; used vines and roots to weave their nets; cut a few bundles of grasses for their shelter's roof; powered their canoe with the strength of their arms; and smoked their catch with a few chunks of driftwood. This versus the barrels and barrels of oil for my dried pear.

It made me feel selfish, kind of a jerk, greedily grabbing more than my share—far more—at the guest table. It felt fatuous, frivolous, self-indulgent, and extremely expensive to be riding along in this fancy plastic kayak that was also imported from halfway around the world. Why was I doing this anyway? There was the question again.

Answer yourself honestly! I demanded of myself. *It's a disservice to that Makua family not to!*

I tried to answer myself with total candor: I'm doing this because it helps satisfy some romantic notion I have about exploration, about my self-image as an adventurer. And whenever I'm not sure why I'm here, whenever I'm having self-doubts, I tell myself that I'm doing something important by bringing attention to wilderness preservation in general and the Niassa Reserve in particular.

We picked up our paddles and stroked again toward the bluish mountain and Luwire Camp. The Makua fisher family disappeared upriver. *What a paradox!* I thought. We from the West, meaning me, are telling these people to *save the wilderness?* I'd heard the sentiment before, but I'd never felt it so viscerally. We in North America, Europe, and Japan who have already consumed the great majority of our *own* wilderness and each day suck up more forests, oil, and farmland, and who have paved thousands of square miles of parking lots for our convenience at our giant consumer goods stores? We're telling these people in dugout canoes and with vine-woven nets not to hunt, not to cut trees, not to touch *anything* because we *need* that wilderness?

What a bunch of fucking hypocrites we are!

Soon Clinton angled to river right. I noticed several big thatched roofs cloistered among the trees at the top of the short steep riverbank, with a few dugout canoes tethered to stakes at the river's muddy edge. As Clinton's kayak eased into shore, the riverbank exploded with activity: Fifteen or twenty African villagers ran down to greet him.

Luwire Camp!

We beached on the muddy shore amid the commotion of greeting. Among the black villagers were a few white faces. As Steve and I climbed from our kayak, bare-chested like Clinton and Rod, I was suddenly struck by how browned and burned, sinewy and muscular, mud-splattered and sun-bleached every single one of us looked, including Cherri. I hadn't noticed on the river, but now we five were almost closer in appearance to the sinewy black fishermen and villagers than to the soft white flesh nurtured by "civilization" like milk-fed veal calves confined to the barn. I wondered: Is this how all whites in the bush looked to the black Africans there?

The dining room at Luwire Camp.

Peter and Josh.

Lance, having flown in with the supplies on Jamie's plane, stood there on the riverbank, shaking hands triumphantly for our mutual progress thus far. So were two or three other young whites whose hands I shook but whose names I didn't catch, although I noted that none were the Luwire Camp hunters Jamie and Derek. One's identity I guessed immediately although I'd never met him. He wore a floppy canvas hat, looked pale and thin, and moved quickly and almost nervously, his eyes darting to take in everything. Here were New York mannerisms transported deep into the African bush. There was Josh the photographer.

I introduced myself. We shook hands. We instantly started jabbering to each other, asking and answering questions, exchanging hunks of information as if it were dried meat. We'd be working together; he'd be shooting photos and I'd be writing, plus he'd be riding in the bow of my boat in Steve's place. (Steve was long overdue at his Phoenix sales job.) It felt as if we had a tremendous amount of catching up to do even though we had never laid eyes on each other.

"I've been hanging around in Pemba for five days waiting to get flown in," he said. "It's been really frustrating."

Our logistical snafus on the Lugenda had trapped him in that fishing port and fledgling resort town on the Indian Ocean, about two hundred

Peter writing notes in camp luxury.

miles to the east of Luwire Camp. A helicopter was originally supposed to bring Josh in, resupply our food, and fly Steve out, using an opening in the forest for a landing pad. But we had lost use of the Kenyan-based helicopter even before the expedition began. So then the plan was altered to make the resupply and exchange at a crude bush strip that could handle Jamie's fixed-wing plane. But our progress downriver had been slower than we expected, and then we'd paddled past that first bush strip by accident. So the exchange and resupply had to wait for our arrival at Luwire Camp and its bush strip. We had been on the river eleven days, paddling down the Lugenda from our put-in at Belem.

Josh and I, instantly comrades-in-arms—at least I felt that way—were the last to climb into Luwire Camp. As I mounted the top, an excited thrill went through me like a child entering the gates of an amusement park. *Elegant, primitive luxury!*

The camp's centerpiece was a big thatched-roof pavilion framed out of bamboo and sitting on posts of peeled tree trunks. It had no walls except for a waist-high balustrade of vertical bamboo strips. From its rafters hung all manner of African artifacts: a graceful dugout canoe, the bleached skulls of crocodiles, and the curved horns of sables. The massive jaws of hippos sat near the entry. Bookcases stood to the pavilion's one side. Volumes about Africa and its wildlife lined their shelves. In the center ran the best part of all: a huge table laden with platters of mashed potatoes, pots of stewed chicken, cauldrons of soup, bowls of beans, and plates of bread.

A white-jacketed waiter—a member of the warrior Makonde tribe, I later learned—delivered platters of food to the table. Other members of the camp and our expedition were already seated around the big table, amid a scattering of tall cans.

"Pe-*tah*, would you like a be-*ah*?" Rod asked me politely, standing up.

"Yes. Definitely. *Please!*"

He padded barefoot and bare-chested across the pavilion to a refrigerator that sat in one corner behind a small bar and was obviously run off a generator hidden somewhere in the compound. A short distance down a riverfront path I could see a few wall tents under the trees. Just upstream from the dining pavilion stood a kitchen area of thatched huts and open fires screened off by a woven fence.

At the head of the table sat a short, roundish, but powerful-looking man.

"You must be Jamie or Derek," I said, going up to him and introducing myself.

"I'm Jamie," he replied.

We shook hands. He didn't get up. He kept eating. He didn't seem particularly interested in meeting me. His hunting partner, Derek—tall, broad-shouldered, with a weather-beaten face—seemed more forthcoming. We shook hands. I sat in an empty chair halfway along the table. There were a total of ten or eleven people at the table, all whites and all males with the exception of Cherri. Rod padded back across the shady pavilion, thigh muscles rippling below his river shorts, and handed me a cold pint can of Castle beer.

I cracked it open and took a sip. It was delicious.

That was around 2:30 p.m. The rest of the sparkling, sunlit afternoon in the shade of the pavilion beside the Lugenda quickly slipped away into a beery haze. I remember Clinton, his scars showing on his hard brown belly, loudly recounting with great enthusiasm stories of our high adventures, heroics, and mishaps on the Lugenda. We watched videos from

Cherri's camera of bits of our trip. I talked to Josh for a long time about our task ahead and about his background. Son of a professor of Latin American literature, he had traveled extensively in South America and so was no stranger to rugged going. I felt good about having him as a companion, but it remained to be seen how he'd do on the river itself. I talked to Derek a long time about hunting.

By then the sun was down, and it was maybe six o'clock. Soft yellow lights came on, hanging from the rafters and screened by fishnets. Dinner was served by Lilepe, the Makonde waiter. The cold beer ran out. Still the party raged on. We all scrounged from the bar whatever drink we could locate: gin, wine, and then finally Kahlua and tequila. It was pure pleasure simply to melt away from thinking so hard about what lay ahead, about the dangers and the risks, and melt away from the hard paddling and endless note-taking and constant observing. We were surrounded by the dark forested wilderness. It felt wonderful to be in this little warmly lit oasis. If humans had in fact built an elaborate and fortified wall between themselves and the wilds, I was very much enjoying being on this side of it.

The volume grew louder and the conversation more disjointed. I remember Josh intensely interrogating Clinton at one end of the table, and Clinton shouting at him over the drunken din: "I don't fucking know why I like to do what I like to do! I only know I don't like to be fucking psychoanalyzed!"

I had to laugh. Josh had no idea what he was in for—with Clinton, with Rod, with Cherri, and especially with the Lugenda River itself.

DAY TWELVE

The next morning the entire camp was up by 6:30. Even hungover, no one slept late in the African bush. In the dawn-chilled air we gathered on camp chairs and logs around a fire pit of glowing orange logs near the pavilion and sipped mugs of coffee or tea while talking and laughing laconically about the night's misadventures.

The party had faded the night before when the generator and pavilion lights shut down for the night about 10:30. The camp staff had prepared for us ahead of time. I walked—staggered—down a path with softly glowing lanterns set in a row on the ground alongside, throwing their gentle light into the underbranches of the big trees along the riverbank. This lantern-lit path guided me to a safari tent I shared with Josh—screened in, twin beds made up with blankets and sheets and pillows, bookshelves and small tables. Most amazing of all was a fully functioning bathroom attached to the back of the tent in a kind of bamboo enclosure that sported a flush toilet and shower. These, I later discovered, were supplied by two 50-gallon drums—one for hot and one for cold—mounted on a little tower in back. Each morning the kitchen staff filled the tanks by climbing a ladder while balancing buckets of cold or fire-heated warm water on their heads.

The tent felt to me like a luxury suite at the Pierre. For paying hunting-safari guests it would cost $1,200 per night per person and would probably seem quaintly rustic.

After so many nights in a bag, it felt strange to sleep between sheets and almost formal to get up by swinging my feet downward and then sit in a chair near the fire. We were called from the fire pit to the pavilion table for a breakfast of porridge smothered with sweet onion sauce. The day's plan wasn't clear, nor were our plans for the days ahead. Rather, there were several possible plans, all of which depended on Jamie the hunter/pilot's cooperation.

It was difficult to read how easily this would come. Today he would fly Steve out to the coastal town of Pemba. That much was clear. But then what? Originally, according to Cherri's carefully scripted schedule for the expedition, we would stop here at Luwire Camp for a week or so. During this time Jamie would fly Josh and me some 50 kilometers north to the Niassa Reserve's headquarters camp, a few tents and structures in the bush. Here we were to interview the staff in order to write about the reserve, plus photograph it. But now there was a new sense of urgency to our expedition because Paul Connolly was paddling down the river behind us. If we wanted to claim first descent of the Lugenda River, we couldn't afford to spend a week hanging out here—not with another 150 kilometers of river ahead of us to the Lugenda's confluence with the Rovuma.

"Look," I told Cherri, "if we're in a hurry, I can just spend a day at Niassa headquarters interviewing people. Even just an hour or two will be enough if they're the right people. Then we can get back on the river."

I felt that we were working as a team again, especially with the specter of Paul Connolly upon us. But I couldn't tell how this proposal went over, either. Cherri said something noncommittal like "Let's see what happens." Everything seemed in flux. I got the sense that Cherri didn't want to push Jamie too hard; he clearly had his own ideas about how things should be done.

"Time to go!" Jamie suddenly announced, getting up from the breakfast table.

I was stirring up another mug of heavily sugared tea. I ran to my tent to fetch some money stashed in a dry bag to give to Rod, who would accompany Jamie on the flight to Pemba.

"Get some fresh meat and seafood for the whole camp," I said to Rod. "A *lot* of red meat! And more beer. *Plenty* of beer!"

I didn't care what it cost, I was so hungry for protein. Luwire Camp, despite being a hunting camp, was just opening for the season and had no meat in its stores. I handed Rod a fistful of U.S. twenties. They climbed into a small truck—Jamie, Rod, Lance, plus another young white guy who was working at a Pemba hotel and had come to Luwire for the fun of it. All sorts of Luwire staff were piled in the back of the truck. Only after the truck had jounced down a forest path and disappeared did it occur to me that Steve was in there somewhere, too. We hadn't even said good-bye.

I went back to my mug of sugared tea at the red-checked pavilion dining table that was covered with a checkered cloth. Derek was sitting there, too.

"That was a great conversation we had last night about hunting," I said.

"Was it?" he said, raising his eyebrows quizzically.

We laughed. Neither of us could remember clearly, but it certainly had *seemed* insightful to me at the time. The conversation had to do with hunting and human instinct. Surely we touched on those Paleolithic hunter-gatherers and their intuitive understanding of what we now call wilderness.

I asked Derek if I could interview him about hunting. This time I'd take notes, I said. He agreed. What I really wanted to know was how organized hunting came to be part of a nature reserve, a concept alien to the U.S. idea of what makes a nature reserve.

In some ways Derek was the archetype of the Great White Safari Hunter. Articulate, well spoken, and ruggedly handsome, he had been educated at African boarding schools (as Jamie, Clinton, and, I believe, Rod were, too). His good British-system education showed as strongly as did his passion for African wildlife. He first told me some of the Niassa Reserve's history. This I later supplemented with my own research.

In 1992 a wealthy Norwegian businessman and conservationist named Halvor Astrup and his friend, a Zambian conservationist named Philip Nel, decided to fly over northern Mozambique after reading old trackers' accounts of elephant herds there. Few outsiders had entered the region for years due to Mozambique's war for independence and its long civil war. Astrup and Nel spotted tremendous numbers of elephants from the air. This was an animal for which Astrup had a special affection, and he was particularly impressed by the very large bull elephants. Securing permission to return by helicopter, Astrup and Nel were astounded by the region's beauty and wildlife, which had been protected from war and poaching by its extreme remoteness. Nel spent months approaching the Mozambican government, just then getting itself on its feet after the war, about protecting some of the region as a wildlife reserve. He was told that in 1954 the old Portuguese colonial government had drawn on paper the boundaries of a reserve in the farthest northern part of Mozambique that they called Niassa but that nothing further had been done with it since marking it out.

With Astrup as its primary benefactor, for the impoverished Mozambican government had no money to contribute, the Niassa Reserve was officially resurrected in the late 1990s. It was doubled in size to forty-two thousand square kilometers, roughly the size of Wales, Switzerland, the Netherlands, Taiwan, or Massachusetts. It is surrounded by tens of thousands of square kilometers of additional wilderness not designated as reserve lands. The reserve itself contains an estimated twelve thousand elephants, plus lions, elands, buffalo, high concentrations of leopards, and many other species. When it expanded in the late 1990s, the reserve also created a "buffer zone" around its core, intended to stymie troublesome outsiders—primarily meat and ivory poachers from far-off cities. One way in which the reserve controls the buffer zone is by allowing carefully monitored safari hunting in that area.

"Hunting is a very good resource for wildlife management," Derek said.

Later I would hear the same argument from wildlife biologists and reserve managers I met in Africa: Safari hunting brings in tremendously high revenues that can go toward maintaining wildlife reserves, staffing antipoaching units, and paying for research and monitoring of the herds. At Luwire, for example, two weeks of hunting is as much as $35,000, ten to twenty times what clients pay on "photographic safaris" to a wildlife reserve, generally around $200 per day. This means fewer visitors are needed to pay for reserve costs and the reserve needs far less tourist infrastructure such as roads, vehicles, and buildings. In this way hunting safaris create less environmental impact than photographic safaris. Of course, animals are killed. The number killed is very limited, however, and is carefully controlled to remain within what the populations can easily sustain. Often, it benefits certain species to be culled due to overpopulation, while other, more endangered populations are helped in their recovery by the money that goes into antipoaching units.

"Who gets the thirty-five thousand U.S. dollars?" I asked Derek.

"Part goes to salaries, part to capital improvements—vehicles and things. Part goes to fees for the reserve and part to the communities. Communities play a very big role. What we are doing is buying them things: grinding mills for corn, electrified fences to put around crops to keep the animals out. Most of the communities in the reserve are behind the idea of the reserve and hunting. It provides these communities with schools and roads. The government doesn't have the resources to do it."

So goes the argument for safari hunting.

The camp had quieted down by midmorning after Derek and I talked. Clinton said he couldn't just sit around Luwire all day; he had to be *doing* something. So he hopped with Derek into the camp's diesel Land Rover and headed out on bush trails toward a distant mountaintop where Jamie and Derek were considering building another camp. The Luwire staff, meanwhile, washed clothes, my clothes among them, in soapy tubs over the open fires of the kitchen compound. I laid out my tent and bag and wet gear to dry in the sun. It felt so good simply to pad around on dry, warm land. Unlike Clinton, I was more than happy to hang out at Luwire all day.

In late morning Cherri, Josh, and I mounted an excursion by kayak across the Lugenda to the nearest village, named Mbemba. Janeiro, a young Mbemba villager who worked at Luwire, guided us, paddling the bow of my kayak while Cherri and Josh paddled together. We avoided sandbar shallows and a few resident hippos, then beached at a steep clay-like bank. Scrambling to its open grassy top, we walked briskly under the hot midday sun along a hard-baked path two miles to the village itself.

We passed small fields—garden patches, really—with flimsy-looking crops poking from the clay: dry corn stalks, leafy manioc, bushy African beans ("ervihla," Janeiro called them). The wet season had ended and the dry begun, imparting a desiccated look to everything. The villagers had burned away the forest vegetation in irregular patches beneath the trees, creating mosaics of gray ash and black cinders, to clear more garden patches. Known by anthropologists as "swidden" or "slash and burn," this type of farming constantly moved the gardens about in the forest and allowed the soils—very poor here in the miombo woodlands—to lie fallow and regenerate.

We passed through an open grove of spindly trees and under an electric elephant fence—two strands of wire hung so high that we didn't even have to duck. Powered by solar cells, the fence wasn't working at the moment, said Janeiro. Here was an example of Halvor Astrup's beneficence and hunting safari revenues, although out of order.

Past the grove we entered the village itself: a pleasant opening in the woodlands with big spreading wild fig trees that reminded me of old oaks.

The scattered houses had thatched roofs and bamboo-framed walls filled in with baked clay balls, like something made of soda straws and peas. Very small, each hut appeared to be a separate bedroom, with most of the cooking and living done outside. When I asked to poke my head into one, I saw they were cool and dark with a simple pallet for a bed.

Janeiro led us to the headquarters of the "game protection unit," the antipoaching unit affiliated with the reserve. Its compound consisted of a few thatched pavilions and crumbling stucco buildings. Several young men wore uniforms and carried 7.7-millimeter rifles, considered necessary against armed and dangerous poachers. Antipoaching appeared to be the village's only cash employment, but poachers weren't as much of an issue as troublesome wildlife.

"The elephants are the biggest game problem," they told us through Janeiro. "They come into the village and trample the crops. That's why we have the fence."

Word of our presence traveled fast. Children swarmed around us. Cherri lined up the mothers and children and took still photographs with her video camera. She showed them the results in the camera's little viewing screen, to much laughter and delight. We walked down the path to the school, a bare, stucco-walled room with simple openings for windows. Then we visited the small mud-walled mosque and went on to the "hospital." This clinic was a plain room with little more than a table and a small supply of medicines. Stepping into it and thinking, *This is probably the best care available for miles around,* I realized how far Mbemba village lay from my own world. Again I felt the material privilege that sets us Westerners apart from the people here. How minor the difficulties, medical and otherwise, I faced in my own life compared to this primitive room that represented their last, best hope.

The "doctor" was a handsome, gentle man in early middle age who carefully, almost proudly, showed us the little equipment he had to work with.

"What are the biggest medical problems you have here?" Cherri asked kindly.

I was so taken aback by the clinic itself that I didn't even think to ask. Her tenderness and compassion with the local people surprised me sometimes, suddenly surfacing in the hardheaded organizer, the group leader, the ambitious businesswoman, the adventuress and explorer that I was used to being around.

"Malaria," he replied, "and pneumonia."

"Do you have much AIDS here?" she asked.

"Not here," he said. "But outside"—he made a gesture to the world out there—"yes."

"Do you have enough medicine?" she asked.

"We have medicine for malaria," he replied, "but never enough."

We headed back on the long walk to the kayaks, past the desiccated garden plots, through the grove of trees, under the elephant fence, and past more burned-off patches and gardens, toward the oasis of Luwire Camp and its electricity and beds and flush toilets and hot showers and the promise of hunks of red meat and cold beer. The camp, I now realized, was an African fantasy for Westerners. So much was imported—food, beer, fuel for generators, and on and on—and all of it upheld by a vast support system of Western money, transportation, and communication. It even had a computer in the bamboo-and-thatch pavilion with a simple email connection via radio or satellite. But here, just across the river in Mbemba village, was the real thing, about as close to bare bones life as you could get. There was the forest and the earth and the wild animals (tsetse-fly–borne sleeping sickness prevented raising livestock in the entire region). There was the sunshine and the rain, the river with its fish to be netted, and one's own manual labor to make things grow. That was the support system.

The people of Mbemba village lived completely surrounded by what we Westerners would call wilderness. Though separated by only a short canoe ride and a two-mile walk through the bush, Mbemba village and Luwire Camp actually lay thousands of miles apart. Did we Westerners come to the African bush, to these wilds, thinking we sought something as elemental as Mbemba village? But did we really vastly prefer something safe and comfortable and familiar like Luwire Camp that simply gave us the illusion of being up to our necks in the wilds? I loved Luwire Camp instantly, but it was a kind of midway oasis between wilderness and civilization.

Like walking into that little clinic, I was coming to believe that one is hit by a sudden, naked shock of recognition when one enters the wilderness—truly enters it. Or at least that was one way to understand wilderness, maybe one among a thousand ways. The sudden flash that here only a very thin margin separates life from death. The people of Mbemba village didn't need to be reminded of that, but maybe we in the Western world do. *This is how people die,* I had thought as I had panted on the slabs of granite, surrounded by a forest filled with predators, while Steve, struggling through the big rapids, disappeared around the bend into the unknown. Do we come to the wilderness seeking these essential moments? These moments verify that we are alive and also that we are mortal. We are animals on the face of this planet and, like all animals, vulnerable in so many ways. Our animal vulnerability is hidden from us in our civilized cities but not here, not during these essential moments, not when one truly enters the wilderness.

Moses summoned the tribe of Israelites out of slavery in Pharaoh's Egypt—summoned them from the fertile, green Nile Valley and led them into the wilderness of the nearby Sinai Peninsula. There, in the desert, life was stripped down to its barest essentials, to the simple, fierce need for water and for food. It was a land where the margin between life and death was very thin. The Israelites, like so many travelers into the wilderness before and since, bewailed that they had ever left security and comfort behind, slaves though they may have been.

> The people thirsted for water there, and grumbled against Moses, crying, "Why did you bring us out of Egypt, only to kill us and our children and our cattle with thirst? (Exodus 17:3) "O, for flesh to eat! We remember the flesh we ate free in Egypt, and the cucumbers and melons and leeks and onions and garlic. But now our appetite is starved." (Numbers 11:4–6)

Yet it was here in the desert wilderness that God appeared to the Israelites, manifested as a mountaintop cloud shot through with lightning and thunder, and delivered to Moses the Ten Commandments. It was the wilderness—this place where life is stripped to its barest essentials—that allowed the Israelites, who would wander for forty years in the desert, to grasp their frailty and insignificance in the vast scope of creation and thus, when he helped them survive, understand the power of God's word.

> "[T]he Eternal your God led you through the desert during these forty years, to teach you your need of him, to prove you, to find out if it was your purpose to obey his orders or not. So he made you feel your need of him, he let you hunger and then fed you with manna . . . that he might make

you know that man lives not only by food but by every word that comes out of the lips of the Eternal." (Deuteronomy 13:2–3)

We've internalized this Old Testament concept of wilderness, those of us of the Western Judeo-Christian tradition, for three thousand years, since 1440 B.C. when Moses wandered into the Sinai Desert. The Old Testament surely picked up many sentiments about wilderness that existed among the "civilized" peoples of the time, such as the Egyptians, and codified these sentiments into this text that became so central to the Judeo-Christian outlook. Wilderness here represents a refuge from oppressors like the Pharaoh; a place of hardship, testing, and proving oneself, especially before God; a place that brings one closer to the spiritual life but also a place where monsters and evil spirits can lurk.[28] According to the Old Testament it is finally man's role to overcome the wilderness and its wild beasts, to dominate it, to cultivate it, to make it suitable for human habitation. As some wilderness scholars have noted, it is a text not of a Paleolithic hunter-gatherer mind-set in which animals and humans are nearly interchangeable but of agriculturalists who see themselves as entirely separate from and in opposition to "wild nature."

How different this is from many Eastern religions. Tibetan Buddhism, about which I knew from previous travels and readings, reveres all forms of life and believes that the human form is only one incarnation on the way to enlightenment. Taoism, instead of trying to overcome "wild nature," looks to it for metaphors that instruct one in how to follow the Way—such as the image of water flowing around a rock. For literally thousands of years Chinese poets, painters, and thinkers have sought out the wilderness as a place of contemplation. The great Tang Dynasty poet Tu Fu lived in the wilds of the Yangtze River gorges to escape the tumultuous wars of the mid-eighth century A.D.: "Evening colors linger on mountain paths / . . . At the cliff's edge, frail clouds stay / All night. Among waves, a lone, shuddering / Moon."[29]

Compare Tu Fu's delicate nature imagery to the bulldozer approach of the Judeo-Christian tradition. In the very opening passages of Genesis we are told in the boldest possible way that God created humans to have mastery over every wild beast, fish and fowl, and gave humans fruit to eat and seeds to plant. And then there is that famous order issued directly from on high:

And God blessed them; God said to them, "Be fruitful and multiply, fill the earth and subdue it." (Genesis 1:26–29)

Cherri, Josh, Janeiro, and I paddled back across the river to Luwire Camp. The camp lay absolutely still in the sunny, lazy warmth of midafternoon except for faint smoke rising from the banked kitchen fires. The staff probably napped. Without the normal human activity to push it back, the weight of the vast forest that surrounded the camp pressed in on it. Humans did not dominate here. Man had not subdued the earth, not here. This little camp carved from the forest existed in a time before agriculture, a pre-biblical time, a time before the great cities rose in the Near East. In Mbemba village man had not really subdued the earth, either. He had cleared a small, shifting patch in the great forest where he could scatter his seeds and bring his netted fish. Despite its difficulties and many uncertainties, there was something about that preagricultural life that beckoned me powerfully. That is why I'd come here so deep in the bush. I sought out those primal moments—those moments when life was stripped to its bare essentials, those moments that returned us to our preurban, preagricultural past. I wanted to know the earth before it was subdued.

I went to my tent and lay on the bed. It felt delicious simply to lie there in the safari tent unmoving—not paddling, not portaging, not walking, not gathering firewood, not packing or unpacking a kayak, not pitching or unpitching a tent, not taking notes. With Jamie still not back from Pemba, it was now growing too late in the day for me to fly off with him to Niassa headquarters even briefly to interview staff people there. That was fine with me. I closed my eyes and napped amid flitting dreams of sunlit rivers and flashing paddles. When I woke, groggy, the sun had dropped low and was bathing the river and the inselbergs downstream in rich, golden, late-afternoon light. Josh prepared his big old box camera— he liked the softness the old lenses gave the photos—and had me, the only male kayaker around, strip off my shirt and paddle Clinton's single a short way out from shore. He stood on a rock and shot photos of me paddling in the great light against the serene backdrop of bush and river and inselbergs. I had the contradictory feeling again of explorer-as-poseur, explorer-as-model. *Maybe so, but, Jesus, it had been a hard haul to get here to pose.* The way some people might value a photo of themselves standing before the Eiffel Tower or the Great Wall of China, I knew I'd treasure this photo of myself paddling in the obscurest region of the African bush.

We heard the faint buzz of an airplane. By the time we finished shooting and climbed back to the camp, Jamie and Rod had returned from the airstrip, bouncing through the bush in the truck bearing goods—among them two toilets, two cases of Castle beer, a fifty-pound sack of flour, and bags of seafood for dinner. That night Lilepe served us prawns and calamari fresh from the Indian Ocean, fried potatoes, salads, and bread, and we helped ourselves to cold Castle beer.

Derek and Clinton rolled in late, accompanied by a headlight-illuminated cloud of dust that surrounded the diesel Land Rover. They had been driving almost solidly for ten hours through the forest. This night there was no party. Everyone was tired. Besides, we knew that tomorrow we'd be paddling.

DAY THIRTEEN

"Hari! Hari! Hari!" Clinton yelled into Josh's and my tent, imitating an African villager's pronunciation of "Hurry." "Get up! Get up! There's paddling to be done today!"

It was 5:30 a.m. We'd had one day's rest. I grunted sleepily, half amused. It was so Clintonian to wake the camp this way, yelling his way down the path.

Josh and I dragged ourselves from our beds, stuffed clothes into dry bags, and walked under the leafy trees along the river to breakfast in the big thatched pavilion. Tea and coffee, peanut butter and honey on toast—better than energy bars but well short of bacon and eggs. We couldn't wait around today for something more elaborate to appear from the open fires of the kitchen compound. I could feel the tension to get on the river from Rod and Clinton, and Cherri, too.

Paul Connolly was somewhere upriver. That's all we knew. He could come paddling around the bend any minute pushing hard toward the Rovuma confluence—ahead of us. Clinton and Rod said we'd try to make the confluence in three days' paddling. It was going to be a hard haul. I knew that there would now be no stopping at villages, no chance to learn more about the local people, at least not without a major protest. Our journey had taken on yet another of its many personalities: from exploration to race to be first.

But everybody conceded to a quick aerial-photo shoot for Josh while the bush plane was available. He and Jamie jounced off to the strip while the rest of us paddled the kayaks out into the Lugenda. First they circled high above as Josh shot photos of three tiny boats nearly lost in the huge landscape of braided silvery river, here maybe four hundred yards wide, of hazy inselbergs, and of endless forest. Then they dropped down for close-ups.

The plane roared downriver at us, a head-on silhouette of wings and landing gear—bigger, bigger, low, *very* low, like an Alfred Hitchcock movie.

We instinctively ducked.

Whoosshh . . . zzzoommm!

They flew so low over us that I could have reached up and hit the landing gear with my paddle. Josh poked his head out the window with his camera, his longish hair streaming back on the one-hundred-mile-per-hour slipstream like a dog with its head out the car window on an extremely high-speed interstate.

The prop wash blasted over us. The plane wheeled around downriver for another pass, lifted up over the forest, banked, dropped low and flat over the river, and bore down at us.

Whoosshh . . . zzzoommm!

"How low can you go?" Josh had asked Jamie at breakfast.

"I can touch the wheels on the water if that's what you want," Jamie had replied.

I thought he was joking at the time. Now I didn't doubt him. I had always admired the cool confidence of bush pilots. Jamie struck me as a true specimen of the breed.

This prop wash photo session over, we reassembled in camp and began ferrying gear from the safari tents down the riverbank to the boats. Derek and Jamie watched, squatting on the mud bank in the African style of waiting. As we returned to the tents for another load, they hopped up and surreptitiously loaded big rocks into the hull compartments of Clinton's kayak—good-old-boy camp humor among white Africans in the bush. It took Clinton only a minute to discover the extra ballast as he loaded in his gear, and we all had a good laugh.

Josh took a long time packing his camera equipment and film, making sure it was carefully stowed in waterproof bags, and I was slow in packing it into our kayak. Every piece of gear had a specific place when I packed the boat with Steve's and my belongings. Now I had to rearrange my careful system to accommodate Josh's gear, at the same time keeping his cameras and film accessible. I sensed the impatience of the others growing as they waited beside their boats on the riverbank while Josh and I tried to cram a dry bag containing one hundred rolls of film into the narrow opening of the forehull.

"Come on, girls!" Clinton shouted to Josh and me.

"Bastards!" Josh whispered under his breath as we stuffed.

I started thinking, *This new partnership might not go well.*

It didn't—at least at first. Clinton and Rod rode Josh hard, as if they were hazing the citified new boy who had arrived at a tough boarding school. They had reasons to be impatient. We fell behind immediately. Josh's limp stroke didn't possess nearly the power of Steve's. In fact, it felt as if I single-handedly powered the boat forward. His photographer's eyes scanned the banks, the sky, and the river, his head swiveling like a radar dish, taking in this strange, wild, new environment, rapidly talking to me, asking questions. I was used to long silences of rhythmic and hypnotic paddling with Steve. Josh reminded me a little of the photographer character in *Apocalypse Now* played by Dennis Hopper whom Marlowe discovers at Kurtz's compound on the riverbank deep in the jungle: pale, jumpy, full of the need to talk to someone, anyone.

I tried to delicately mention his paddling.

"Josh, you could put a little more power in your strokes."

Clinton and Rod didn't bother with the subtlety.

"Paddle!" they shouted back to us. "Start paddling!"

This approach just pissed me off. I obstinately refused to put any more effort into my own paddling. We lagged even further.

The river remained broad and flat until we reached the first set of inselbergs about eight or ten kilometers downriver from Luwire Camp—known as Mbemba Mountains, Janeiro had told me. The river swerved right of the mountains, which threw a kind of granite hill into the Lugenda's course, kicking up rapids. We scouted them. The first section formed an easy chute with nice, manageable waves at the bottom and a quiet pool for a runout. I felt fine about running it. I offered to take us through the rapids first so Josh could photograph the other two boats coming through. This minor delay was fine with them. Everyone knew that for proper documentation of our expedition, for our glory, the photographer needed opportunities to shoot.

Josh and I paddled across the calm pool above the rapids, tilted over the edge, and raced down the chute in sparkling sunlight under blue sky.

The kayak plunged deeply through the foaming green waves. Whitewater slammed into Josh's arms and chest, and the boat wallowed, then resurfaced. I steadied our course as we slammed through another wave, inundating Josh again, and bellied out into the calm pool below. The sound of cascading water dimmed as I steered us to the granite slabs of shore. There were openings of grass in the forest beyond the slabs, almost savannah here.

We climbed out of the boat. I was so used to running rapids that I hardly thought about this one. But Josh seemed taken aback.

"Is that a big one?" he asked.

"Not very big," I replied as we clambered up the granite slab with his cameras. "We've been through a lot of those."

He didn't look reassured.

"So we'll have more like that?"

"I don't know. Probably."

I could imagine what he was going through, confronted with the sudden reality of the river itself. Clinton had given him the abbreviated "safety talk" about swimming away from angry, chomping hippos and beating the shit out of aggressive crocs. He had added an extra bit of advice for Josh's time on dry land.

"If you see a lion, make yourself look big. If you see an elephant, make yourself look small."

Delivered with Clinton's "the sky is blue today" matter-of-factness, none of this was exactly comforting. One could just as easily have the opposite reaction: *What have I gotten myself into?* Josh had also met a South African man back in Johannesburg or someplace who had given him dire warnings about hippos. The man said he'd carried in his own arms a friend's son who had been killed by one.

When we got back in the kayak after the photo shoot, the river picked up its pace, plunged through more easy chutes, braided, and jumped and bounced through many smallish rapids and narrow channels—plenty of river action.

"This is pretty intense!" Josh kept calling back to me from the bow.

"Yeah, it felt that way to me at first," I replied, grizzled old hand of the Lugenda that I was. "You'll get used to it."

We whipped down more channels and small rapids, maneuvering tightly. Already I could see Josh getting the hang of paddling in these tight spots, first pulling the bow of the boat over with his paddle at my instruction and then doing it without my having to tell him. Steve had never really caught on. I was feeling much better that Josh was handling himself well in these tight spots despite his weak stroke on the flats. Probably weighing forty pounds less than Steve, Josh was much lighter in the bow, and my big tandem kayak suddenly felt much more maneuverable—almost another carefree day in the rapids. My misgivings of the morning were fading as we kept up with the others more easily in the fast water.

Still, we lagged behind on the flat sections where both of us lacked power. The river braided. We paddled around a small, willowy island into a quiet pool surrounded by vine-hung trees. The others were already well across the pool. Two hippos suddenly erupted from the pool's center and charged upstream in Josh's and my direction with tremendous splashes.

"Backpaddle! Backpaddle!" shouted Clinton with alarm, furiously backpaddling himself in order to get out of the pool.

Josh and I windmilled backward. The hippos cascaded past just to our left, looking like they were galloping, apparently running over the shallows while throwing off wakes like a couple of churning paddle-wheel steamboats. Fortunately, a small clump of willows at the island's foot intervened for a moment and screened us from them.

"Paddle!" screamed Clinton. "Paddle!"

I knew he now meant forward. As the hippos charged upstream on the other side of the willow clump, Josh and I reversed direction and forepaddled madly to get downstream and out of their reach. The hippos suddenly hit deeper water and submerged in a snorting splash, spreading waves that washed over the willow shallows like a boat's wake suddenly hitting the shore of a quiet lake.

Without breaking our furious pace, Josh and I reached the others at the pool's foot. We all looked back anxiously. The pool was now quiet.

"You have to stay closer!" Clinton rebuked Josh and me.

"You have to wait for us!" I replied.

"Paddle harder!" Clinton said.

"Paddle harder!" Rod echoed.

"Come *on*!" I said, both angry and contemptuously dismissive of the suggestion, feeling suddenly protective of Josh, my ward. "We're trying to break Josh in!"

"You can paddle harder!" both Clinton and Rod said almost in unison.

Now I was pissed again, doubly so, because I felt they were being too hard on Josh who was just getting on the river and had hardly had a chance to get used to it. I felt as if we were back at the river's start all over again, the tension between us suddenly back.

"Part of the problem," I said angrily, "is that when we all take a toonda break or whatever, you all take off before we're ready, and you're two hundred meters downriver by the time we start and we can't catch up. So will you wait until we're ready?"

Clinton gave a kind of grunt, floating nearby in his kayak. This pissed me off more. I could see he hated to be rebuked, as did I. I felt as if I was now talking to one of our children, disciplining them. I wanted Clinton to answer me instead of grunt. He had his head down, staring at his foredeck, as I spoke forcefully to him.

"Is that a deal, Clinton, that you'll wait?"

"Yes, that's fine," he said quietly.

"And for our part of the deal," I said, "we'll paddle harder."

We paddled on. I was still angry—Clinton had such attitude sometimes—but it helped to talk it out. I felt on more equal footing with Clinton and Rod than I had in those early days. Josh was now the odd man out, and I, solely by virtue of having come this far, nearly ranked as part of the inner circle.

The braiding river now kept up a crazy antic pace. It dipped us through quick rapids, ricocheted us into narrow channels, bounced us over shallow rocks, and banged us into low-hanging branches. Crocs leaped off the banks. Hippos snorted in side channels.

"This is really pretty dangerous!" Josh exclaimed as we banged along.

I had to laugh to myself. *If it's not a rapid,* I thought, *it's a hippo, and if it's not a hippo, it's a croc, and if it's not a croc, it's a waterfall. Something is always happening on the Lugenda River!*

I was having a good time, however. It all felt so manageable. Plus, it was fascinating to see it through Josh's eyes. I felt better about my reactions, too. It wasn't simply that I'd been an alarmist earlier when I'd reacted to rapids and other hazards while Clinton and Rod seemed so self-assured. Josh was plenty alarmed, too.

"Anytime you want to take photos, just let me know," I said to Josh. "You can put down your paddle and shoot from the bow, and I'll steer us through."

"That's okay," Josh said. "I think I'd better get used to this first."

We skirted a pod of hippos in a quiet pool, ducking under branches along the bank.

I felt something going *clunkety, clunkety, clunkety* against the plastic hull.

"What the hell is that bumping us?" I exclaimed.

"That's just my knee," Josh said. "It's trembling against the boat. I don't do very well around hippos."

I thought he was being a little overcautious by not taking any photos from the boat, but soon, of course, the river caught us. We whipped around a bend, Clinton ahead. The channel split around an island into two narrower, faster channels. A big tree was dragging its tangle of limbs in the river at the island's head. Clinton squeezed by the fallen tree into the left channel and tilted down its small rapids. Following him, I wheeled our big boat left as hard as I could. I didn't want to plow into that nasty-looking strainer, but our boat didn't swivel as quickly. *Smash!* Broadside into a boulder just upstream of the fallen tree. It hit us amidships. The swift current pressing equally on bow and stern pinned it against the rock, acting like the fulcrum of a teeter-totter; the kayak balanced there for long seconds. I leaned into the rock to counter the tendency for the current to undercut us and flip us upstream. It felt as if we were riding the spindle of a roulette wheel and waiting for the ball to drop. *Maybe the boat will pivot downstream, the current will release us from the rock, and we can go happily on our way.*

The ball dropped. The boat pivoted the wrong way. Its bow swung upstream, into the current, pinning us even harder against the rock. Slowly, very slowly the water surged over our upstream gunnel, burying it. The current's pressure now shoved the gunnel down like a powerful arm from above. The kayak slowly tipped. Slowly, very slowly Josh and I tumbled from the cockpits into the Lugenda River as if some mischievous river spirit had purposefully dumped us out.

The swamped kayak swung free from the boulder. The current now shoved it into the branches of the fallen tree, entangling it. I quickly snatched up the paddles—holding them in a white-knuckle grip—and managed to give the boat a shove to free it. Now it started floating down the left channel into the rapids. Josh tried to grab it as it floated past him but lost his grip.

Our kayak hit a rock, flipped upside down, and lurched heavily over rapids and boulders like an overloaded pickup truck on a potholed country road. Our sleeping bags bungeed to the deck were ripped off by the impacts and bobbed merrily down the whitewater. Clinton, waiting in an eddy halfway down, stroked hard into the narrow channel and tried to stop our overturned boat by shoving it toward shore with his bow. It kept going, down the next little chute, although he managed to snag the sleeping bags.

I stood on rocks at the rapid's head and meditatively watched our boat go, knowing there was nothing I could do to stop it, and refusing to relinquish my death grip on the paddles, our last paddles. I felt almost Ahabesque standing there ankle-deep in the rushing river with a kayak paddle like a harpoon in each hand as my great white boat made its run for freedom. Josh surely wondered what the hell was going on.

The boat careened through the last small chute and came to rest upside down in a quiet pool below. I started wading down toward it, with Josh following behind.

"Well, now you've had your baptism in the Lugenda," I said pensively.

Whatever he said in reply, I didn't hear it. I continued slogging through shallow rapids toward our boat, its great white belly exposed to the sky.

We emptied the water out, lashed things down again, and paddled around the next bend. The river braided intricately into tiny swift channels. Clinton entered one that cut through tight brush and branches. Josh and I followed, but where his boat glided easily over the rocks, our much heavier one wedged to a stop. I hopped out, grabbed the cockpit cowling, and dragged us forward while Josh sat in the bow pushing against the bottom with his paddle. He gave me a strange look.

We scraped past the rocks and bushes and limbs, and I hopped back in. The channel spilled into a slightly wider one.

"Did you see that big white snake back there?" said Josh.

"No, I didn't. Where was it?"

"On a branch about a foot from your shoulder," he said. "I thought maybe I shouldn't say anything right then."

"Jesus!" I said. "Josh, there are some things I don't need to know."

Cherri and Rod now pulled up behind us.

"Did you see all those crocs back in the braided section!" Cherri called out. "It was just full of them, diving into the water everywhere."

Something else I probably didn't need or want to know. On we went.

The river felt crazy here, ripping down narrow channels in the vast forest. It felt wild, with snakes and crocs thrusting out from the banks. It felt Edenesque. Five small humans among vine-hung pools full of hippos.

No, this was somewhere beyond Eden. Supposedly, Eden was overseen by a benign and guiding force. This wasn't. Here, a random, even hectic, quality characterized the occurrences, the threats, the pleasures of the place. It brought to mind a quote from the early Portuguese mariners. They had to struggle to reconcile their benign and graceful vision of the Eden they had hoped to find with the fierce actuality of the Africa they encountered:

> But it seems that for our sins, or for some inscrutable judgment of God, in all the entrances of this great Ethiopia that we navigate along, He has placed a striking angel with a flaming sword of deadly fevers, who prevents us from penetrating into the interior to the springs of this garden, whence proceed rivers of gold that flow to the sea.[30]

The Garden of Eden for centuries was rumored to lie "out there" somewhere—in the Orient or far to the west of Europe across the Western Ocean or on a lush South Seas isle. The explorers may have expected a more elaborate version of their walled gardens back in Portugal or England or Spain, with the addition of gold and other riches for the taking lying about under the fruit trees. But when these first explorers and colonists from Europe finally rowed ashore after weeks or months at sea, they stepped not into walled gardens but onto entire continents, land masses of unfathomable size cloaked with nearly impenetrable forest and inhabited by tribes who often greeted them with arrows, spears, or hurled rocks, and in the tropics they confronted jungles and swamps that hid mysterious and fatal diseases.

That the Garden of Eden lay on those shores became a very difficult fantasy to sustain. (There were exceptions: Early sailors to the South Seas did find a version of paradise in those tropical islands with their fruit trees and native women, while in South and Central America the Spaniards indeed discovered gold for the taking—although not without slaughtering the people who possessed it.) But in Africa and North America those optimistic visions of Eden dissipated rapidly. The Portuguese staked out a Christian outpost in the Congo in the 1500s, but it was eventually swallowed up by local tribes, and they remained largely confined to their island trading fortresses like Mozambique.

In North America the disillusionment of arrival left a permanent impression on the national psyche that has done much to shape our attitude toward the wilds. The Jamestown colonists of Virginia stopped en route at "very faire" and fragrant islands in the Caribbean. On their initial landings at Chesapeake Bay in May 1607, these first permanent English colonists in North America, perhaps with an eye to impressing their investors back home, described woods full of sweet-smelling cypress and cedar trees, wild strawberries far bigger than England's, and flower-strewn paths like a garden or an orchard or a paradise.[31] However, by August of that same year, a mere three months later, they were dropping dead from starvation and disease. By January when a relief ship finally arrived from England, only 38 of the original 144 colonists were alive to meet it.

Thirteen years later, when the *Mayflower* anchored in 1620 off an autumnal Cape Cod, William Bradford wasn't under any illusion of entering Eden. But he did frame the plight of these "pilgrims" as he biblically referred to his group of religiously-inspired colonists, in Old Testament terms:

> [W]hat could they see but a hideous and desolate wilderness, full of wild beasts and wild men—and what multitudes there might be of them they knew not. Neither could they, as it were, go up to the top of Pisgah to view from this wilderness a more goodly country to feed their hopes; for which way soever they turned their eyes (save upward to the heavens) they could have little solace. . . . For summer being done, all things stand upon them with a weatherbeaten face, and the whole country, full of woods and thickets, represented a wild and savage hue.[32]

The new lands in both Africa and North America transmuted into staging grounds for a vast Old Testament epic. As the early Portuguese in Africa faced that sword-wielding angel who blocked the Garden, the Plymouth colonists became the tribes of Israel wandering in the wilderness, lacking even a Mount Pisgah for Moses to climb and gaze toward the far-off Promised Land. In 1652 the first Dutch arrivals settled in a small station to service passing ships at Africa's Cape of Good Hope. Within a few decades many had broken from the little colony and became the nomadic herdsmen called the Boers. They, too, saw themselves wandering in the wilderness in patriarchal tribes styled after those of the Old Testament, and they ruthlessly took the land and enslaved the native people.

Thus began in Africa, North America, and elsewhere the battle between light and dark, good and evil, to root out the Devil who inhabited the heathens, to subdue the wilderness, and to make the new lands fruitful in the name of God and civilization.[33]

In early afternoon it felt like an omen when Jamie's plane flew low overhead. It was easy to see omens everywhere in the wilderness—easy for lack of any other reference point, for lack of any solid information other than guesswork. You're so eager for a sign, any sign, that augurs what might lie ahead. The Portuguese and Pilgrims and Boers relied for their interpretation of omens on the stories of the Bible, which they superimposed on the wilds they encountered. Our omens came from the sky: from satellites, from airplanes, from handheld telephones and radio receivers whose frequencies searched out signals from high above.

Rod pulled the radio from the orange Pelican case strapped to his deck and managed to make contact as we drifted in a cluster down a channel. The message from Jamie circling overhead was simple. Indeed, it sounded like an omen, ominous.

"The other chap," we heard Jamie say over the crackling radio, referring to Paul Connolly, "passed the fly-in camp at one o'clock today."

The fly-in camp was our original resupply point, but we had missed it and reached Luwire Camp only the next day. Jamie's staff at the fly-in camp apparently had seen Paul Connolly paddle by an hour or two earlier and had relayed word by radio to Jamie, who took to the air to relay it to us. We had just left Luwire Camp that morning, so this meant that Connolly was less than two days' paddling behind us and moving fast. A wave of alarm swept through our group. Could he catch us? He was now very close.

"We'll try to delay him," Jamie said, signing off.

Rod stowed the radio and battened down the case. We all picked up our paddles. Instantly, the pace accelerated. Everybody was revved up. I wanted not to care if we got to the confluence first, but I *did* care. It was hard to tell if Josh was revved up, too, or simply trying to sort out all the things coming at him so fast today.

"We'll be paddling late today," Rod announced.

It was all I could do to paddle hard enough to stay reasonably close to the other two boats. Rod's blades shoveled mounds of water to his stern, his back muscles flexing like a racehorse's flanks. Cherri determinedly dug in her paddle from the bow. Clinton's graceful, rhythmic back-and-forth quickened like a metronome hitting an allegro tempo. *Shoop, shoop, shoop.* Josh put more muscle into his strokes, too, although he didn't have nearly the strength of Steve.

For two hours we paddled hard with frantic energy, attempting to put distance between us and the spectre of super-kayaker Paul Connolly—racing us, chasing us, whatever he was doing coming down the river fast behind us. Maybe he merely wished to join us collegially. Had he intentionally given us a week's head start as a challenge? Or maybe he just wanted to paddle the river himself, unencumbered by our group. Did he really want the prize for himself? Who knew? I got the impression from Clinton and Cherri that Connolly was a highly competitive person. Clinton said that Connolly was a marathoner and a former lawyer, and his children were multilingual. Then again, we were competitive types, too.

"There's enough glory on the Lugenda River for us all," I said aloud more than once as we paddled hard.

There was silence from the others. Apparently they didn't think so. I wasn't sure I thought so, either. Rather, it was as if I was trying to convince myself that I wasn't competitive, that I was somehow more charitable than that, that it wasn't important who got there *first*. This had been a theme and a tension in African exploration at least since James Bruce claimed to be the first to "discover" the source of the Blue Nile. The Portuguese, in fact, had arrived there 150 years before him. Livingstone made himself crazy—almost suicidal, it seemed to me—to be first, and like Bruce he deliberately excised the Portuguese who had come to his various "discoveries" before. Second didn't count. It may have been just as difficult to reach the same spot—maybe even more difficult—but the way was known. It was the *unknown* that counted, as if the psychological barrier of the unknown loomed larger than the physical obstacles. That had been my own experience on the Lugenda River. The truly frightening part was *not knowing*. It was as if the European "civilized" world that conferred the honors of exploration and the gold medals for arriving first implicitly understood without having been there the power of the unknown.

I wanted to be better than James Bruce and David Livingstone and

Henry Stanley, Richard Burton and John Speke, Alexander Laing and René Caillié and Heinrich Barth, and all those other explorers scrambling to be first—to find the Niger, to Timbuktu, to the Nile source, across the Sahara, down the Congo. But, really, I was no different. Like Cherri and Rod and Clinton, I didn't at all want Paul Connolly to beat us to the confluence if that's what he was trying to do. I would paddle to exhaustion to get there first.

Down the Lugenda River we charged. Broad flat stretches alternated with narrow braids through the forest. Here the current quickened. We maintained our hard-charging pace as the channels dodged and ducked and dropped over small sets of rapids. Our hulls banged the rocky bottom, our paddles whapped through the underbrush on the banks, and our boats swiveled this way, spun that way, and slalomed down the channels.

Josh was really excelling at paddling in these tight spots. Maybe it was his photographer's keen eyes and hair-trigger reactions. He quickly got the hang of maneuvering the boat's bow in the direction it needed to go without my telling him first, while I concentrated on our overall course and brought the stern around. We passed Rod and Cherri. We were flying down the river after Clinton's rabbit-quick yellow stern, just slamming through rocky channels, ducking under low-hanging branches, whipping into hairpin turns, dodging down another tiny brushy channel over a drop, sliding down rocks into another tiny rushing channel that braided off through willow thickets, hopping out for a moment to push, hopping back in.

I was having a ball. Josh and I felt like a synchronized duet, doing a kind of dance. I hardly had to say anything to him other than "take the left channel ahead" or "let's duck into this one." There was hardly time to say anything, it was happening so quickly as we played a giant game of pinball with the kayak caroming off rocks and down channels while the two of us worked the flippers together in total concentration. Most of the time we couldn't even see Clinton ahead, the channels were so small, tight, fast, and brushy. I had to guess which way he'd gone. Rod and Cherri were somewhere behind us. We couldn't see them, either.

If we all get separated here in different channels, I thought, *we might not see one another for days.*

Still, we kept the frantic adrenaline-charged pace. I loved it. It was as if we finally had a truly focused mission: Beat Paul Connolly. It wasn't a mission from God, like the Portuguese or the Puritans or the Spaniards or the Boers imagined their mission, but it would do. It was a reason for being here, a very clear, graspable reason amid all the other much less tangible ones that I was trying to work out. For the moment I needed no other.

I heard a roar ahead. I saw Clinton's yellow boat being pulled to the left, weaving through narrow channels, while he probed for a larger channel to the right. But still the swift current in a small channel funneled us left. I guessed the river was pushing up against another left-trending band of rock. I knew what this meant.

The little channel suddenly piled into a big mound of granite surrounded by brush and forest, sieving around it. Clinton hopped onto the low dome followed by Josh and me.

"How are you two doing?" Clinton asked.

"We're doing fine," I replied. "But we're nearing the end."

"As soon as we get out of this, we'll look for a place to camp," he replied.

We peered over the dome's top. The river spread out into a hundred small channels and poured in countless thin white rivulets over an amphitheater-shaped waterfall, a giant horseshoe about ten or fifteen feet high. Ringed by dense forest, it was a beautiful wild spot.

But we didn't stop to admire it. Rod and Cherri landed behind us. Dragging the boats by the bowlines one at a time, with Josh shooting photos of the portage, we hauled the kayaks quickly up and over the dome and down its far side. We grunted them across patches of sand and willow brush, and emerged on a sandy beach below the falls.

We stood there, panting. It was now almost sunset. The falling water looked phosphorescent white against the darkening black forest. We jumped back in the boats. We could see a sandy island across the river just below the falls. We paddled to it. A single acacia tree protruded from its center, like the palm tree of the classic desert island. It looked inviting. We beached our boats and quickly pitched tents.

A half-moon made lacy shadows from the acacia tree on the sand. Rod instructed Josh about not going too close to the shore, where there was deep water, due to the crocodiles. The waterfall *shush*ed white in the moonlight backed by black forest. We sat around the fire and sipped our small rations from our renewed whiskey canteen.

"It's outrageous that he's chasing us or racing us," Cherri said.

She was upset partly because she had given Connolly maps of the region that had taken her many months to extract from the Mozambican government.

Clinton was on the satellite phone to Lance back in Pemba on the Indian Ocean. Dispatched on what we called "an intelligence mission," Lance had hung out the previous night at a Pemba travelers' bar with Connolly's backup driver to try to extract information. I now appreciated Rod's background in reconnaissance if he was indeed the one who had assigned Lance the task. Clinton lived intensely for the moment; Rod always seemed to be thinking ahead.

Clinton debriefed Lance and signed off. He reported to us around the fire that Connolly had put in at the second bridge downriver four or five days from where we had put in near Belem. That is partly why he could catch up to us so quickly even though he had started a week later.

"I don't think he's racing us," Clinton said reflectively into the fire. "I think he's just trying to join us. It's in our mind."

DAY FOURTEEN

"Let's go!" Cherri was yelling.

We had almost finished packing the boats. The sun wasn't even up yet. We had woken at five and it was now just past six, and she was impatient to start paddling.

"Clinton thinks Paul Connolly isn't trying to beat us but simply join us," I said, stuffing the last of Josh's and my gear into hull openings.

Cherri would have none of it.

"There is absolutely no way I'm going to let Paul Connolly get to the confluence before we do! Not after all the work I've put into organizing this trip! Not after two years!"

We climbed into our boats, pushed off with our paddles, and backed out into the river. I didn't want to leave the beautiful amphitheater waterfall with its hundreds of white tendrils splashing down the wet, dark rock, but there was no stopping. The expedition had developed its own momentum like a boulder tumbling faster and faster down a hill.

Within a few kilometers our surroundings had melded into a blur of shiny river and golden sandbars, dark forest and grassy banks, sun and blue sky.

Stroke . . . stroke . . . stroke . . . stroke . . .

There were no rapids, only the broad river winding among sandbars. Josh and I talked some—about photography, about writing, about traveling.

I realized that on long, uncomfortable journeys I had a way of falling into a kind of mesmerized, timeless state. No expectations. Not marking time or distance. Here I let my mind drift off with the hypnotic rhythm of the paddle while one node of my consciousness continued to assess the landscape. Often I did not even know where my mind had gone when it came back. Was this "traveling hypnosis" an ability I had inherited from long, long ago, honed when humans started to migrate across the earth? There were no immediate dangers. The way was long. One had to rest one's senses. It was almost like sleeping while walking or while paddling.

My mind returned to the kayak when Josh spoke or Clinton paused to regroup, or we had to push with paddles or wade barefoot and drag the boats over broad, sandy shallows to find a deeper channel. Sandbars edged into the river everywhere. The wildlife appeared rich on this lower part of the Lugenda. We skirted pods of hippos, snorting and grunting in the deeper channels, but here the river spread so broad that it was easy to give them hundreds of yards of leeway.

Clinton and Rod pointed out three Egyptian geese standing on a sandbar, a female calling to two males. The geese took their name from the Egyptian tombs on which they are portrayed in hieroglyphics from thousands of years ago, Clinton said.

We spotted other species new to us: purple herons, wattled plovers, honey buzzards. A vulture soared high overhead, wings extended, riding the air.

"Vultures are a cool bird," said Clinton.

He paused paddling—he didn't often stop spontaneously—to explain how different types of vultures fly at different altitudes. They watch for others of their species and can see one another riding the air currents as far as fifteen or twenty kilometers away. When one vulture spots a kill lying on the ground below, it signals to the other vultures by putting down its talons as it soars. Their eyes are so good, Clinton said, that from the altitude of a kilometer they can spot a piece of meat lying on the ground that is a mere six centimeters in diameter.

I liked to hear Clinton and his enthusiasm when describing animals. There was something appealingly boyish about it and professorial at the same time. We paddled on . . . and on. The sandbars grew more numerous, and it became difficult to find channels between them, forcing us to push against the shallow bottom with our paddles or climb out and drag the boats. We finally stopped for breakfast where a broad, dried-up streambed joined the Lugenda. Though it was only 11 a.m., the sun felt very hot and was directly overhead, as if we had traveled that much nearer to the equator. That morning we had in fact crossed another line of latitude, putting us at twelve degrees south. We walked over the baked mud of the streambed's delta toward the forest's edge, looking for a bit of shade in which to make our fire and cook our oatmeal. Without a spot of shadow, the dried mudflat looked almost white in the direct overhead sun, like weathered bones. Huge elephant prints were pressed into it like potholes, creating ripped-up edges that I tripped across. I paused and gazed over the expanse, toward the ragged forest edge a few hundred yards away.

It looked beat-up, ancient, worn. Whatever it was, it wasn't beautiful, not by the standard definition, but there was something compelling. Animals carried out strange rituals here that humans would never understand. They knew this terrain. I looked up the dried, sunbaked streambed cutting far back into the anonymous forest, winding like a giant path. It would be terrifying to walk up there alone into obscurity. Terrifying and exciting both. Part of me wanted to go there, and part of me wanted to stay away.

Was this what they used to call *sublime,* a place like this, this sensation? Not beautiful. Sublime was a category that lay beyond beauty, the way this sunbaked streambed leading into the forest lay beyond the human realm.

"Whatever is fitted in any sort to excite the ideas of pain and danger" is how the English philosopher and essayist Edmund Burke defined "the sublime" in 1756.

This adjective, *sublime,* was affixed with delicious terror by late-eighteenth-century English and Continental travelers to the "wild" land-scapes they encountered in the Alps and on the moors: deep forests, river chasms, precipitous mountains. Not beautiful but sublime, filling the viewer with the place's power, with astonishment.

While Burke was writing his pamphlets in London, over in France a clever and tempestuous vagabond-turned-musician-turned-essayist named Jean-Jacques Rousseau grew disgusted with the artificiality of intellectual society in glamorous Parisian *salons.* For a writing contest he composed his famous contrarian essay in which he argued that the so-called advancements in the arts and sciences have actually corrupted man's natural state and that the simpler rustic life was spiritually healthier and more honest. Born in Geneva, Rousseau himself loved mountain walks and the rural life in Alpine villages.[34]

His essay won the Dijon Academy prize. A few years later, in 1761, having written his soon-to-be-famous tracts on political and social inequality that would fuel revolution in America and France, Rousseau published a novel that swept literary Europe, *Julie, ou la Nouvelle Héloïse*. It celebrated wild places and the simple pastoral life away from the artificiality of the cities. The novel is in the form of a series of letters between two young lovers who live in a town at the "foot of the Alps." In the midst of emotional turbulence, the protagonist, St. Preux, takes to Switzerland's Upper Valais where he unexpectedly finds the mountains' power and pure air infusing him with serenity. He writes to his lover:

> I had set out, sad with my woes. . . . I climbed slowly, and on foot, paths that were fairly rugged, led by a man I had engaged to be my guide. . . . Sometimes huge cliffs hung like ruins above my head. Sometimes high and thundering waterfalls drenched me in their thick fog. Sometimes a perpetual mountain stream opened by my side an abyss the depth of which my eyes dared not fathom. On occasion I got lost in the darkness of a dense wood. . . . I reached that [second] day [the crest of] some of the least high mountains. . . . Meditations there take on an indescribably grand and sublime character, in proportion with the objects that strike us. . . . It seems that by rising above the habitation of men one leaves all base and earthly sentiments behind, and in proportion as one approaches ethereal spaces the soul contracts something of their inalterable purity.[35]

Only 140 years earlier America's "howling wilderness" had terrified and disgusted the Pilgrims on their landfall at Cape Cod, in 1620. Now the wilds—at least some manageable Continental version of them—were growing fashionable. Instead of the lair of monsters and the Devil's creatures, the wilds, the forests and chasms, mountains and moors, were *sublime*.

So much had changed in the European outlook in those 140 years. Science, mathematics, and rationalism were ascendant. Galileo and his telescope had confirmed Copernicus's theory that the earth revolves around the sun, not vice versa, with the religious implication that man was no longer the central hub of creation. Isaac Newton published his *Mathematical Principles of Natural Philosophy*. The universe came to be viewed as a giant clocklike machine. A market economy had replaced the old feudal system. With it arrived new demands for transport to take goods to market, and then the Industrial Revolution geared up, its whirling cogs spun by a fantastic new source of power: the steam engine. The engine would be fueled mostly by coal. The great forests of western Europe had been lev-eled centuries earlier for firewood and building materials and to cultivate.

As the Industrial Revolution gained footing, the rural populations of western Europe flocked to the cities. The less there was of "wild nature" and the fewer the people who had access to it, the more valuable it became. Wealthy city dwellers sought out "wild nature" on walking tours and Alpine jaunts. A backlash developed to the mechanistic, mathemati-cal view of the universe, with some impassioned souls refusing to view all of creation as a giant machine. They embraced Nature itself—the wilder, the better—to inspire their deepest passions and reveal the presence of a deity—an Absolute, some called it—both in nature and the human soul.

German philosophers, with Immanuel Kant initially laying the groundwork but then backing away, pioneered this thinking in the late 1700s. Friedrich von Schiller, who wrote *Wilhelm Tell* among many other works, laid out in his essay "On the Sublime" what could have served as a manifesto for these impassioned souls who were later known as the Romantics.

Once man escaped the daily fight to wrestle food from nature, Schiller wrote, he could embrace the spiritual qualities nature embodied:

> [N]o sooner has free contemplation set him at a distance from the blind assault of natural forces . . . than the savage bulk of nature about him begins to speak another language to his heart; and the relative grandeur out-side him is the mirror in which he perceives the absolute grandeur within himself. . . . The sight of unlimited distance, and heights lost to view, the vast ocean at his feet and the vaster ocean above him, pluck his spirit out of the narrow sphere of the actual. . . . Who knows how many illumined thoughts of heroic decisions that could never have been born in a cell-like study or a society salon have been produced by this bold struggle of the mind with the great spirit of nature while wandering about.[36]

"Wandering about" wasn't exactly the phrase that came to mind as we paddled on. This was no walk in the Lake District or Alpine idyll. By 3 p.m. we had paddled some forty kilometers measured in a straight line, the best distance so far. It began to look as if we might actually make the Rovuma confluence by the next day. That was assuming, of course, that we could keep up the fierce pace and that an even fiercer-paddling Paul Connolly didn't suddenly pull up behind and pass us by.

Clinton paddled up beside Josh and me with his steady powerful stroke.

"How are you feeling?" he asked Josh.

"Pretty worked," Josh replied, maintaining his own rhythmic paddling.

"Just think of it as spending a full day at the gym," Clinton said, digging in his blades and powering ahead.

Puffy afternoon thunderheads massed above the northern forest line, billowing fifty or one hundred miles away over the plains of Tanzania. The lowering sun cast them in an ivory hue against the blue sky, roiling upward invisibly at this great distance. Josh stopped us briefly, and I maneuvered our kayak so he could take photos of bare-chested Rod and sun-hatted Cherri powering their double and Clinton muscling his single down the wide Lugenda against the endless rim of dark forest and the massive towers of ivory cloud. Here Schiller surely would have plucked his spirit out of the narrow sphere of the actual.

But the actual kept intruding in the form of our rigorous demands for time and distance. Instead of glorying in the sight, we resumed paddling. We skirted a pod of hippos, sticking close to the bank, and a three-foot-long lizard dropped from a tree branch and nearly landed in Josh's cockpit, plunging beside him with a large splash. Josh appeared oddly calm about it. Maybe he was getting used to the Lugenda, too.

An hour later we passed three fishermen standing on a midriver sandbar beside their beached dugout canoes.

"Do you think we can stop to shoot?" asked Josh, eyeing Clinton and Rod and Cherri's kayaks ahead of us.

"Go ahead," I said.

We paddled up beside them. The three stared back at us. There was always this tension in the moment of first contact. *Who were we?* We were something so alien to the Lugenda River. Once we started talking, however, the threesome became very friendly and animated. Josh picked up his camera and asked if it was okay to take some photos. They said yes. He hopped out on the sand. I kept talking to the three to distract them while he shot, to relax their expressions; I told them that we were two Africans and three Americans paddling to the Rovuma. I explained that our boats were made of *plástico* and showed how the rudder worked. This demonstration was greeted, as usual, with hilarious laughter. It reminded me again of the utter frivolousness of our mission compared with these three who were working the river with nets and dugouts for fish to feed their children. They were too busy thinking about where the fish might be to engage in Schiller's "free contemplation" of the "savage bulk" of nature.

"*Cigarro?*" they asked when Josh had finished.

We wanted to give them something but explained the cigarettes were in Clinton's boat, out of sight far down the river.

"Do we have any food?" Josh asked me.

I remembered that we had a bag of dried peaches in one of the dry bags, snack food that Cherri had distributed earlier in the day. I dug it out and handed it to them along with a bag of nuts. They seemed pleased with the gift.

Through Portuguese phrases and gestures they gave us a parting warning about elephants: Watch out that they don't trample you when you're sleeping.

"It's good to sleep on the open sand," one said.

We pushed off. Far ahead, a kilometer or two downstream, we saw a glint from the lowering sun on the side of a kayak. Josh and I paddled hard down the dark blue current that reflected the purplish sky. The sun would set soon. We rounded the point of a big sandbar on river right. We spotted Clinton, Rod, and Cherri pulling their boats across the sandy shallows to make camp on the open sandbar.

It was a relief to stop. We quickly pitched tents and each took a bath in the sand shallows, unconcerned about crocs because the water wasn't deep enough. We scrubbed ourselves clean of the sand and sweat and dirt of the last hard couple of days. It felt wonderful simply to let my body fall limp and drift along in the coolish-warmish current, bumping over the sandy bottom in the last bit of golden sun. As I watched the big ivory thunderheads hovering on the horizon, I realized I was beginning to feel at home here in Africa.

In the dark, Rod lay faceup on the sand beside the campfire, his lower back hurting too much from paddling to cook dinner. Cherri had taken over the duties. Our bodies were finally giving out. Mine hurt everywhere, and my heels had become excruciatingly raw and bleeding from rubbing against the sandy inner hull of the boat as I worked the rudder pedals. By daylight I had noticed how everyone except Josh, fresh and newly arrived, was looking stringy, tattered, worn, and very thin. We all had a kind of beef jerky quality to our physiques from paddling so many days on so little food. Before he lay down, Rod had checked the GPS—we had gone a huge distance today, over fifty kilometers—and his satellite phone for email messages. We had hoped to hear from Jamie, but there was no word about the whereabouts of Paul Connolly.

"The plan is to get up at five and be on the river by six-thirty like today," Rod announced. "So get your boats ready tonight."

Our dinner of pasta and sauce finished simmering in the black pot over the fire. Clinton got up to serve a plate for Rod, who remained prone on the sand in the dark, as if summoning strength for the push tomorrow.

It was pleasant to sit on the expanse of powdery dry sand in the cool evening with the jumping flames, eat our dinner, and sip our grog, exhausted as we were. Cherri raised her mug by headlamp.

"I propose a toast to Rod and Clinton for saving us hundreds of times!" she announced.

"To Rod and Clinton!" we called out, and drank.

It was our own little awards ceremony, although the event wasn't yet over and Paul Connolly remained unaccounted for. Cherri thanked me for "being great," which I appreciated. I, in turn, thanked Rod and Clinton, saying they did a great job, and I thanked Cherri for all her organization. There were so many other things to say, but I left them unsaid. We all acknowledged Josh for his contribution and for being so game.

Dishes done, Clinton asked me for the customary "bedtime story." By headlamp I walked over the cool sand to my tent and fetched *Wild Africa*.

I sat down beside the fire and cracked the slightly damp volume to the excerpt titled "The Death of Hugh Clapperton."

Clapperton, the intense Scottish explorer who had engaged in the famous running feud across the Sahara Desert with his expedition mate Major Dixon Denham (see Day One), had returned to England in 1825 after the death of his other companion, Walter Oudney. Within months of arriving in Britain, and eager to go back to Africa, he was again dispatched by Lord Bathurst in yet another attempt to "ascertain the source, progress and termination of the mysterious Niger." With the easygoing and adventurous son of a Cornish innkeeper, Richard Lander, accompanying him as manservant, Clapperton made it about four hundred miles inland before dysentery struck him down. Lander recorded in intimate detail the last hours of his beloved master's foray into Africa's interior:

I fanned the invalid nearly the whole of the day, and this seemed to cool the burning of his body, of which he repeatedly complained. Almost the whole of the conversation reverted to his country and friends, although I never heard him regret having left them. . . . [O]n the morning of the 13th, being awake, I was greatly alarmed on hearing a peculiar rattling noise issuing from my master's throat. . . . [O]n his calling out "Richard!" in a low, hurried, and singular tone, I was instantly at his side, and was astonished beyond measure on beholding him sitting upright in his bed. . . . I clasped him in my arms . . . some indistinct expressions quivered on his lips, and whilst he vainly strove to give them utterance, his heart ceased to vibrate, and his eyes closed forever!

. . . The grave was dug on an unremarkable naked piece of ground, with no remarkable object near it to invite attention;—no mournful cypress or yew weeps over the lonely spot—no sculptured marble shines above all that remains of heroic enterprise and daring adventure! But the sleeper needs no funeral emblem to perpetuate his name and actions, having erected for

Peter, Rod (with GPS), and Cherri checking position on map, Day Fourteen.

himself a nobler and far more imperishable mausoleum in the breasts of his countrymen and the civilized world, than all the artists of the universe could rear over his ashes.

Clinton was already in his sleeping bag under the tarp suspended on paddles. Everyone seemed to approve of the Clapperton excerpt, but, as usual, they were too tired to say much about it. Rod put away a few last things.

"There's some boiled water here in the pot," he said. "Anyone want it for their water bottle?"

I was running low on iodine tablets to purify my water. I poured the water from the pot into my spare bottle. I took a sip. It tasted greasy and smoky and thick, and slightly nauseating. It would be my backup water.

Josh, Cherri, and I headed to our tents pitched on the sand a short distance from the fire. I unzipped my flap, crawled into my bag, and removed my gritty contacts. While lying on my elbow, I pushed the pen across the damp notebook pages and wrote more of the day's notes. I noticed my stomach start to grind. I tried to ignore it. I wrote more. The grinding spread down into my intestines. I kept writing.

I had been struck by the passage I'd read at the campfire about the death of Hugh Clapperton. Occurring in the late 1820s, Clapperton's death in the African interior and Lander's description of it felt so much a piece of the Romantic era, then near its height in England. "But the sleeper needs no funereal emblem to perpetuate his name and actions, having erected for himself a nobler and far more imperishable mausoleum in the breasts of his countrymen."

Was it the Romantic spirit that propelled some young explorers on their quests to Africa? A British, German, or French adventurer lost in the bush surely could experience Schiller's "bold struggle of the mind with the great spirit of nature while wandering about." The word *Romantick* itself, according to Samuel Johnson's 1755 dictionary, could mean "wild" or "full of wild scenery." One of the English Romantic movement's earliest and most influential figures, Samuel Taylor Coleridge, drew on African exploration literature for his poetic imagery.

He highly recommended to his friends *Travels to Discover the Source of the Nile* by James Bruce, that proud and eccentric Scottish explorer of Abyssinia in the 1770s. Coleridge also devoured William Bartram's descriptions of the forest wilderness of the American Southeast. With images of wild nature taken from Bruce (the Nile springs) and Bartram (cedar forests), and writing under the influence of opium, Coleridge in 1797 composed *Kubla Khan,* his great hallucinatory poem about the power of the imagination and nature's even greater creative power as embodied in a mighty Nile-like springs.

> *But, oh! that deep romantic chasm which slanted*
> *Down the green hill athwart a cedarn cover!*
> *A savage place! as holy and enchanted*
> *As e'er beneath a waning moon was haunted*
> *By woman wailing for her demon-lover!*
> *And from this chasm, with ceaseless turmoil seething,*
> *As if this earth in fast quick pants were breathing,*
> *A mighty fountain momentarily was forced . . .*
> *Five miles meandering with a mazy motion*
> *Through wood and dale the sacred river ran,*
> *Then reached the caverns measureless to man . . .*[37]

Did the Romantic spirit infect all those young explorers who took off for Africa after James Bruce, and did their accounts of the savage wilds, in turn, further fuel the Romantic poets back home? I could easily understand how the constrained life of a would-be New England lawyer (John Ledyard) or a Scottish doctor (Mungo Park, Walter Oudney) would pale against the sublime grandeur of the Romantic vision of the wilds. The knowledge on the part of the public back home that these young men perished on their quests (Clapperton and all of the above plus many more) could serve only to inflame the Romantic love affair (usually conducted at a safe distance) with the savage wild.

No, it wasn't the simple lure of African gold—even if it did, in fact, pave the streets of Timbuktu as the African Association hoped when it funded some of these adventurers. But for young men of a certain Romantic bent there were far weightier things than gold to be had deep in the African wilds: Unimaginable truths. Profound emotions. Soulful loneliness. Eternal fame.

I understood all this because I, too, had experienced some of its draw.

I couldn't hang on any longer. I pushed aside my pen and notebook, slid from my bag, unzipped the tent, and crawled out into the darkness. Frogs croaking. Crickets chirping. The cool powdery sand beneath my

Peter taking notes, Day Fourteen.

bare feet. But then there was something else, faintly at first, then gathering strength, rising and fading as if on a breeze although the night was calm—the thumping of drums somewhere across the wide sandbar, back in the forest.

Dah . . . dah . . . dah . . . Dum! Dum! Dum! . . . dah . . . dah . . . dah . . . Dum! Dum! Dum!

I saw a spark of faint yellow light glimmering far back in the trees. Was it a bonfire?

Carrying a water bottle and flashing my headlamp over the sand, I walked to a patch of willow bushes fifty feet from my tent. Should I be worried about lions? I didn't know and didn't really care. With my foot I scraped a hole in the sand. Swearing as I did, I squatted, washed myself, and refilled the hole.

Dah . . . dah . . . dah . . . Dum! Dum! Dum!

You wanted African exploration, I told myself, *and here it is—being sick in the willow bushes in the middle of the night along an unmapped river while mysterious drums thump from the forest.* Romantic? It was indeed romantic even while extremely uncomfortable and unnerving. Hugh Clapperton and his manservant Richard Lander had captured just that, framing dysentery and death out in the African bush as high art, erecting that "imperishable mausoleum" in the breasts of their countrymen. Is this what I, too, was trying to do? Was I in some way a Romantic? Were we all—anyone who had ever entertained the notion of "exploring" Africa?

I walked back to my tent and crawled in. My stomach and intestines started to grind again almost immediately. Ten minutes later I was back at the willow patch. Now I heard a strange breathy noise from the forest in the direction of the drums. It sounded amplified, as if the village had installed a sound system and the village chief had taken up the microphone and was blowing into it in long huffs. But where did they get the electricity?

Back to the tent, then out again. What was going on with my body? I wondered how anxious I should be about it. Was it merely something I ate, like the semi-raw onions in the pasta sauce or the double ration of whiskey or the piece of chocolate we'd been saving or the antimalaria medicine hitting my stomach hard? Or was it one of those infinite tropical diseases that can decimate the European constitution—a run-in with the "disease barrier," as the European explorers came to call it? At least I wasn't losing blood; that was somewhat encouraging.

Back in the tent, too uncomfortable to sleep, I picked up *Wild Africa.* I first read Mary Kingsley's 1893 account of West African mangrove swamps. She found both "grandeur" and, quoting Coleridge's *The Rime of the Ancient Mariner,* "slimy things [that] did crawl with legs / Upon a slimy sea." I put down the book and headed out into the willow bushes again. Back in my bag, I turned to the excerpt in *Wild Africa* from Conrad's "Heart of Darkness." Marlowe was describing what he saw as he headed by small steamship up the Congo River:

> It made you feel very small, very lost, and yet it was not altogether depressing, that feeling. . . . The reaches opened before us and closed behind, as if the forest had stepped leisurely across the water to bar the way for our return. We penetrated deeper and deeper into the heart of darkness. It was very quiet there. At night sometimes the roll of drums behind the curtain

of trees would run up the river and remain sustained faintly, as if hovering in the air high over our heads, till the first break of day. Whether it meant war, peace, or prayer, we could not tell.

Dah . . . dah . . . dah . . . Dum! Dum! Dum! . . . dah . . . dah . . . dah . . . Dum! Dum! Dum! Then that *huff, huff, huff*ing of the strange loudspeaker. Yes, Romantic.

DAY FIFTEEN

At about 11 p.m. I swallowed a sleeping pill. I dozed briefly and woke suddenly around 1 a.m. overwhelmed by nausea. Wrapped in my bag, I flipped to my hands and knees, struggled for the zipper of the tent's mosquito netting, and yanked it down. My stomach clenched. On hands and knees, my legs still in my bag, I frantically pawed a hole in the sand at the door and thrust my head from the tent.

I vomited a long, hard, hot stream into the hole. I sucked in a breath, vomited again. Then once more.

My stomach paused. I spat into the large pool I'd made in the sand. I waited. Nothing more.

I sat back on my haunches and wiped away the tears squeezed from my eyes by the effort. I started to scrape big handfuls of dry sand over the hole, still half in my sleeping bag.

"Josh?" I heard Rod call out from the tarp shelter near the darkened fire.

"No, it's Peter," I said in a hushed voice.

"Are you all right?" Rod asked.

"I just threw up. I've been really nauseous, but now I'm feeling a bit better. I'm out of iodine pills to purify water. Do you have any? I've been having diarrhea and lost a lot of liquid. I'm going to be really thirsty before long."

"I'll find some tablets," Rod said.

I saw his headlamp click on.

I walked shakily across the sand toward the darkened shapes of the tarp and gear piles. Rod was kneeling in the sand and searching by headlamp through his gear.

"Did you hear the lion last night?" he asked as he looked.

"You mean that strange breathing sound during the drums?"

"That was a lion," he said, "about a mile away."

"Really? I thought it was some guy breathing through a loudspeaker. But then I thought, 'They can't have electricity way out here.' "

Clinton was now up helping Rod look.

"I'm sorry to wake you guys in the middle of the night," I said.

"No trouble at all," they replied.

Rod found the tablets and handed me a couple of small packets.

"Do you have any idea what might have caused it?" he asked.

"I'm hoping it's just something I ate."

He and Clinton climbed back in their bags. I walked to the edge of the sandbar and dipped my water bottle into the dark river, dropped an iodine tablet in it, and went back to my tent. I crawled out a moment later to squat yet again at my willow clump, wondering if the lion had moved on or moved closer.

Back in my bag, I felt spent. I wanted to drink water, gulps and gulps of water. I opened the canteen and allowed myself three tiny sips and then screwed the lid on. I lay on my side and switched off my headlamp. The camp was dead quiet. No drums, no lion huffing, no crickets, no frogs, no hushed voices over the powdery sand. Only the African darkness. I drifted into that hallucinatory stage between waking and sleeping, Coleridge's state when writing his opium-induced *Kubla Khan*. I felt my limbs twitch and fell deeper, an empty shell drifting down, as if some powerful force had rolled through my body and then rolled on into the depths of the African night.

The Romantics would have appreciated this overpowered state. Yearning for nature to transport them with its sublime terror, they pitched themselves headlong into the forces of the Universe in hopes of being filled by Grand Emotion and Absolute Truth. They were Romantics, these African explorers. I had begun to understand that. There was James Bruce and his exquisite despair on reaching the Blue Nile's springs after tremendous hardship and realizing he had now completed only half his journey—and for what? There was John Ledyard dropping out of Dartmouth College and hewing his canoe from a giant pine on the banks of the Connecticut River to paddle into the years of grand adventure that ended in death by emetic at the Sahara's edge. There was Mungo Park faced with the prospect of a stormy night in the branches of a tree and his profound, tearful gratitude for the kindly woman who took him home and cooked him a simple grilled fish and sang him songs. There was the fever-stricken Hugh Clapperton with his unmarked grave in the bush who had nevertheless erected a "tower of heroism" in the breasts of his countrymen.

I am a Romantic, too. I was coming to understand that as well. I had sought the remote places of the world, remote from the "civilization" that I knew. After my father's first suicide attempt I had dropped out of college—John Ledyard's college on the banks of the Connecticut River—and traveled overland to the Himalayas. I wanted to remove myself as far as I could from my life as I knew it. Looking down with Himalayan clarity, I sought to sort out my confusion and my responsibilities. They were to whom? I hoped the profound power of those mountains would strip me down to some absolute core. It actually worked. In some way that I never suspected, but over a much longer period of time instead of *right then*, it actually worked.

But that is the subject of a different story.

I am a child of Romantics. My father was a Romantic in so many, many ways. On a Romantic impulse he made a voyage around Cape Horn as an ordinary seaman on the last commercial windjammer to make the rounding. On coming ashore he reconstructed a pioneer's log cabin in the Wisconsin woods that was his and my mother's first house. He loved the power of nature. Later, when our family moved to a house on the shores of a lake, he loved to venture out by canoe or small sailboat into big storms—the driving wind and rain pelting him, the thunder and lightning crashing around him, the waves smashing into the bow, nature blowing through him, throwing him into the mercy of its grand power. My father's love of storms on the lake reminds me that the great Romantic poet Shelley (who happened to be reading Rousseau's *The New Heloise* with Byron while rowing about Lake Geneva some years earlier) died in precisely this manner: His small sailboat capsized during a storm a few miles off the Tuscany coast in 1822. Byron and his other grieving literary friends incinerated Shelley's body in a funeral pyre on the Tuscany beach, at the very last extracting his still-intact heart from the flames.

When it came to nature, my grandfather was a Romantic, too. He loved the peacefulness of Wisconsin's North Woods, the slowly sliding river under his canoe, the sheer exuberance of flinging his body—still powerful in his sixties when I first knew him—into outdoor sports: swimming, diving from cliffs, climbing trees, ice skating. He loved the escape from his business life in the city. I can trace my grandfather's attitude toward nature in a direct line of descent back to Coleridge and Schiller and others of the Romantic era although my grandfather would have laughed at the notion—if he even bothered to understand it. He was born in the 1890s when the "Fresh Air" and outdoor exercise movement were getting under way in the United States, and charitable programs sprang up to take youth out of the unhealthful, ever-swelling, immigrant-and-disease-choked cities for rejuvenation in nature. Other outdoor youth programs started in Germany while the English hero of Africa's Boer War, Robert Baden-Powell, founded the Boy Scouts in England, followed by American outdoorsman Ernest Thompson Seton in the United States.

My grandfather benefited from all this. Son of the Prussian candymaker and his English wife, my city-bred grandfather's first exposure to the outdoors—to the canoeing that played such a big part in my upbringing—was through YMCA camps designed to bring city children in contact with healthful nature. This nature movement had many forebears, but one key figure—a figure whom others revolve around and whom through my grandfather I can trace my own love of the outdoors and wild places—is "the original hippie of Concord, Massachusetts" (as I once heard him described by my college literature professor), Henry David Thoreau.

It was in April 1851 that Thoreau, then in his early thirties, stood at a podium in the Concord lecture hall "to speak a word for Nature." Refined and delivered many times in subsequent years under the title "The Wild," his address contained the short remark that captured a sentiment that was novel at the time but resounded powerfully today: *"[I]n Wildness is the preservation of the world."*

Son of the proprietor of a small pencil factory in Concord, then a village outside Boston surrounded by woods and fields, and a garrulous and reformist mother, Thoreau's family scraped together the tuition to send him to Harvard. Here, Thoreau was known as a genial, talkative, but rather peculiar student who traversed Harvard Yard, as one of his classmates remembered years later, with a "grave Indian stride."[38] Reading voraciously in the classics and works of Eastern religion, Thoreau wrote prolifically (including an essay on Burke's "sublime") and gained a reputation as a close observer of nature. The college librarian, a serious amateur entomologist, later remarked that Thoreau would have made a good entomologist if Emerson hadn't spoiled him.

Ralph Waldo Emerson, the entomologist's spoiler, was another preacher in an unbroken line of Massachusetts preachers going straight back to Puritan days, a direct spiritual descendant of those who had found a "godless" Wilderness on the North American continent. After his wife's early death from tuberculosis, Emerson had come to question his faith, quit the ministry, and traveled to Europe in the early 1830s where he met and was deeply influenced by the great Romantic poets—Coleridge and Wordsworth among them—and encountered German philosophy. On his return to America, Emerson settled in pastoral Concord, Thoreau's hometown, at a time when Thoreau was still in college. Thoreau's first entry in his two-million-word-long *Journals* evidently was inspired by one of his early encounters with Emerson in Concord, shortly after Thoreau's 1837 Harvard graduation.

"What are you doing now?" he asked. "Do you keep a journal?" So I make my first entry today.

Unlike his Puritan forebears, who spotted Satan in the tangled thickets, Emerson believed that the divine existed in all of nature as well as inside oneself. He thought that one could experience it by looking inward or by reading the natural world properly. "[N]ature is the symbol of the spirit," he wrote.[39]

A group of young intellectuals congregated around Emerson in Concord, becoming known in the late 1830s as the Transcendentalists, among them the young Henry David Thoreau at loose ends. After unhappy stints as a schoolteacher and a pencil-maker, and a revelatory boat trip into the woods on the Concord and Merrimack rivers, Thoreau dedicated himself to being a poet of nature. In exchange for room and board at Emerson's house, he worked as Emerson's gardener and began publishing poems and essays in the literary magazine founded by Emerson, *The Dial.* "[He is] a young man with much of wild, original Nature still remaining in him," wrote novelist Nathaniel Hawthorne, also newly arrived in Concord, after meeting Thoreau. "He is as ugly as sin . . . and with uncouth and somewhat rustic manners . . . and seems inclined to lead a sort of Indian life. . . . He is a keen and delicate observer of Nature."[40]

Thoreau soon built his shack in the woods at Walden Pond and planted his bean field, embarking on his famous two-year experiment in self-sufficiency and life with nature that would form the basis of *Walden, or Life in the Woods.* "I went to the woods because I wished to live deliberately, to front only the essential facts of life." Hardly deep in the impenetrable wilderness, Walden Pond lay near enough to Concord that Thoreau could easily walk into the village for Sunday dinner at his mentor's house. It was here in the confines of Walden and elsewhere around Concord village that Thoreau, until his early death of tuberculosis at forty-four, documented in the most intimate detail and poetic language the processes of the natural world as observed in a small area. He had predecessors: Gilbert White, curate of Selborne, England, in the 1700s wrote intimately of the natural history of his parish. An admirer of White's, Thoreau brought natural observations to an entirely new level, employing them to illuminate the human spirit—mostly his own—and vice versa. A kind of one-man Paleolithic Revolution in reverse, his carefully honed prose breached the wall, the same wall erected by Gilgamesh around Uruk at the Agricultural Revolution's outset, between Man and Nature, Civilization and Wilderness.

On several occasions Thoreau did trek from the Concord environs into wilder nature, with surprising results. Halfway through his Walden stay he journeyed to the deep wilderness of the Maine woods with friends and attempted to climb five-thousand-foot-high Mount Katahdin, the highest peak in Maine. His companions having retreated from the summit attempt, Thoreau forged ahead and found himself alone on a barren, rocky, windswept ridge short of the summit. Beset by "hostile ranks of clouds," he was unable to go on. One senses that Thoreau was genuinely frightened by the sheer power of this much wilder manifestation of nature than that generally found in pastoral Concord:

Occasionally, when the wind columns broke in to me, I caught sight of a dark, damp crag to the right or left; the mist driving ceaselessly between it and me. It reminded me of the creations of the old epic and dramatic poets, of Atlas, Vulcan. . . . It was vast, Titanic, and such as man never inhabits. Some part of the beholder, even some vital part, seems to escape through the loose grating of his ribs as he ascends. He is more lone than you can imagine. There is less of substantial thought and fair understanding in him than in the plains where men inhabit. His reason is dispersed and shadowy, more thin and subtile, like the air. Vast, Titanic, inhuman Nature has got him at disadvantage, caught him alone, and pilfers him of some of his divine faculty. She does not smile at him as on the plains. She seems to say sternly, Why came ye here before your time. . . . This was the Earth of which we have heard, made out of Chaos and Old Nights. . . . Man was not to be associated with it. . . . Talk of mysteries! . . . *Contact! Contact! Who* are we? *Where* are we?[41]

Rod's bird whistle came, as promised, at 5 a.m. I opened my eyes. It was still quite dark. I turned over in my bag for what felt like the hundredth time since the middle of the night, wanting very much to lie inert. Every square inch of my body ached. After throwing up past midnight, I had slept fitfully, waking every twenty minutes or so to turn over painfully and take three tiny sips of water from my canteen to slake my deepening thirst. I had confronted not the hostile ranks of Thoreau's clouds but the hostile ranks of some unknown bacterium that inhabited what the old explorers called Africa's "disease barrier."

I inserted gritty contacts, stuffed my bag and pad, and crawled out onto the sand. I staggered when I stood, lightheaded, then caught myself. It took a conscious effort to propel my body upright across the flat sandbar, as if climbing a dune.

Rod and Clinton looked up from where they squatted beside the just-kindled fire, feeding driftwood twigs into the tiny flames.

"How are you feeling this morning, Pe-*tah*?" Rod said.

"Better. Kind of weak and shaky, but my stomach's better."

"Here's some rehydration mix," Rod said, handing me a couple of packets. "Stir a packet into your water bottle."

"And have some Nutrina," Clinton added. "You'll need something in your stomach."

I had no interest whatsoever in putting Nutrina, South African breakfast cereal, into my stomach. I went down to the river in the soft pink and orange dawn, refilled my water bottle, and dropped in an iodine tablet. While waiting for it to dissolve, I collapsed my tent and then sat beside my gear pile with a small roll of duct tape. I wrapped the raw, painful sores on my heels, pressing the adhesive directly onto the oozing flesh. I didn't care. I just wanted to get through the day. That's all I needed to do.

As the pot of water heated on the yellow flames, Rod pulled out the sat phone and checked his email messages on the little screen. There was one from Jamie at Luwire Camp. It said that Paul Connolly and a paddling companion, someone named Bruno, had stayed last night at Luwire Camp. They planned to leave this morning and paddle toward the river's mouth. That put them two days behind us.

Rod announced the news to the four of us. I felt a wave of relief. Surely all of us did. The pressure was off. What a problem it would have been if suddenly Paul Connolly and Bruno came steaming around the bend in their tandem—or their singles or whatever they were paddling—bent on reaching the confluence before we did! Cherri had worked out a plan in that event: Clinton and Rod would jump into Rod's double and simply sprint for the confluence, leaving all the gear and everyone else behind. This assumed, of course, that Paul Connolly cared about scoring the first descent of the Lugenda as much as Cherri did. But what a scene it would make if he did! A sprint by Westerners in kayaks in the African wilds, paddles windmilling and shooting spray in the sunlight, the fishermen in their dugout canoes along the sandbanks looking utterly perplexed. Whatever is their *hurry*?

But now the chances of that happening were almost nil. Leaving from Luwire Camp this morning, there was no way that Connolly and the mysterious Bruno—I imagined biceps on him the size of the Incredible Hulk's—could catch us before we reached the Rovuma confluence, which we estimated was about twenty kilometers away, unless something delayed us unexpectedly along this last stretch of river.

The first pale gold rays of sun sieved through ragged treetops at the forest's edge across the wide expanse of sand and willow brush. I knelt in the sand, opened my water bottle, and poured in the packet of rehydration drink. I looked forward to drinking it as much as anything I could remember, anticipating the sweetish and slightly salty liquid that would restore my vital fluids. I pulled my river knife from its sheath on my shorts and carefully stirred the powder into the water, not wanting to lose a speck.

I happened to glance up toward the rising sun. I stopped my stirring. Four sinewy African men strode toward us in a row across the expanse of sand and willow. They wore deep frowns—even fierce frowns. One turned slightly as he strode, and I noticed the sun's rays glint on something strapped over his shoulder. A gun. I was closest to them, near my tent site at the edge of camp. I glanced back toward the fire. Clinton, Rod, and Cherri were busy packing the boats at the water's edge. Josh stood off to my side, dismantling his own tent. He stopped suddenly to watch the four men, too. He later told me that as they approached, from his angle he saw one of them raise his shirt, pull a pistol from a holster hidden there, and hold the gun behind his back, at the ready.

Here's trouble! I thought.

I quickly sheathed my knife and stood up from my water bottle and my precious rehydration mix

"Look who's here!" I called out to the others, trying to sound the alarm while appearing nonchalant, and then I turned to face the four men.

"Bom dia!" I called out to them with a smile and a wave. I went up and shook each of their hands, smiling broadly. They didn't smile back.

Clinton, Rod, and Cherri paused to watch these introductions, then kept packing—hurriedly.

"Hey, do you see what this guy has strapped on his back?" I called out to Clinton behind me, still trying to sound casual.

I could now see that it was a stubby, lethal-looking AK-47, one so well worn that its finish had rubbed off and it shone like dull silver in the early sun. This gun had seen some use.

"It's okay!" Clinton called back, looking up briefly from stuffing things quickly into the kayaks. "Find out what they want!"

Because I spoke a little Portuguese, I knew I could be most useful by running interference with the four men. I'd steer the conversation before they steered it—and possibly us—to wherever they wanted to go.

"Do you speak Portuguese?" I asked, chipper and upbeat. "I speak a little."

"Sim," one said.

"What are you doing here?" the one with the fiercest frown interrupted abruptly. "Where are you going?"

"To the Rovuma River," I said. I started explaining that we were paddling the length of the Lugenda to the Rovuma, stumbling over my Portuguese vocabulary and using plenty of hand gestures.

"Chefe, Negomano!" barked out the one with the fierce frown, extending his hand in the direction of the forest and the village from which we'd heard drums in the night.

That's all I could catch in what was clearly an order to us. *Chefe* meant chief, and Negomano was a village that, at least according to the map, lay at the confluence of the Lugenda and Rovuma. I assumed that the chief of Negomano was visiting this village. I also suspected that these four had been dispatched to fetch us to the chief. But I played dumb, stalling for enough time to get the boats packed and hoping to blunder our way out of this.

"Chefe, Negomano!" the leader kept saying fiercely to me, pointing back toward the forest.

"Chefe aqui?" I finally said, acting surprised. "I heard drums last night," I said, using a mixture of sign language and Portuguese, playing an imaginary drum and pointing to my ear. "Were the drums for the chief of Negomano?"

"Sim, sim," they answered.

"Good drum music," I said, giving a cheerful thumbs-up.

"Chefe, Negomano!" the leader barked at me again, pointing to me and toward the village.

I was wondering when the AK-47 was finally going to swing around at me.

"Oh, the chief of Negomano wants to meet us!" I said as if I finally got it.

"Sim! Sim!"

I looked back toward Clinton, Rod, and Cherri. They all worked fast, packing the boats.

"These guys want us to go to the village and meet the chief!" I called out to Clinton. "What should I tell them? They seem awfully serious about it. Maybe we'd better go with them."

"That will take hours and hours at least!" he called back. "Can you tell them we're going to the Rovuma, and we'll come back here and meet the chief because the road passes through here?" he said.

The road he referred to was essentially a forest trail that led from Negomano to another temporary camp of Jamie's some distance back up the Lugenda. We had passed this little camp the previous day. It also had a bush strip. The plan was for Lance to meet us in the Land Rover at the Rovuma confluence at Negomano and take us via Land Rover on the forest trail back to this little camp, where Jamie could fly in and meet us, and then wing us off to various destinations. Meanwhile, Lance and Clinton would drive the Land Rover with the boats and gear back to Pemba on the Indian Ocean. There they could pick up a halfway decent road that would lead them south down the coast and all the way back to Botswana.

"I'm not sure these guys will go for that," I said to Clinton.

I turned back to the four men. I explained with a lot of arm waving and broken phrases about the *carro* that would meet us at the Rovuma and bring us back here later today to meet the chief of Negomano. The three milder men made signs of agreement. The fierce one scowled even more deeply. They didn't move. I went back to the boats, carefully removed my river knife sheath from my shorts, casually picked up the headlamp that lay near my water bottle, and stuffed them into a bag out of sight. I didn't want these four appropriating anything from me as a commission or thinking the knife meant some sign of aggression.

"What did they say?" asked Clinton.

"Three of them seem to think it's okay, but the fourth doesn't look too happy about it. Do we have any cigarettes left to give these guys? That might help."

Rod looked up from where he was lashing things to his deck. "We gave away all the cigarettes."

"We have energy bars," said Cherri. "Give them all an energy bar."

"Do you want to handle that?" I said to Cherri. "I think it would be better coming from you as head of the expedition."

She dug five Clif bars out of our extensive stores. As she did, I quickly stuffed the rest of my gear into our boat, plus Josh's. She walked to where the four men stood at the edge of camp and, with a kind of ceremonious gesture, handed one energy bar to each plus one to take back to the chief of Negomano. The four, clearly perplexed by whatever it was she handed them, turned the sleek, silvery packages over in their fingers as the sun glinted off them.

We hopped into the boats while they examined the packages, moving as fast as we could while trying not to look rushed. We pushed backward off from the sandbar with our paddles. The boats backed into the swifter current, caught the flow, and we were quickly a hundred yards away from them, swept along by the river.

Rod swiveled his head back to me as we all began stroking downstream, out of range of the AK-47.

"*That* was an African credit card, Pe-*tah*!"

We now approached Dr. Livingstone territory. Some thirty miles down the Rovuma from the Lugenda confluence at Negomano, trying to make his way upstream from the Indian Ocean, Livingstone faced one of his lowest moments and greatest setbacks. While they lived oceans apart and entered the wilds from two very different directions, odd parallels existed between Henry Thoreau and David Livingstone. When the young Thoreau was finishing his studies at Harvard, the young Livingstone was graduating from the spinning mills of Blantyre, Scotland, and living in the single room of a row house in which were crammed a family of seven. Livingstone had worked in the mills since age ten but, like Thoreau at Concord Academy, had shown promise and determination as a student in the after-hours mill schools, in part because his deeply Christian father had taught him early to read. Livingstone soon was studying Latin.[42] When a plea went out to train British medical missionaries for work in China, Livingstone saw both an escape from the spinning mills and a way to put his education and strong religious background to use. African exploration—at least at first—had nothing to do with it.

As Henry Thoreau was Indian-striding through his Harvard senior year, David Livingstone entered medical studies at Anderson's College in Glasgow, followed by training with the London Missionary Society. But when the outbreak of the Opium War in 1839 nixed China for his missionary work, the society's directors suggested the West Indies. Livingstone, whose ambition to be first showed early and intensely, rejected the Caribbean and its colonial past as too Europeanized and opted instead for southern Africa. By the 1830s, Europeans had barely settled there except in a few outposts such as the British Colony around Capetown.

Landing in the spring of 1841 at Port Elizabeth, Livingstone made the two-month, five-hundred-mile journey inland by oxcart to the remotest mission in southern Africa, Kuruman. He instantly loved the freedom of traveling in the African bush after his rigorous routines in spinning mills and medical studies. But Kuruman itself came as a crashing disappointment. It had been lauded in British fund-raising circles as the jewel in the crown of the London Missionary Society's fieldwork, headed by the famed missionary Robert Moffat, but in reality Livingstone found Kuruman to be a small village surrounded by near desert where in twenty years of hard work Moffat and his wife had made a mere forty converts.

Livingstone quickly resolved that he would not remain at Kuruman. Instead, he sought to start his own mission among "untouched" tribes that lay to the north. "I would never build on another man's foundation," he wrote in a telling letter to his sisters back in Scotland. "I shall preach the gospel beyond every other man's line of things."

Here was a sentiment that just as easily could have been written by Henry Thoreau, who had just then abandoned his teaching career to become a poet of nature. Thoreau, too, sought to preach his own brand of gospel beyond every other man's line of things.

Four hours. If I could just hang on for four hours. That's how long I figured it would take us to make the confluence with the Rovuma and the expedition's end. I'd had quite enough with going beyond the other man's line of things. We had started paddling just past 6:30 a.m. As the men with the guns faded into the distance, Rod and Clinton held an animated discussion about whether the men actually had any bullets for the AK-47. I didn't give a damn about the finer points of their armament. I could think only of time and distance. About twenty Ks. Twenty kilometers. At five or six Ks an hour we should be there by 10:30 a.m. But it stretched ahead of me as long as the distance we'd already come in fourteen days on the river.

I felt terribly weak sitting in the rear cockpit, paddling lamely and trying to steer. A thin bank of clouds slid over the sun, sending a deep chill through me. I was almost shaking. Then the sun reappeared. I broke into a feverish sweat. Josh was doing most of the paddling. We managed to keep reasonably close to the others because the going was slow. Clinton was picking our way through sand shallows in search of deeper channels in the broad river. Often we had to pole with our paddles. Shoving the heavy kayak forward, I heard the muted crunch of paddle blade in sand reverberate up the paddle shaft like a dialogue I was holding with the river bottom. *Stay,* it was telling me, *stay, stay.* I kept sipping from my canteen to rehydrate. Sometimes we had to climb out and drag the boats through ankle-deep water. Mostly I held on to the deck while I walked, using it for support like some waterborne walking cane, as Josh did the pulling from the bow.

"I'm sorry, Josh," I apologized. "I'm not much help."

After a while my body felt too heavy and lightheaded to climb out at all.

"Do you mind doing the dragging?" I asked.

"That's fine," Josh said, getting out yet again.

I slowly chewed half an energy bar, on top of the few spoonfuls of Nutrina that Clinton and Rod had made me eat back in camp, but it didn't help my utter weakness. Clinton drifted along a grassy bank, with Cherri and Rod floating near him, waiting for Josh and me to catch up.

"Don't die on us now, Pe-*tah.* You can die after you get on the plane."

It wasn't quite clear to me if he meant it figuratively or literally. We soon lagged again.

"Don't die yet," Rod reiterated gently.

Both very solicitous of me, they didn't push as hard as they had the days before. We were now so close to the finish.

But after two hours I wasn't sure I could keep going. I thought I might pass out. I almost needed to hang on to the cockpit cowling in order to sit upright.

"If I could just lie down for a while," I said to Josh.

"I could use a toonda break anyway," he said.

He called out to the others for a pit stop. They pulled over to a mid-river sandbar, muddy and flat along the edges, rising to a small hump of dry sand. Without a word I climbed shakily from the boat. It was too much effort to explain. I walked slowly to the dry pillow of sand, lay down on it, and closed my eyes. The warm sun felt delicious on my body. I wanted to lie just like this, on this warm spot of dry sand, for a long, long time. It didn't matter to me in the least that it was in the midst of the African bush and I was spread-eagled on a muddy, sandy bit of island in a little-known river. It was a fine place. It offered everything I wanted in that moment: quiet, calm, warmth, and rest. I had a glimmer of understanding how the Hugh Clappertons and David Livingstones had expired in the midst of the African wilds. It wouldn't be too difficult. The difficult thing would be to bother to carry on at all.

But carry on they did until they simply couldn't go.

It was in the year 1845 that both David Livingstone and Henry David Thoreau truly ventured "beyond the other man's line of things." That spring, Thoreau felled the big pines along the shores of Walden Pond for his cabin's foundation. That January, David Livingstone married Mary Moffat, the famous missionary's unpretty but sturdy daughter (more out of convenience and duty on both their parts, seemingly, than for any deep romance). As Thoreau finished his cabin, Livingstone and Mary took the first step into the unknown north to establish their own mission at a place called Chonuane. Earlier, Livingstone had founded a mission farther south with a man named Roger Edwards, but the two had quarreled bitterly after Livingstone tried to claim all credit for its founding in his letters home to the London Missionary Society.

As Thoreau planted his bean field to experiment with living deliberately at Walden Pond, Livingstone boasted in letters home to friends that his new Chonuane mission was the most remote in all of southern Africa and "a blank on the map." But situated in an area that lacked rainfall, the mission didn't last long. The local chieftain, Sechele, and his people of the Bakwain tribe moved farther north to a place called Kolobeng. Livingstone, lacking any possibility of converts without Sechele, moved his mission after the chief, who was mainly interested in the European's access to guns and didn't want to give up his multiple wives plus face the scorn of his people in order to become Christian. This was the third mission Livingstone had started in as many years.

After two years of trying at Kolobeng, Livingstone managed to convert Sechele, his single convert. But five months after the baptism Livingstone noticed one of the rejected wives growing pregnant, and Sechele confessed that he had relapsed. This sent Livingstone into despondency. Unlike Robert Moffat, Livingstone could not see himself spending a lifetime in a single place to make a handful of converts. It is easy to understand his trapped feeling: He was in a passionless marriage with two small children, his career was at a standstill at the last mission of the line, and he was without a convert to his name. It was at this impasse that Livingstone formulated ideas about "itinerant missionaries" who would move on if the seeds of Christianity didn't find fertile soil among a tribe. He had heard of a large lake lying hundreds of miles northwest, across the Kalahari Desert, that no white man had seen. When a wealthy English hunter and traveler, William Cotton Oswell, came through the missions of southern Africa, Livingstone convinced him to underwrite an expedition to the unknown lake. He wrote to the directors of the missionary society back in London that Sechele and the Bakwains were not offering fertile ground for converts but, far to the north, thousands of souls could be saved. "It is therefore imperatively necessary to extend the *gospel to all* surrounding tribes."

It was 1849. Thoreau was just then embarking on the Herculean task of drafting and redrafting and re-redrafting his Walden Pond journals into a view of nature and wildness that no one had ever expressed before. David Livingstone—whether from pure Christian charity, from an unquenchable ambition to be first, or from a simple wish to escape an unhappy domestic situation—left behind Mary and their two small children and three-month-old son, and embarked on the first leg of his celebrated career in African exploration.

"Pe-*tah*?"

I could hear him calling from far away.

"Pe-*tah*? You need to get up. We need to go."

I didn't want to move. I didn't want to open my eyes to compromise

An ailing Peter lies on a sandbar, Day Fifteen.

this perfect point of repose I had found floating in warm, soft, darkness lit by a golden glow beyond the black.

"We've got to go."

I stirred my legs. I felt sand and dried mud. I lay still again.

With the wealthy hunter William Cotton Oswell providing twenty horses, eighty oxen, and two wagons, Livingstone, Oswell, and a friend of Oswell's crossed the Kalahari Desert and were the first Europeans to see the large expanse of Lake Ngami. Livingstone made sure in his letters home to Britain that he got credited for being the initiator of the expedition—that is, the lake's discoverer—and he would win a gold medal and a cash prize from the British Royal Geographical Society for it. What really excited Livingstone, however, was less the lake than the information from the local people of a large system of rivers lying north of Lake Ngami. He wrote the directors of the London Missionary Society that this river system "opens out the prospect of a highway capable of being quickly traversed by boats to a large section of well-peopled territory."

Here was Livingstone's epiphany, the one that would shape his life: Large rivers could serve as highways to bring "Christianity, Commerce, and Civilization" to the otherwise impenetrable and pagan heart of the African continent.

Six months after returning to Kolobeng mission and his family from Lake Ngami, Livingstone set out in an attempt to reach the river system, this time traveling with Mary, pregnant again, and the three children: Robert, age four; Agnes, age three; and Thomas, age one. Oswell was supposed to join him, bringing a portable boat to ford rivers, but Livingstone didn't wait around for Oswell and the agreed departure date, apparently unwilling to share credit for the river's discovery. The Livingstone family, however, had barely reached Lake Ngami before turning back; their oxen were dying from the tsetse fly, and the children had contracted malaria (which Livingstone treated with quinine, then a new remedy). They went four months without eating vegetables, two days at one point without water, and generally declined in health until the two youngest became too weak to stand. Mary Livingstone managed to give birth to a baby daughter a week after their return to the Kolobeng mission, but the baby, Elizabeth, contracted a bronchial infection that the other Livingstone children had picked up from the Bakwain tribe and died within a month.

"It was the first death in our family," wrote Livingstone, "but [was] just as likely to have happened if we had remained at home, and now we have one of our number in heaven."

They spent three months recovering from the trek, which had also caused a temporary paralysis in Mary's face, at the Moffat's Kuruman mission. Back at Kolobeng, Livingstone again proposed heading north with Mary (pregnant again) and children to seek the undiscovered river system.

"O Livingstone, what do you mean?" his mother-in-law wrote him angrily. "Was it not enough that you lost one lovely babe, and scarcely saved the other, while the mother came home threatened with Paralysis? And will you again expose her & them in those sickly regions on an exploring expedition? All the world will condemn the *cruelty* of the thing."

This didn't stop him. Setting north with the entire family in April 1851 (at the same time that Thoreau was taking the podium in the Concord Lyceum), David Livingstone, with Oswell at his side, arrived four months later on the wide banks of the Upper Zambezi River. With local information, Livingstone and Oswell correctly deduced it was the same river that emptied into the Indian Ocean near the Portuguese outpost at Mozambique Island many hundreds of miles east. In fact, a Portuguese trader named Silva Porto had already reached the Upper Zambezi several years before Livingstone. But Livingstone would dismiss Silva Porto (incorrectly) as a half-caste and stake his own claim as the Upper Zambezi's first European discoverer. Here, finally, at the moment Thoreau was extolling the benefits of wildness—that in it lay the preservation of the world—and was bemoaning the earth's fast-shrinking component of it, Livingstone had found his great Highway of Commerce, Christianity, and Civilization to tame the wild pagan heart of Africa.

Livingstone promptly dispatched his wife and their four small children (Mary had given birth during the expedition) back to Britain where they led an itinerant existence scraping by on the charity of relatives and friends and on handouts from the missionary society. Mary expected Livingstone to return in two years. His absence stretched to four years. Mary started to drink. She made bitter remarks about missionary work. Meanwhile, Livingstone crossed the entirety of southern Africa to the west coast and then to the east coast, tracing the Zambezi River a good part of the way and renaming "the smoke that thunders," as the local people called the great waterfall, Victoria Falls after the Queen.

Having left England an obscure missionary, Livingstone returned in 1856 a national hero. He spent two years traveling around Britain on speaking engagements and collecting honors, and writing a book, *Missionary Travels,* that became a publishing sensation. With his book royalties he set up accounts for his impoverished wife and children, then left again for Africa, writing to Robert, his eldest son: "While I was in England I was so busy that I could not enjoy much the company of my children."

Now he would put his grand plans into action. Abandoning the cautious and tight-fisted constraints of the London Missionary Society, he arrived in Africa in 1858 with the full support of the British government, which outfitted him with a small steamer and a contingent of British personnel and naval officers. But the pressure was on. Livingstone had promised to open a river route up the Zambezi to the interior highlands. Here in a healthful climate above the malarial swamps British entrepreneurs could profit mightily by growing cotton. At the same time the native Africans, their recalcitrant tribal institutions undermined, would be enlightened by their exposure to Commerce and Christianity, which together, of course, equaled Civilization. All this would serve to abolish the despicable African slave trade, which by the mid-1800s was vehemently opposed by the British. The slave trade was then flourishing in the Zambezi region, however, conducted by Arab, Portuguese, and native African slave traders.

It was a lot for Livingstone to deliver—far too much. Quarrels broke out from the very start at the Zambezi's mouth between Livingstone and the British personnel. It quickly became clear that the Zambezi was a very shallow river even for so small a steamer and that Livingstone, so capable traveling alone and good with the African natives, knew little of navigation or how to get along with European expedition mates, who finally saw him as deceitful, ungrateful, manipulative, and prone to engage in vicious campaigns of character assassination against anyone who challenged him. They had to winch the little steamer over sandbars. Commander Bedingfeld of the Royal Navy, the Zambezi expedition's second-in-command, was dismissed or quit over ongoing arguments with Livingstone. Then, in a several-hundred-mile section of the Zambezi's loop that Livingstone had hastily skipped on his African traverse, their progress upstream was blocked by a major rapids he hadn't foreseen, impassable by the steamer. Beyond the rapids lay a further obstacle: a thirty-foot-high waterfall.

His expedition mates could not believe what they considered Livingstone's outright lie when, in letters back to the foreign secretary, he claimed that a more powerful steamer could complete the upriver journey when the Zambezi was in flood. Meanwhile, Livingstone searched desperately for a way to salvage his vision. He would try the Shiré River instead, a tributary of the Zambezi that fed in from the north. A Portuguese trader had told him that it drained from an enormous lake surrounded by highlands, but those great hopes unraveled into disaster, too. The Shiré was blocked by big rapids as well. Reached by Livingstone on foot, the highlands near the enormous lake, which he named Nyassa, looked good for British settlement. But when a Universities' Mission party, inspired by Livingstone's lectures at Cambridge, arrived at the Zambezi and Livingstone pointed them toward these Shiré Highlands, they fell victim to malaria and disease—including the death of the celebrated mission leader Bishop Charles Mackenzie—and got caught up in tribal warfare over the slave trade. Meanwhile, Mary Livingstone, drinking heavily and badly overweight, arrived by ship to rejoin her husband after ten years away from Africa. She promptly died of fever near the malarial Zambezi mouth.

It was after Mary's death, and with Livingstone's much-hailed Zambezi expedition fast running out of options, that Livingstone set off on a serious attempt (he'd tried a casual one earlier) to ascend the Rovuma River hoping to find an easier river route than the Shiré River to Lake Nyassa and the

Shiré Highlands. Maybe the Rovuma, not the Zambezi, would serve as his beloved Highway of Christianity and Commerce. After five days heading upstream in two small boats his expedition mates concluded that the river was too shallow to be of any use in reaching Lake Nyassa. Livingstone obsessively pushed them on as if to purge the disasters he had suffered with the death of the missionaries and his wife, and the failure of his highway. Soon they were ducking poisoned arrows from tribes who feared Arab slavers. Still Livingstone pushed the little party up the Rovuma.

"I can come to no other conclusion than that Dr. L. is out of his mind," wrote Dr. John Kirk, doctor, botanist, and fellow Scotsman who had stuck with the good Dr. L. for the Zambezi expedition's entire four and a half years but now called him "cracked." "[He] is a most unsafe leader. It is useless making any remark to him."

Late on the afternoon of September 26, 1862, about thirty miles below Negomano and the Lugenda confluence, the two little boats arrived at the foot of a cataract. It formed the end of Livingstone's final hope for a new highway.

As the Zambezi expedition fell into a shambles of bitter personnel resignations and impassable rapids, Foreign Secretary Lord John Russell sent out a dispatch recalling it to England.

Livingstone's grand vision had failed.

"Pe-*tah*! We need to go!"

I felt someone standing over me. I opened my eyes. Sunlight and blue sky. I rolled over on the sand, got up on hands and knees, and slowly raised myself. I was barefoot, shirtless, and wearing only river shorts and knife. I stood on a small sand, mud, and willow bar in a river surrounded by forest.

But after my brief rest I felt a little better.

A fisherman had poled his dugout canoe up to the sandbar. He got out and sat down on the sand, watching us. Someone gave him a Clif Bar. He was friendly and smiling. The rest of us sat beside him. Josh took photos. Again I felt that weird dichotomy between making an expedition and documenting the making of it. Which were we really doing? It was as if none of these explorations—like the Portuguese traders' discoveries of the Upper Zambezi and Lake Nyassa that Livingstone had coopted—existed without the account.

"How far is it to the Rovuma River?" I asked the fisherman in Portuguese. I was hoping for the best. *"Dois horas?"*

"Uma hora," he responded.

I very much hoped he was right. One hour. I was pretty sure I could paddle, however lamely, for one hour.

We climbed back into the boats. I still felt weak but not nearly as much as before. We stroked downstream at an easy pace. Very soon the riverbanks began to pull back. Now sandy and covered with tall grass, they looked almost like dunes at a seashore. The forest receded to the distance, far back from the banks. The sky seemed huge and blue and beautiful after so many days in the closed-in forest, and enormous tall muted clouds floated in the distance over Tanzania.

Our own success felt very near, modest as it may have been. Poor Livingstone. He failed right here, turning back thirty miles downstream on the Rovuma. I didn't like him, but I felt sorry for him. An impossible person, he seemed noble in his stated aims to spread Christianity and eradicate the slave trade, and also incredibly needy and selfish. He wanted to remake all of Africa and get full credit for it, but he couldn't love his own family. His eldest son, Robert, a difficult and rebellious adolescent for Mary, had changed his name (in order not to dishonor it, he explained in a letter to his always-rebuking father) and died in 1864 at age eighteen fighting against slavery on the northern side in the American Civil War.

Livingstone returned to England after the Zambezi failure and, getting caught up in the feverish debate between Burton and Speke over the Nile's true source, set out once again, this time to find the source himself. It was in the midst of this seven-year odyssey that Henry Morton Stanley, in what was actually a newspaper publicity stunt, "found" the badly ailing Livingstone at Lake Tanganyika. Generously resupplied with food and medicine by Stanley, whom he liked as a kind of surrogate son, Livingstone continued alone on his Nile quest. With his faithful African retainers at his side, he finally expired, probably of severe blood loss from hemorrhoids and possibly dysentery, in the swamps of Lake Bangweolo at age sixty. Some of his last writings were unsent drafts of letters to the foreign secretary that announced his discovery of the true springs of the Nile, springs that he never found.

Overall, I liked Thoreau a lot better. He was difficult, too, but in a genial and self-secure way. Where Livingstone cast his net wide over an enormous swath of Africa largely unexplored by Europeans, Thoreau went deep. While Livingstone searched over thousands of square miles, Thoreau stuck mainly to an area around the village of Concord that measured seven miles from north to south. But both clearly were searching for something in their respective wild or not-so-wild territories; both were living out some deep need. Otherwise, why ever would they bother?

In Livingstone what I mostly saw was a desperate need to prove himself. The wilds of Africa provided a grand tableau over which to do it—to make a name for himself and at the same time make good by helping others, as his father's strict religion drove into him very young. In Thoreau I saw a profound—*desperate* seems too extreme a word for him—need to understand himself or his place in the universe. His tiny place in the universe, as it turned out. But he profoundly grasped that his tiny place in the universe was connected to all other organisms, all other matter. He called

The Lugenda expedition at Luwire Camp: Peter, Clinton, Steve, Rod, Cherri, and camp staff in background.

A happy arrival at Luwire: Rod (foreground), Steve, Cherri, Peter, and Clinton.

himself a "co-inhabitant" of Concord's plant life, while the stars were his "fellow-creatures"; and the fish known locally as striped bream was, for Thoreau, "my contemporary and my neighbor."[43]

That's what the miniature wilds of Concord taught Henry Thoreau. David Livingstone had all the grand wilds of Africa—where early in his missionary career he had even survived a mauling by a goat-killing lion that he'd wounded with his gun—and he still didn't understand how small he really was and how he was connected. He still didn't understand that he, too, was a neighbor of the bream. Livingstone fought desperately to make himself larger right up to his very last days when he was losing blood during the rains while wandering lost in the swamps of Lake Bangweolo. There were those very sad letter drafts to the foreign secretary announcing his discovery of the Nile springs, with intimate descriptions of how they looked rising from the base of a hill, except that he left blank spaces in the letters for latitude and longitude.

Then again, maybe Livingstone had learned one great lesson of Africa's wilds as opposed to Concord's wilds: In Africa you had to make yourself look bigger (as Clinton had instructed if confronted by a lion) in order to survive.

I believed that man had, to one degree or another, a deep instinct to roam, to move beyond where he was and see what was over the next hill, if only for simple survival and the prospect of finding more promising sources of food. *Homo erectus* and then *Homo sapiens* had made those grand journeys out of Africa into what was then the wild unpeopled world. But I was convinced, too, that not just physical necessity compels us. Spiritual necessity compels us as well to seek out the wild places of the Earth. Exact contemporaries, Livingstone and Thoreau were two very different manifestations of that spiritual need for the wilds. They both sought out the wilds in order to measure themselves and their place in the universe.

I realized that that was exactly what I was doing.

The river opened up further. We passed a series of slender grassy islands midstream. The Lugenda now appeared at least half a mile across. For several miles ahead we could see shimmery flat water reflecting the pale blue sky.

Then we spotted it. A mile off to the right on a wide sandbank sat the tiny, boxy shape of Cherri's Land Rover, dwarfed by the immensity of water and sand and sky. Rod grabbed the air horn bungeed to his rear deck. He let loose two long blasts that rang across the water. We saw a tiny figure appear. Lance had found his way to the confluence, and we had found Lance and the Lugenda's end.

EPILOGUE

The next few days are a blur in my memory. I was very tired and very hungry. We later learned that in the expedition's course, Rod had lost around twenty-five pounds; Clinton, Steve, and I had each shrunk by about fifteen pounds; while Cherri, trim to start, looked scarecrow-skinny by the end.

I felt a lump in my throat as we paddled under the luminous skies with tall-grass and sand-dune riverbanks stretching to the distance, aiming toward the little Land Rover on the broad white sandbank.

We'd done it! I'd done it! I'd survived all the dangers! We'd all survived! We'd all done it together!

As we paddled closer, I thought about how much I'd missed my family. I thought that I'd now be with them again. A huge sense of relief rose in me. It was as if I'd headed into the unknown for them so that I could come back with something to offer them. Now I had succeeded. I thought of Amy smiling widely at my accomplishment.

"I'm so proud of you," I could hear her say.

That choked me up even more.

Cherri's and Rod's boat beached. Clinton's boat slid onto the sand. Last of all came Josh and me. Josh hurriedly dug out his cameras. Cherri jumped from her cockpit into the shallow water to give Lance, standing there to greet us, a big hug. She gave us all hugs as we came out of the boats, and there were congratulatory handshakes all around—Lance, Clinton, Rod, Josh, and me. Rod gave me a bear hug. We all had worked together very well, finally, despite the tensions and irritations. Each member had brought his or her expertise and generously shared it for the benefit of the whole group as we threaded our way through so many, many obstacles. A warm sense of that teamwork was implicit in every hug and handshake.

Lance, Clinton, and Rod hurried a few hundred feet to the Land Rover. Already villagers—dozens of them, the women in their bright capulana wraps—were gathering around the boats and the Land Rover. The threesome returned with tall cans of Castle beer and passed them around. We toasted one another and the expedition's success, standing beside the beached kayaks under the lustrous shimmery clouds that floated over the Rovuma and Tanzania. Beyond the horizon lay the Indian Ocean where the mixed waters of the Lugenda and Rovuma joined the world's seas.

The rest of the day vanished in a long, lurching drive upriver on the faintest of forest tracks. At the end was Jamie's lower camp and its bush airstrip. I lay in the back of the Land Rover once again atop the layer cake of petrol cans, coolers, and camping gear, wedged with Clinton and Josh, then Rod and Josh. Soon empty beer cans were stashed in every crevice of the gear pile. Still very weak and tired, I let myself loll with the lurches. After the second or third beer I slipped away into something like sleep. It was neither unpleasant nor pleasant, just a feeling of being absolutely spent, of nothing left. I could sense myself lift into the air as the Rover bounced over dried-up streambeds, then fall back down on my impro- vised bed.

Toward the end of the afternoon we reached the camp, a smaller and simpler version of Luwire Camp that was undergoing rethatching and repairs. Lance cooked up steaks for us on his camping stove. Then he, Clinton, and a villager guide climbed back into the Land Rover. Clinton was still in a tremendous hurry. He wanted to get going right now. I still couldn't understand why—whether to make safari commitments or so he and Lance could get back to their girlfriends (as Cherri theorized) or sim- ply due to his general high-energy impatience. He and Lance faced many days of driving—first east to the Mozambican coast, then looping south around the miombo forest, and finally aiming across southern Africa to Botswana. Cherri and Rod, meanwhile, were to fly out the next morning to Pemba in Jamie's bush plane. Rod would fly commercially from Pemba down to Johannesburg and back to Botswana; Cherri was due to head off for a few days' rest and relaxation at a South African luxury lodge with her boyfriend Richard. Before he flew Cherri and Rod out to Pemba, Jamie would fly Josh and me to the Headquarters Camp of the Niassa Reserve.

Our plan was to spend a week or so looking around the reserve and seeing some of the terrain we had just paddled past.

It was sad to separate out our piles of personal gear. The long, hard journey together was ending so abruptly and our little team was breaking up so quickly after we had reached our goal. Everybody was tired of the river, tired of paddling, tired of one another. At least I was. My petty irritations were starting to surface again. I could see it happening in the others, too. It pissed me off that Cherri wouldn't let me keep my life jacket, which I wanted out of sentimentality, although I'd brought all the life jackets from the States and given them to her as a donation from the magazine.

"That's all I'm getting out of this trip," she had said as I handed over my trusty red kayaker's life jacket, "that and bills."

Still, some deep bond remained among us or, again, at least it did for me, one that I wouldn't fully appreciate until later. When they climbed into the Land Rover, I felt sad saying good-bye to both Clinton and Lance. Clinton's irrepressible spirit lay at the very heart of the expedition, and Lance had been totally selfless in his support of the expedition with no pay but many days of difficult driving in the bush. At the takeout that morning, Clinton and Rod, as well as Lance, had presented me with a toy

At the journey's end, Peter, Josh, and Rod celebrate in the Land Rover rear.

Land Rover beautifully carved out of different kinds of wood that they'd bought from a craftsman way back in Malawi during their drive with the kayaks to Lake Nyasa. I was very touched by their thoughtfulness.

"You have to keep it on your desk," Clinton said.

"I will," I replied.

The doors slammed shut in the dusk. The Land Rover's engine revved. Then it disappeared down the darkening forest path.

Cherri, Rod, Josh, and I sat in camp chairs on the Lugenda's high bank quietly watching the river slide by in the twilight. We spoke of what an amazing river it was and what a thing we'd done. Cherri spoke of her ambition to explore, which she'd had since she was a small girl. It was a peaceful, bittersweet moment for me. I felt warmly toward her and toward Rod. I wished I could be more present and respond to her and Rod, too. But I was so tired, I could hardly speak.

By 6 p.m. we were all in our tents asleep.

The following morning Jamie dropped Josh and me at the Niassa Reserve bush airstrip. Cherri and Rod accompanied us this far, and we said good-bye with more hugs and handshakes. Then they climbed back into the Cessna, and the plane roared down the bumpy strip, lifted easily over the treetops, and disappeared over the forest.

Then there was silence again.

Josh and I spent the next week in the Niassa Reserve. We had heard that due to the thick vegetation of the miombo forest, the Niassa Reserve was a difficult place to "see" animals in the course of a few days, unlike the savannah reserves elsewhere in Africa. There was no tourist infrastructure or regular guide service to take anyone sightseeing. There were no tourists. There was only a headquarters camp of a few safari tents for visiting guests and scientists, a small dining pavilion, and a few outbuildings. When we arrived, a miniature conference was under way: Two German wildlife scientists were visiting from reserves in neighboring Tanzania and comparing notes with the two managers of Niassa Reserve.

With the meeting going on and no animals to see without a great deal of work, they didn't quite know what to do with Josh and me. We pitched our tent on the camp's edge. We then spent that first day driving around with a staffer named Batista in one of the reserve's few vehicles. At my request we visited villages to get more of a sense of how people lived. After several hours of meandering on a dirt track, Batista, Josh, and I happened to end up at Mussoma village. It was near here, I remembered, that the local men had portaged our kayaks around a big waterfall.

"Is there a big *catarata* near here?" I asked in my Portuguese/Spanish as we stepped from the Land Rover into the center of a small collection of mud buildings.

"Yes," said a young man. "There is a big *catarata*. I can guide you there."

A tiny outdoor market was going on in Mussoma's center: A few small piles of salt, tobacco twists, edible roots, tomatoes, and peanuts were spread on ground cloths. This was the Mussoma economy. As I eyed the produce, another young villager approached Josh and me, speaking eagerly in broken English as if we were Mussoma's best hope for a future.

"I have a plan. You can help us build a dam at the *catarata,* and we can make electricity and sell it for a profit!"

I gave some polite acknowledgment although in fact I thought it a terrible idea to dam a beautiful waterfall gorge in a newly designated wildlife reserve. Once again in the Rover, we bounced along a bush path for nearly an hour toward the waterfall. We stopped at a smaller village en route to obtain the chief's permission to pass. A slender, gracious older man, the chief was sitting in front of his ochre-colored mud-and-thatch house. He came out and we exchanged warm greetings. He readily gave permission to Batista to proceed to the waterfall. One of our young guides from Mussoma, clinging to the back of the Land Rover, asked the chief for a light for the cigarette he'd rolled from a few shreds of homegrown tobacco. The chief summoned his wizened wife, who emerged from their darkened doorway gripping a smoldering log in her gnarled hand. The chief held the log graciously for the young man as he lit his cigarette against its glowing coals; then he handed it back to his wife, who returned it inside the house.

I imagined the mayor of a U.S. or European town greeting an official guest who asked for a light by handing him a burning log fetched by his wife from inside his house. It was suddenly a lot harder to think *No, you people shouldn't have a dam here. A smoldering log should remain your source of heat and light.*

But what about Thoreau? What about my own passion for wild places? What about *in wildness is the preservation of the World*?

Thoreau would have loved to talk about the prospect of a dam here.

What good is it, he had asked, to jack up everything to a faster pace with your steam-powered locomotives, your electricity, your whatever? Faster means more complex. Faster means more fragmented and less graspable. *Simplify, simplify,* said Thoreau. He wanted to go deeper instead of faster or farther. He wanted essence instead of abundance.

Would these people—these occupants of mud-and-thatch huts in forest villages—have understood that? I wanted to think so. I wanted to think they had an instinctive understanding that electricity or automobiles, concrete walls or cash money, weren't really going to solve much at all. Or these conveniences might solve some things—a lack of medicine, health care, and schoolbooks, for instance—but the circumstances that brought these things might also create a whole different and more intractable set of problems, problems that run to humankind's spiritual core. I wanted to think they might be able to find some other way besides building a dam to give them what they felt they lacked.

But I really didn't know if they thought that, and I feared there wasn't going to be another way except a dam or its equivalent.

At the waterfall Josh and I scrambled over the huge granite shield, taking photos of the *catarata* and poking around. Just upstream from here, I recalled, we had really started to encounter people and villages again after several days very deep in the wilds. Some of the local young fishermen followed us over the rocks, and I asked them, with help from Batista and the Mussoma guides, and through the Jawa tribal language and Portuguese, the name of the waterfall.

"*Ndilima,*" one replied.

"What does that mean?"

"It means 'echo,' " he said. "The sound the water makes."

I asked them if they knew the names of any other *cataratas* upstream. They spoke of one twelve kilometers upriver called *Kandema,* translated as "long and fast current," and one roughly forty kilometers up that they knew as *Maveliga,* "whirlpool." After that they really didn't know. This forty kilometers upriver covered only a few of the last rapids and drops we had run on the Lugenda; I knew there were many, many more above that, such as that big, beautiful waterfall with the blue-colored river entering on the left bank.

I carefully wrote the names that they did know in my notebook. I thought that probably no one, certainly no Westerner, has ever recorded these names before. It gave me the sense again of truly exploring, this time recording major geographical features for the first time, however inaccurately.

But then later, back at Niassa Reserve Headquarters Camp, we had dinner under the thatched pavilion with the reserve's two highest-ranking staff, Baldeu Chande, wildlife technician, and Anabela Rodrigues, general manager. They told Josh and me that they thought a Portuguese crocodile hunter and his wife had descended the Lugenda River by small boat in the 1950s and that the wife had written a book about it.

Could this be true? That there was a "first descent" of the Lugenda before our "first descent"? That the *cataratas* whose names I'd so carefully recorded that day had already been named and described?

It was very difficult for me to imagine that this couple had run the river's whole length as we did, especially in what must have been a small open boat. I could believe they might have run the lower third or half of the Lugenda. I'd already heard of a British explorer, Joseph Thompson, who had come a short distance *up* the lower Lugenda in 1881, maybe as far as we'd paddled in the last day or two, looking for a seam of coal that Livingstone had speculated lay somewhere in the region.

But who knows? Maybe the Portuguese crocodile-hunting couple really did run the river's length. Maybe we weren't the first ones down the Lugenda at all. Maybe I was being just like Bruce and Livingstone and all those other jealous explorers who, preceded by Portuguese traders and missionaries, couldn't bear the thought that they hadn't been first.

On our third and fourth days inside the reserve we joined a hunt to shoot a Cape buffalo.

The buffalo hunt seemed appropriate in one sense. Hunting played a key role in the extinction and preservation of wildlife both in Africa and North America. So many parallel events have unfolded on the two continents to determine the fate of the wilds, usually a few decades later in Africa than in the United States. As Livingstone made his final foray into the swamps in quest of the Nile springs, the United States established the world's first large-scale wilderness preserve: Yellowstone National Park. Originally designated by Congress to protect the hot springs and geysers from commercial exploitation, Yellowstone in the decades following would serve as a model for other parks and reserves in North America, Africa, and indeed the world over.

By then, the 1870s, the Western United States had been largely explored. Settlers swarmed in by the tens of thousands, and an alarm went up that the last wildernesses were vanishing along with the great herds of buffalo that once roamed the grasslands. A similar lament began to be heard among the aristocrats of the British Empire who no longer could find the abundance of game animals that they once had hunted in southern Africa. White settlement expanded rapidly northward in Africa, as did the "gun frontier" that put lethal modern weapons in the hands of native hunters, with devastating results for game.

Within a mere decade of Livingstone's death, the colonial land grab known as "The Great Scramble for Africa" had begun. Rival European powers—France, Germany, Britain, and Belgium—snatched up huge chunks of the continent during the frenzied 1880s and 1890s. The Germans, similarly alarmed at the rapid disappearance of game, initially led the way in hunting regulation and game reserves in their new colony of German East Africa (later Tanganyika, now Tanzania). As in England, hunting in Germany had long been the domain of aristocrats. The Germans further had centuries of experience in the close management of forests and game. It was therefore not a great leap for the Germans to impose land management on their African colonies.

But the Boers, vigorous subsistence hunters, actually established the first reserve on the continent, Pongolo, in 1894, followed soon by the Sabi Reserve (which eventually became the renowned Kruger National Park). They realized that unless they acted fast, there would be no wildlife left at all. The British aristocrats, concerned about preserving animals for their own hunt, quickly jumped on board the conservation bandwagon. In response to the "appalling" destruction of wild animals, in 1903 they created The Society for the Preservation of the Wild Fauna of the Empire, which would have great influence in the years to come both in Africa and India.[44]

Many of its members were wealthy hunters who wanted to preserve the big game animals for themselves. As in England, the local African people suddenly were no longer indigenous hunters. Instead, they were branded as "poachers."

The hunt that Josh and I joined to shoot a Cape buffalo occurred under special circumstances within the Niassa Reserve itself—quite unlike the paid safari hunting that Derek and Jamie guided for wealthy clients in the buffer zone. While individual hunting by the local people is banned in Niassa Reserve as in most African reserves, the villages within the reserve receive an annual allotment of game to hunt for meat and special occasions. Two weeks earlier a village had dispatched one of its hunters for a Cape buffalo. His shot wounded a running buffalo and the buffalo veered at the hunter and gored him to death with its horns. Now the village had asked Derek and Jamie, with their powerful rifles and long experience, to shoot a Cape buffalo for them. Derek had invited Josh and me along as observers. With the trackers standing on the truck bed in back, he had driven six hours or so in a Land Rover from Luwire Camp to pick us up at Niassa Headquarters Camp, close to the area where the buffalo gored the hunter.

We spent all afternoon driving on forest tracks looking for signs of buffalo. In late afternoon we reached a village where a woman reported that every night, very late, five or six buffalo trampled through her garden patch. She'd be pleased if we got rid of them. Derek looked up at the twilit sky and pronounced that it would be a full moon tonight—enough light to see. The hunt was on. The woman gave our little party a place to sleep in her compound beneath a thatched roof held up by peeled tree trunks. The men built a big fire for us—it was almost cold here near the inselberg

Stalking Cape buffalo for villagers in Niassa Reserve: the teacher Samorra, apprentice hunter Chris, and hunter Derek.

mountains—and we rolled out sleeping bags. Derek surveyed the buffalo run and returned to report that it crossed an area of head-high grass.

"At night if we lose the animals in this tall grass," he said with classic British-Empire-in-the-bush understatement, "that could prove to be quite entertaining."

I decided right then that I wouldn't be one of the entertainees. I stayed behind late that night as the trackers, after quite a party somewhere in the village imbibing the local home brew, headed out with Derek to find the buffalo.

I surfaced and submerged, in and out of sleep, as dawn turned to daylight. I loved lying there, secure in my bag under the thatched pavilion, eyes closed and listening to the village's sounds of waking: the chirping of birds, the crowing of roosters, the clank of iron pots over cookfires, the pouring of water, the cooing of mothers, the sleepy voices of children, and the swish of twig brooms sweeping packed earth. *Simplify*, said Thoreau. Here I heard the clear, plain rhythms of people who were deeply bound to

The Cape buffalo that Derek shot, where it fell in the bamboo grove.

the earth. Secure in my bag in this woman's compound, I felt my own powerful sense of contentment and *belonging.*

The rising warmth of the sun then touched my bag. I opened my eyes and found myself being watched by a handful of curious women and children.

A young tracker arrived from the hunt. They had found the buffalo and made a kill. He led Josh and me a mile or so to the kill—a huge dark mound of a beast lying on its side in a dense green bamboo thicket. Derek and the others were now off tracking the rest.

I heard a trickling sound amid the stalks of bamboo.

"Sangre," said the tracker.

I looked down and saw the red pool dripping beneath the carcass and between the slender fallen bamboo leaves in the cool green grove.

Here was the harsh, sad reality hidden in the emerald bamboo grove. For us to live, something—whether animal or vegetable—had to die. I had learned that lesson with jolting impact with the first deer I shot when I was almost forty. Molly, back at home with Amy, was then two years old. I knew my life and her life were intimately bound to the death of this deer lying sprawled still warm before me on the sage-covered bluffside. Here was food for her. But amid the harsh sadness there was gracefulness, too. For us to live, many other organisms had to live, too: the sagebrush and grasses that fed the deer, the birds that spread the seed, the microorganisms that made the soil, the star that warmed it—on into the great interconnectedness of things.

I first learned these lessons with emotional certainty when I became a hands-on predator. Now here lay that same lesson in the shape of a great dark hump trickling *sangre* in the emerald bamboo grove of the Niassa Reserve. It is no accident that the twentieth century's leading American prophet of that interconnectedness of living things was first a passionate hunter: Aldo Leopold. The Niassa Reserve and places like it—great expanses of wildlife-rich wilderness that have been set aside—owe a great deal to Aldo Leopold and to his predecessor as a wilderness advocate, John Muir. Both were in some ways protégés of Henry David Thoreau.

I already knew a good deal about them because they both had deep Wisconsin roots. The eleven-year-old Muir arrived from Scotland in 1849 (just as Thoreau was writing *Walden*). At the order of his strict Calvinist father, Muir spent much of his youth memorizing the Bible and chopping down trees to clear the family farm from the central Wisconsin wilderness. During a stint at Wisconsin's state university, he read Emerson, Wordsworth, and the newly published Thoreau. It was a crucial moment in the natural sciences. Muir happened to be studying botany and geology at the university just as Darwin's *Origin of Species,* published in 1859, was shaking the concept that God had created the Earth and all its creatures in a single stroke for the use of man. As if in revolt against all his Calvinist and land-clearing upbringing, Muir walked into the woods—quite literally—for what became a life's work as an advocate for wilderness, which for him was a religious temple and a baptism in God's divinity.

"The clearest way into the Universe," he wrote, "is through a forest wilderness."

Muir made a huge popular impact starting in the 1890s as a writer on wilderness, the founder and head of the Sierra Club, and an advisor to conservation figures such as President Theodore Roosevelt. Just getting under way were the Fresh Air movement, Boy Scouts, and other youth groups advocating the health benefits of nature and wilderness; national parks were being set aside, and large tracts of U.S. woodlands were being designated as Forest Reserves (now called National Forests). One beneficiary of Muir's work and all this nature-oriented youth activity was my grandfather who headed off each summer from the city to a YMCA camp where he learned to love canoeing and the silence of the woods, a love that he handed on to my father and then to me. Another beneficiary was a young man from nearby Iowa who grew up hunting with his family along the wildlife-rich Mississippi River bottom lands before heading east to prep school and college: Aldo Leopold.

Graduating in 1909 from the newly founded Yale School of Forestry, Leopold's first job was as an assistant forester on the new National Forest lands in Arizona and New Mexico. Distressed to find that streams were clouding with erosion from grazing and timber-cutting and that the game was getting wiped out, Leopold passionately enforced hunting regulations, restocked streams, and exterminated deer-killing predators such as coyotes and wolves. But he soon concluded that in this age of encroaching automobile roads, what was really needed were large tracts of wilderness, areas open to hunting and fishing and "big enough to absorb a two weeks' pack trip."

Leopold's own thinking evolved dramatically over the next two decades, absorbing a new concept: *ecology.* A German scientist had coined the word itself decades before, but the field-to-be was just then being explored and defined as a concept through the work of thinkers like Cambridge University's young Charles Elton, author of *Animal Ecology*, who saw the natural world as a community. Meanwhile, Aldo Leopold, having left the Forest Service to become a professor of game management at the University of Wisconsin, groped for a new approach to land and game management beyond the goal of simply maximizing productivity of animals and trees. In 1935 he purchased an abandoned farm and shack in Sand County near Baraboo, Wisconsin, where he would do some of his deepest thinking and writing on ecology, as Thoreau had at Walden Pond.[45]

Maybe it was pure coincidence, or maybe not, that this was the area where my grandfather had done some of his favorite canoeing as a young man and had taken me as a boy, on the Baraboo and Wisconsin rivers. Leopold's shack was also not far from the Muir family's farm where young John Muir had memorized the Bible and cleared the Wisconsin wilderness. And Leopold's shack was very near that spot on the Wisconsin River where my grandfather, when I was on my first overnight canoe trip at the age of four, had pointed over the campfire flames to the forest across the river and told me about the coming highway bridge.

"When you're grown up, this will all be gone."

Leopold had his own deep issues with automobile roads that cut through wild country and the "Fords" that drove over them. To the ecological concept of nature as an interdependent community, Leopold added a new component. He addressed what he saw as a desperate need for ethical behavior when dealing with that natural community. In this he was influenced by the writings of Albert Schweitzer, who on an upriver journey into Africa's interior in the early 1900s had had the epiphany that any valid ethical system must extend beyond human-to-human relations to embrace a reverence for all forms of life. Leopold distilled his own thinking about ethics and ecology into a simple, powerful statement he called "The Land Ethic," which has since become a touchstone for ecological consciousness:

> A thing is right when it tends to preserve the integrity, stability, and beauty
> of the biotic community. It is wrong when it tends otherwise.

Had I ignored the "biotic community"? All the way down the Lugenda River I'd been obsessed with the dangers from rapids, waterfalls, hidden obstacles, and large animals. Had I been too focused on these hazards to appreciate in a subtler way the ecological interconnectedness of things? It was true that I had come to a profound understanding of myself as an animal on the face of this Earth, but I'd come to that understanding mainly through a sense of my vulnerability. I now understood viscerally what it felt like to be low down on the food chain (a concept first introduced by Charles Elton in his *Animal Ecology* that had so influenced Aldo Leopold). For those fifteen days on the river I had been like a deer that was constantly monitoring the hazards around it, nervously lifting its head from browsing to sniff the wind, twitch its ears, and be ready to bolt.

But maybe I had overemphasized what is popularly known as Africa's "tooth and claw" aspects. After two days of buffalo hunting, Josh and I had returned with Derek and the trackers in the Land Rover to Luwire Camp. Once again I sat happily at its pavilion dining table as darkness descended on the Lugenda, this time over a dinner of wild boar and beer, following two days of virtually nothing to eat except a few handfuls of the cornmeal mush known as *nshima* that was offered to us in a village. I asked Derek to level with me.

"Really, how dangerous is it to go walking around out here in the African bush by yourself and without a gun?"

It really wasn't that great a problem, according to Derek.

"The lions will pretty much leave you alone, and as for elephants, you just have to stay well clear of them," he replied, or words to that effect. (I wasn't taking notes at the time.)

"What about snakes? Do you have to think of them with every step in tall grass?"

"You don't think about rattlesnakes with every step in the tall grass in Montana, do you?" he asked.

"Not usually."

"That's the same here."

He then told a story of how a black mamba, a highly venomous snake that is very aggressive in defending its territory and the most feared in Africa, had come charging at him and another game ranger when they had provoked it.

Derek went on to qualify his relatively benign assessment of Africa's tooth-and-claw dangers.

"During the day you wouldn't have much problem walking around in the bush, but at night, that's different. At night you just don't go walking around. The local people don't go walking in the bush at night, either."

"Why is that?" I asked.

"At night the animals see you differently."

There was no reason for me to worry then the next day when in broad daylight we bounced through the forest in the Land Rover. Jamie sat behind the wheel, which was on the right side of the vehicle in the British-style Rover. I sat on his left in the bucket-style passenger seat and asked him questions about the reserve's wildlife, taking a few bump-jostled notes. In the truck bed behind us stood Josh plus the trackers, and a young white from Zimbabwe named Chris who was apprenticing at Luwire, and the trackers. We finally stopped at a dry streambed deep in the forest where the trackers quickly constructed a leopard blind, an enclosure made out of dried reeds. The plan was to return that night and watch a leopard feed on a dead baboon the trackers had wired to a tree limb over the streambed.

We all returned to the Land Rover parked in the woods. The trackers were diverted for a few minutes by the song of a "honey guide." This is a bird that has evolved a weirdly symbiotic relationship with humans by directing them with its call to trees that hide honey. The humans then smoke out the bees, break open the hive, and take the honey while the bird happily feeds on the larvae. Here was a prime example of Aldo Leopold's biotic community, including its human components, in all its interdependent glory.

With the grizzled old tracker they called Samorra and the bird literally whistling back and forth to each other, the trackers located the tree. But apparently there were too many of us, too close. We disturbed the bees before the trackers got a smoky fire going. The bees swarmed out and we all hurried away, but not before one of them stung me on the ear. It burned.

"You're not allergic to bees, are you?" Jamie asked once we were back in the Land Rover and driving down a faint forest path toward Luwire Camp.

"No," I said. "At least I've never had any allergic reaction before. Are these some kind of heavy-duty bees or are they just normal bees?"

"They're just your normal African killer bees," he said.

I laughed. Still, it throbbed intensely and then slowly subsided. It was pleasant, despite the sting, to drive down the faint forest track in the open-air Rover. A hunting vehicle, it had no roof, windshield, or doors. Mounted on the dashboard sat Jamie's high-powered rifle, at the ready. I felt relaxed. I felt safe. I felt I could simply look around, for a change.

We swung around a bend in the path at a brisk clip, maybe a fast run, and headed into a small, sunny clearing. I didn't really think anything about the stick at first. It was on my side of the path, the left side, and was thick and blackish. Curved, it poked up three or four feet from the ground. We were still about one hundred feet away and closing fast on the stick when I realized we had driven through this same clearing an hour earlier and there was no big, curving stick poking up along the path. I recognized the clearing, and I surely would have seen the stick. And the stick could not have fallen from a tree within the last hour on this calm, sunny morning.

My senses instantly went on high alert, a deep instinctive response to that curved stick shape. My focus bore in as the Rover careened toward it. The big, dark stick was growing taller! Now it was shoulder high and was swaying back and forth! The stick had a thickness at the top end like a head! It wasn't a big stick poking up at all, it was a huge snake! In the path! Taking aim! At us! Rather, at me!

Jamie still didn't see it. This whole sequence of events had occurred in no more than three or four seconds. If he noticed it at all, he probably registered it as a big stick, as I had, because I could clearly see that he was planning to stay on the path and drive within two or three feet of it, letting it pass on my side of the Rover. Which might have been okay except for the fact that the Rover did not have a windshield, doors, roof, or anything at all to protect me from its strike or from flinging itself into the open-air front seat. It was clearly taking a bead on us, and I clearly would be the first warm, living object within its reach. But it was far too late and we were moving too fast even to yell "Stop" to Jamie. I hardly had time to react myself.

"Oh, shit!" I shouted, diving away from the snake.

I landed in the gap between the two bucket seats, partly sprawled on Jamie's lap, my head under the dashboard, my bare legs curled up fetal-like away from the open door.

Thwang!

Something hit hard on metal. I thought it was the seat belt clasp between the seats banging the Rover's floor as I dove down. Jamie, now realizing something was badly amiss or seeing the snake himself at the last instant, punched the accelerator down. The engine raced and the Rover bounced wildly down the path and across the clearing. Sprawled on the floor and over Jamie's lap I expected to feel the huge snake writhing around my bare legs.

Nothing.

Jamie braked to a stop.

The trackers jumped down from the rear bed. They were shouting and pointing back down the path.

"*Mamba!*" they were shouting. "*Mamba!*"

I didn't want to get out of the Rover. Chris, the young white from Zimbabwe, climbed down from the bed, as did Josh.

The trackers now were examining the outside of the Rover on my side. One of them pointed with his finger just in front of the open door where I sat. The others gathered around, talking excitedly, leaning closer, repeating "mamba!"

I got out. They pointed for me. There it was just in front of my open door where my bare leg had been sitting exposed: two exactly parallel scratches about an inch apart and three or so inches long in the Rover's hard greenish enamel. That was where the black mamba's fangs had struck.

The trackers pointed at the marks and then at me, as if to say, "That was really close! You were really lucky!"

"Did you hear it hit the car?" said Chris excitedly. "Bang!"

"I thought that was me sitting on the seat belt holder," I said.

"No, that was the snake hitting the metal."

With its lightning speed and its habit of striking its prey repeatedly until it drops, the snake apparently had tried to hit again as the Rover's rear went past. Josh was standing barelegged on the Rover bed right behind me.

"I would have been next in line," he said.

We climbed back in. Jamie drove on. He seemed as taken aback as anyone, speculating that the mamba must have been twelve or thirteen feet long to stand up that high.

"If that had hit you, we'd be driving at high speed to the landing strip right now."

It gradually dawned on me how close I'd come to dying. So maybe I hadn't been overly obsessed with Africa's tooth-and-claw aspects after all. Still, I was glad that Jamie hadn't tried to shoot the snake. We were fellow members of Leopold's "biotic community." Like Thoreau's striped bream, the mamba was my neighbor and contemporary. But I'd discovered with almost fatal results that he was a neighbor with a very cranky temperament. I preferred to leave him well alone.

Two days later Jamie drove Derek, Josh, and me in the fang-scratched Rover to Luwire's bush strip. We stowed our gear, and I climbed into the rear seat of the Cessna 206. Cameras at the ready for aerial shots, Josh climbed into the seat beside Jamie. Kicking over the bush plane's powerful engine, Jamie taxied down the dirt strip, swung around, and opened the throttle. Clouds of dust spewed behind as the plane accelerated, bouncing. Derek sat on the hood of the Rover at the bush strip's edge. He waved farewell with arm extended high as we roared past, which I tried to return with a little wave in my rear window. I'd liked Derek a lot. He was thoughtful, very competent, and articulate. Now I might never see him again, I thought as the tiny figure disappeared below.

We lifted over the forest and soon cruised at thirty-five hundred feet. The braided Lugenda glimmered hazily in the morning sun, winding off to the northeast until it appeared to spread out and evaporate where hazy horizon met bright sky. Bluish inselbergs thrust up like the volcanoes in depictions of the dinosaur age. The forest extended in every direction as far as I could see—greenish gray and nubbly-looking, peeled back in patches to reveal a bright green swampy place, a brownish bit of savannah, or a veinlike network of darker green forest that marked river courses and feeder streams. There was absolutely no sign of a human presence.

It was enormous, and I knew I was seeing only a tiny portion of it.

I wanted the forest to go on and on, be even bigger than I knew it was. I stared out the window looking for signs of humans, of "civilization," wanting not to see them. We flew on. I saw only the faintest reddish path in the forest and maybe one or two places that looked like a tiny cluster of thatched huts.

That was okay.

I didn't want to see a road going to that tiny cluster of thatched huts. I wanted it to remain what it was, like my grandfather's river before they built the highway bridge. Who was this all for, finally, this vast stretch of forest, this wilderness? Was it for me? Was it for the people who lived in those thatched huts? Was it for the animals? Was it for the entirety of Leopold's biotic community?

Like the Earth itself, this vast wilderness was used by each species and each individual of each species in its own way. I could finally understand it best in the way I had used it. I had used it by attempting to understand what drew me to it, what drew explorers from *Homo erectus* to Mungo Park onward into the unknown. The Niassa Reserve, I now saw, was a line drawn on a map designating a piece of geography devoted to the exercise of this compelling human curiosity about what lies "out there." But by drawing boundaries around it, the reserve and places like it constrained that urge, too—corralled it. I was grateful that most of our river trip had taken place in the wilderness outside the Niassa Reserve. Once we had reached its borders, I felt that we had entered a region that had been somehow, though only slightly, tamed.[46]

There were a thousand reasons to enter the wilderness, a thousand reasons that compelled that long line of individuals to explore. But, finally, the single answer that worked best for me was one given voice so succinctly by Thoreau in *Walden*: "Not till we are lost, in other words not till we have lost the world, do we begin to find ourselves, and realize where we are and the infinite extent of our relations."

The Cessna droned eastward, 115 knots at 3,500 feet. Jamie and Josh were talking in front, but sitting in back, I couldn't hear anything over the engine roar. An inselberg rose directly under us. The plane's crucifixlike shadow flashed up its sheer cliffs, over its viney top, and dropped down to the forest again. More dark green veinlike river systems. A plume of smoke on the horizon—a far-off village burning its garden plots in the forest. A range of inselbergs. A tiny village.

Then a dirt road.

More forest again.

Another road, one paved in patches. Square-shaped buildings were strung out along it, as if to service automobile traffic. In the distance a deeper haze of blue. Suddenly, we were skimming low over white sandy beaches, palm trees, the incredible blue of the Indian Ocean, the aquamarine of coral reefs. I saw fishing canoes and thatched huts, rusted corrugated metal roofs and a grid of streets, beach bungalows and a fancy hotel, a harbor, a few sailing yachts.

It all looked so very inviting and so very benign.

That was two years ago. Much has happened since then to all of us who took part in the Lugenda expedition. There have been marriages, as if the wilderness river journey represented, among other things, a last blast of singlehood for its participants. Cherri and Richard married in the Kalahari Desert. Rod married his girlfriend, and Clinton married his at Victoria Falls. And there's been illness, far too much of it. Steve survived a bad bout of colon cancer that surely was sapping him while on the river. He is now recovering, and his ambition when he does is to climb the mountains of Colorado. He recently had a tattoo spelling out the words "Rio Lugenda," in stylized waves, emblazoned on his skin in memory of our trip though the African wilds.

I've spent much of the last two years back in Montana, thinking and writing about those fifteen days on the Lugenda River—about what they meant, about the urge to explore, and about wilderness. Flying into Pemba with Jamie and Josh that morning two years ago, I never could have imagined that someday I'd be living in Mozambique. But that's where we are now as I finish this account, Amy, Molly, Skyler, and I.

We recently rented a house for a year in Maputo, the capital city. This is far south of the Lugenda River. Still, as I write I am only five blocks from that bright blue Indian Ocean that I first saw flying into Pemba. There's a palm tree and a papaya tree and a lemon tree in our garden. Coincidentally, the streets are named after some of the exploration chroniclers. We live on the corner of João de Barros, who wrote of the early Portuguese seagoing expeditions that I've described.

We've come to Mozambique for many reasons. A pragmatic one is that Amy has a year off from teaching, and we wanted to live abroad with Molly and Skyler. Maybe I want to show them, as my grandfather showed

The Miombo Forest and a tributary of the Lugenda River, from the air.

me, something about the world as it was before they built the highway bridges. I want to return to that great wilderness in the far north. Something powerful has drawn me back to Africa.

I keep returning to one image from the river journey. As we drifted along in our fancy plastic boats nibbling dried pears from France, we passed that fishing family with their nets of twisted vines and their canoe hollowed from a tree trunk. I very much want to keep the Lugenda River, and places like it, wilderness.

But what do we say to this family? And what do they have to say to us?

—*Maputo, Mozambique*
October 2004

NOTES

1. Frank McLynn. *Hearts of Darkness: The European Exploration of Africa*. New York: Carroll & Graf, 1993, p. 31.

2. Christopher Hibbert. *Africa Explored: Europeans in the Dark Continent, 1769–1889*. New York: W. W. Norton, 1982, p. 19.

3. Brian M. Fagan. *People of the Earth: An Introduction to World Prehistory*. Upper Saddle River, N.J.: Prentice Hall, 2004, p. 46.

4. See Hibbert, *Africa Explored*.

5. See McLynn, *Hearts of Darkness*, p. 13.

6. McLynn, p. 13.

7. Gaspar Correa. *The Three Voyages of Vasco da Gama and His Viceroyalty, from the Lendas da India of Gaspar Correa*. Ed. and trans. by Henry E. J. Stanley. London: Hakluyt Society, 1869, p. 56.

8. Daniel J. Boorstin. *The Discoverers: A History of Man's Search to Know His World and Himself*. New York: Random House, 1983, pp. 159–60.

9. Gomes Eannes de Zurara. *Chronicle of the Discovery and Conquest of Guinea*. Trans. by C. Raymond Beazley and Edgar Prestage. London: Hakluyt Society, 1896.

10. Paul Bowles. *Their Heads Are Green and Their Hands Are Blue: Scenes from the Non-Christian World*. New York: Ecco Press, 1984, first published 1957, pp. 143–44.

11. *A Journal of the First Voyage of Vasco da Gama, 1497–1499*. Ed. by E. G. Ravenstein. London: Hakluyt Society, 1896, p. 30.

12. See Correa, *The Three Voyages of Vasco da Gama*, p. 331.

13. Ma Huan. *Ying-Yai Sheng-Lan*, or *The Overall Survey of the Ocean's Shores* (originally published in China in 1433). Trans. by J. V. G. Mills. Cambridge, England: Hakluyt Society, 1970, pp. 27–28. Mills quotes measurement figures from, among other sources, Pao Tsen-Peng, *On the Ships of Cheng Ho* (Taipei: 1961).

14. This was the five-masted, 433-foot-long square rigger *Preussen*, built by the German shipping firm Laeisz in 1902 and carrying nitrate from South America to Europe.

15. See Mills, *Ying-Yai Sheng-Lan*, p. 34.

16. See Boorstin, *The Discoverers*, p. 201.

17. *The Travels of Ibn Battuta, A.D. 1325–1354*. Trans. and ed. by C. Defrémery,

B. R. Sanguinetti, and H. A. R. Gibb. Cambridge, U.K.: University Press for the Hakluyt Society, 1958.

18. Quotations and translations from Cyprian Rice, *The Persian Sufis*. London: George Allen and Unwin, 1964.

19. Ross E. Dunn. *The Adventures of Ibn Battuta: A Muslim Traveler of the 14th Century*. Berkeley: University of California Press, 1989, p. 125.

20. Says the Koran: "Whatsoever you take in booty, the fifth of it belongs to God, the Apostle, the relative, the orphans, the poor, and the traveler." Trans. in Gibb, vol. 2, footnote 63, p. 381.

21. Herodotus. *Collected works*. Trans. by Rev. Henry Cary. London: George Bell and Sons, 1904. Book 2, para. 32.

22. Sabatino Moscati. *The World of the Phoenicians*. Trans. by Alastair Hamilton. London: Weidenfeld and Nicolson, 1968, pp. 182–83.

23. Roland Oliver. *The African Experience: Major Themes in African History from Earliest Times to the Present*. New York: HarperCollins Publishers, 1991, p. 20.

24. Max Oelschlaeger. *The Idea of Wilderness*. New Haven, Conn.: Yale University Press, 1991, p. 356.

25. Roderick Nash. *Wilderness and the American Mind*, rev. ed. New Haven, Conn.: Yale University Press, 1973, 2001, pp. 1–2.

26. See Oelschlaeger, *The Idea of Wilderness*, pp. 5, 23.

27. *The Epic of Gilgamesh*. Trans. and ed. by Benjamin R. Foster. New York: W. W. Norton, 2001, p. 47.

28. For a detailed analysis of the uses and definitions of wilderness in the Old Testament, see *Dictionary of Biblical Imagery*, pp. 948–50. The English word *wilderness* itself translates a variety of Hebrew words in the Old Testament, such as *midbār*, which means arid land that can nevertheless at certain times be used for by nomadic herders for pasture, to other Hebrew words for empty, barren, or desert land. See also Nash, *Wilderness and the American Mind*, pp. 15–16.

29. Tu Fu. "Overnight at the Riverside Tower." Trans. from Poetry Archives @ eMule.com.

30. João de Barros. *Ásia: Décadas I & II*, facsimile of 1932 edition of António Baião. Lisbon: INCM, 1988, p. 120 (as cited in Russell, 2001).

31. George Percy. *Observations Gathered out of a Discourse on the Plantation of the Southerne Colonie in Virginia by the English, 1606*. Collected in *Narratives of Early Virginia*, ed. by Lyon Gardiner Tyler. New York: Charles Scribner's Sons, 1907, p. 16.

32. William Bradford. *Of Plymouth Plantation, 1620–1647*. Ed. by Samuel Eliot Morison. New York: Alfred A. Knopf, 1959, p. 62.

33. Roderick Nash in his classic study *Wilderness and the American Mind* treats at length this theme of how the colonists' confrontation with the North American wilderness left a permanent impression on the American psyche.

34. Through Rousseau, a wayward eighteenth-century female aristocrat, Baronne de Warens, exerted a considerable—though unheralded—influence on what became a modernist view of nature. A Swiss native, Madame de Warens had married an aristocrat, taken his money, and run off with the gardener's son and established an estate in Savoy which she operated as a kind of shelter for wayward Protestant youths who had converted to

Catholicism. Rousseau's mother having died in childbirth, he fled his Swiss relatives at age sixteen and, crossing parts of the Alps, converted to Catholicism (he got paid for doing so) and eventually landed at Mme. de Warens's estate. Here he remained for several charmed years as her lover. A naturopath and a Deist—one who believed God manifested himself in nature—as well as a woman of learning, Baronne de Warens tutored the unshaped young adventurer Rousseau in both the classics and in a profound appreciation for the natural world.

35. Jean-Jacques Rousseau. *Julie, or the New Heloise: Letters of Two Lovers Who Live in a Small Town at the Foot of the Alps.* Trans. by Philip Steward and Jean Vaché. Hanover, N.H.: Dartmouth College, University Press of New England, 1997, pp. 63–64.

36. Friedrich von Schiller. *Two Essays: Naive and Sentimental Poetry and On the Sublime.* Trans. by Julius A. Elias. New York: Frederick Ungar, 1966, pp. 203–4.

37. Samuel Taylor Coleridge. *Selected Prose and Poetry of Coleridge.* Ed. by Donald Stauffer. (New York: The Modern Library, 1951). For Coleridge's use of Bruce and Bartram see *The Road to Xanadu: A Study in the Ways of the Imagination* by John Livingston Lowes. Boston: Houghton Mifflin, 1927.

38. Warren Harding. *The Days of Henry Thoreau.* New York: Alfred A. Knopf, 1966, p. 40.

39. Emerson, as quoted in Nash, *Wilderness and the American Mind,* p. 85.

40. F. B. Sanborn. *The Life of Henry David Thoreau.* Boston: Houghton Mifflin, 1917, p. 236–37.

41. Henry David Thoreau. *The Maine Woods.* Boston: Houghton Mifflin, 1893; originally copyrighted 1864.

42. Tim Jeal. *Livingstone.* New York: G. P. Putnam and Sons, 1973. Much of the Livingstone biographical material in this chapter is from Jeal's book.

43. Donald Worster. *Nature's Economy: A History of Ecological Ideas.* Cambridge, U.K.: Cambridge University Press, 1985; first published by Sierra Club Books, 1977, p. 84.

44. John M. Mackenzie. *The Empire of Nature: Hunting, Conservation and British Imperialism.* Manchester, U.K.: Manchester University Press, 1988, p. 211.

45. Aldo Leopold. *A Sand County Almanac with Essays on Conservation from Round River.* New York: Ballantine Books, 1970; first published 1949 and 1953 by Oxford University Press.

46. For more on how formal wilderness preserves diminish the untamed aspect of wilderness see Jack Turner, *The Abstract Wild.* Tucson, AZ: University of Arizona Press, 1996.

BIBLIOGRAPHY

GENERAL

Bevis, Richard. *The Road to Egdon Heath: The Aesthetics of the Great in Nature.* Montreal: McGill-Queen's University Press, 1999.

Boorstin, Daniel. *The Discoverers.* New York: Random House, 1983.

Callicott, J. Baird and Michael P. Nelson, eds. *The Great New Wilderness Debate.* Athens, Ga.: University of Georgia Press, 1998.

Duffy, James. *Portugal in Africa.* Baltimore: Penguin Books, 1962.

———. *Portuguese Africa.* Cambridge, Mass.: Harvard University Press, 1959.

Ehnmark, Anders and Per Wastberg. *Angola and Mozambique: The Case Against Portugal.* Paul Britten-Austin, trans. New York: Roy Publishers, 1963.

Eisenberg, Evan. *The Ecology of Eden.* New York: Knopf, 1998.

Finnegan, William. *A Complicated War: The Harrowing of Mozambique.* Berkeley: University of California Press, 1992.

Glacken, Clarence J. *Traces on the Rhodian Shore: Nature and Culture in Western Thought . . . to the Eighteenth Century.* Berkeley: University of California Press, 1967.

Hallett, Robin. *The Penetration of Africa: European Enterprise and Exploration Principally in Northern and Western Africa Up to 1830* (John Ledyard), vol. I to 1815. London: Routledge and Kegan Paul, 1965.

Hibbert, Christopher. *Africa Explored: Europeans in the Dark Continent, 1769–1889.* New York and London: W. W. Norton & Company, 1982.

McEvedy, Colin. *The Penguin Atlas of African History.* London: Penguin Books, 1980. Rev. ed., 1995.

McGlynn, Frank. *Hearts of Darkness: The European Exploration of Africa.* New York: Carroll & Graf Publishers, Inc., 1992, 1993.

Murray, John A., ed. *Wild Africa.* New York and Oxford, U.K.: Oxford University Press, 1993.

Nash, Roderick Frazier. *Wilderness and the American Mind.* New Haven: Yale University Press, 2001.

Oelschlaeger, Max. *The Idea of Wilderness: From Prehistory to the Age of Ecology.* New Haven and London: Yale University Press, 1991.

Rotberg, Robert I., ed. *Africa and Its Explorers: Motives, Methods and Impact.* Cambridge, Mass.: Harvard University Press, 1970.

Worster, Donald. *Nature's Economy: A History of Ecological Ideas.* Cambridge, U.K.: Cambridge University Press, 2001, and Sierra Club Books, 1977.

Zweig, Paul. *The Adventurer.* New York: Basic Books, 1974.

APPROACH

Boaz, Noel T. and Alan J. Almquist. *Essentials of Biological Anthropology.* Upper Saddle River, N.J.: Prentice-Hall, 1999.

Fagan, Bruce M. *People of the Earth: An Introduction to World Prehistory, 11th ed.* Upper Saddle River, N.J.: Prentice-Hall, 2004.

Seitz, Don C. "First American Traveler" (John Ledyard), *Uncommon Americans: Pencil Portraits of Men and Women Who Have Broken the Rules.* Indianapolis: Bobbs-Merrill Company, 1925.

Wenke, Robert J. *Patterns in Prehistory: Mankind's First Three Million Years.* New York: Oxford University Press, 1980.

DAY ONE

Denham, Major Dixon, Captain Hugh Clapperton, and Dr. Walter Oudney. "Narrative of Travels and Discoveries in Northern and Central Africa in the Years 1822, 1823, and 1824," in *The Bornu Mission, 1822–25: Missions to the Niger,* vol. II, part I, E. W. Bovill. Cambridge, U.K.: Hakluyt Society.

———. "Major Denham's Narrative" in *The Bornu Mission, 1822–25, Missions to the Niger,* vol. III, part II. E. W. Bovill, Cambridge, U.K.: Hakluyt Society, 2nd series, no. 129, University Press, 1965.

DAY TWO

Almeida, Manoel. "The History of High Ethiopia or Abassia" *& Bahrey,* "History of the Galla," from *Some Records of Ethiopia, 1593–1646,* C. F. Beckingham and G. W. B. Huntingford, trans. and eds. Cambridge, U.K.: Hakluyt Society, 2nd series, no. 107, University Press, 1954.

Alvares, Father Francisco. A True Relation of the Lands of the Prester John: Being the Narrative of the Portuguese Embassy to Ethiopia in 1520. *The Prester John of the Indies.* vols. 1 and 2, Lord Stanley of Alderley, trans., 1881, C. F. Beckingham and G. W. B. Huntingford. Cambridge, U.K.: Hakluyt Society, 2nd series, nos. 114 and 115, University Press, 1961.

Bruce, James. *Finding the Source of the Blue Nile: Travels to Discover the Source of the Nile.* London, 1790, John Q. Murray, ed., *Wild Africa,* op. cit.

Castanhoso, Miguel, João Bermudez, and Gaspar Correa. *The Portuguese Expedition to Abyssinia.* R. S. Whiteway, trans. and ed. London: Hakluyt Society, 2nd series, no. 10, 1902.

Crawford, O. G. S., ed. *Ethiopian Itineraries, Circa 1400–1524: Including Those Collected by Alessandro Zorzi at Venice, 1519–24.* Cambridge, U.K.: Hakluyt Society, 2nd series, no. 109, University Press, 1958.

Lobo, Jeronimo. *The Itinerario of Jeronimo Lobo.* Donald M. Lockhart, trans. Introduction by C. F. Beckingham. Cambridge, U.K.: Hakluyt Society, 2nd series, no. 162, University Press, 1984.

DAY THREE

Azurara, Gomes Eannes. *The Discovery and Conquest of Guinea,* vols. 1 and 2. Charles Raymond Beazley and Edgar Prestage, trans. London: Hakluyt Society, 1st series, nos. 95 and 100, 1896 and 1899.

Bowles, Paul. *Their Heads Are Green and Their Hands Are Blue.* New York: Ecco Press, 1984.

Correa, Gaspar. *The Three Voyages of Vasco da Gama and His Viceroyalty, from the Lenas da India.* Henry E. J. Stanley, trans. London: Hakluyt Society, 1st series, no. 42, 1899.

da Gama, Vasco. *A Journal of the First Voyage, 1497–1499.* E. G. Ravenstein, trans. & ed. London: Hakluyt Society, 1st series, no. 99, 1899.

Russell, Peter. *Prince Henry the Navigator: A Life.* New Haven and London: Yale University Press, 2000.

DAY FOUR

Barbosa, Duarte. *The Book of Duarte Barbosa, 1518,* vol. 1. Mansel Longworth Dames, trans. London: Hakluyt Society, 2nd series, no. 44, 1917.

DAY FIVE

Huntington, Madge. *A Traveler's Guide to Chinese History.* New York: Henry Holt, 1984.

Ma Huan. *The Overall Survey of the Ocean's Shores, 1433.* Feng Ch'eng-Chin, trans. Introduction and notes, J. V. G. Mills. Cambridge, U.K.: Hakluyt Society, University Press, 1970.

Ronan, Colin A. *The Shorter Science and Civilization in China: An Abridgement of Joseph Needham's Original Text.* Cambridge, U.K.: Cambridge University Press, 1978.

DAY SIX

Bivar, A. D. H. comp. *The Travels of Ibn Battuta: A.D. 1325–1354,* Index to Volumes 1–4. London: Hakluyt Society, 2nd series, no. 190, British Library, 2000.

Dunn, Ross E. *The Adventures of Ibn Battuta: A Muslim Traveler of the 14th Century.* Berkeley: University of California Press, 1986.

Gibb. H. A. R. *The Travels of Ibn Battuta: A.D. 1325–1354.* C. Defremery, B. R. Sanguinetti, trans. and eds. vol. I, 2nd series, no. 110. Cambridge, U.K.: Cambridge University Press, 1958.

———. *The Travels,* op. cit., Vol. 2. 2nd series, no. 117, 1962.

———. *The Travels,* op. cit., Vol. 3. 2nd series, no. 141, 1971.

———. *The Travels,* op. cit., Vol. 4. 2nd series, no. 178, 1994.

DAY SEVEN

Edey, Maitland A. and the editors of Time-Life Books. *The Sea Traders, The Emergence of Man Series.* New York: Time-Life Books, 1974.

Hardin, Donald. *The Phoenicians,* vol. 26: *Ancient Peoples and Places.* New York: Praeger, 1962.

Herodotus. *Collected Works.* The Rev. Henry Clay, trans., Bohn's Classical Library. London: George Bell & Sons, 1904.

How, W. W. and J. Wells. *A Commentary on Herodotus,* vol. 1, books 1–4, Oxford, U.K.: Clarendon Press, 1912, 1967.

Moscati, Sabatino. *The World of the Phoenicians.* Alastair Hamilton, trans. London: Weidenfeld & Nicolson, 1965, 1968.

DAY EIGHT

Buss, Donald M. *Evolutionary Psychology: The New Science of the Mind.* Boston: Allyn & Bacon, 1999.

Davidson, Basil. *A History of East and Central Africa to the Late Nineteenth Century.* Garden City, N.Y.: Doubleday, 1969.

Gaulin, Steven J. C. and Donald H. McBurney. *Psychology: An Evolutionary Approach.* Upper Saddle River, N.J.; Prentice-Hall, 2001.

Oliver, Roland. *The African Experience.* New York: HarperCollins, 1991.

DAY TEN

Angeloni, Elvio, ed. *Physical Anthropology.* Guilford, Conn.: McGraw-Hill/Dushkin, 2003.

Campbell, Joseph. *The Masks of God: Primitive Mythology.* New York: Penguin, 1959, 1991.

Mithen, Steven. *The Prehistory of the Mind.* London: Thames & Hudson, 1996.

DAY ELEVEN

Foster, Benjamin R. trans. and ed. *The Epic of Gilgamesh.* New York: W. W. Norton, 2001.

Sandars, N. K. *The Epic of Gilgamesh.* London: Penguin, 1960, 1972.

DAY TWELVE

The Old Testament. Vol. I Genesis—Esther. James Moffatt, trans. New York: George H. Doran Co., 1924.

Roche, Paul. *The Bible's Greatest Stories.* New York: Penguin, 1990.

Rowley, H. H. *The Modern Reader's Bible Atlas.* London: English Universities Press, 1960.

Smith, George Adam. *The Historical Geography of the Holy Land.* London: Hodder & Stoughton, 1894. Rev. ed., Harper & Row 1931, 1966.

DAY THIRTEEN

Bradford, William. *Of Plymouth Plantation 1620–1647.* Text, notes, and introduction by Samuel Eliot Morison. New York: Alfred A. Knopf, 1959.

Grove, Richard H. *Green Imperialism: Colonial Expansion, Tropical Island Edens and the Origins of Environmentalism, 1600–1860.* Cambridge, U.K.: Cambridge University Press, 1995.

Morton, Richard L. *Colonial Virginia,* vol. 1, *The Tidewater Period, 1607–1710.* Chapel Hill, N.C.: University of North Carolina Press, 1960.

Tyler, Lyon Gardiner. *Narratives of Early Virginia, 1606–1625.* New York: Charles Scribner's Sons, 1907.

DAY FOURTEEN

Bartram, William. *Travels and Other Writings, 1773–74.* New York: Library of America, 1996.

Burke, Edmund. *[Essays] On Taste; On the Sublime and Beautiful; Reflections on the French Revolution; A Letter to a Noble Lord.* Danbury, Conn.: Harvard Classics, Grolier Enterprises, 1909, 1980.

Burwick, Frederick. *Poetic Madness and the Romantic Imagination.* University Park: Pennsylvania State University Press, 1996.

Coleridge, Samuel Taylor. *Selected Poetry and Prose of Coleridge.* Donald A. Stauffer, ed. New York: Modern Library, 1951.

Lowes, John Livingston. *The Road to Xanadu: A Study in the Ways of the Imagination.* Boston: Houghton Mifflin, 1927.

McFarland, Thomas. *Romanticism and the Heritage of Rousseau.* Oxford: Clarendon Press, 1995.

Peckham, Morse, ed. *Romanticism: The Culture of the Nineteenth Century.* New York: George Braziller, 1965.

Peckham, Morse. *Romanticism and Behavior: Collected Essays II.* Columbia, S.C.: University of South Carolina Press, 1976.

Rousseau, Jean-Jacques. *The Confessions.* W. Conyngham Mallory, trans. New York: Tudor Publishing, 1928.

———. *Julie, or The New Heloise: Letters of Two Lovers in a Small Town at the Foot of the Alps.* Hanover, N.H.: University Press of New England, 1997.

Schiller, Friedrich von. *Naive and Sentimental Poetry* and *On the Sublime.* Julius A. Elias, trans. Introduction by Julius A. Elias. New York: Praeger, 1966.

Stromberg, Roland N. *An Intellectual History of Modern Europe,* 2nd ed. Englewood Cliffs, N.J.: Prentice-Hall, 1975.

Thorsley, Peter L., Jr. *The Byronic Hero: Types and Prototypes.* Minneapolis: University of Minnesota Press, 1962.

DAY FIFTEEN

Africa and Its Exploration As Told by Its Explorers, vols. 1 and 2. London: Samson, Low, & Marston, 1891, 1892.

Dugard, Martin. *Into Africa: The Epic Adventures of Stanley and Livingstone.* New York: Broadway Books, 2003.

Harding, Walter. *The Days of Henry Thoreau.* New York: Knopf, 1966.

Jeal, Tim. *Livingstone.* New York: G. P. Putnam's Sons, 1973.

Jones, Charles H. *Africa: The History of Exploration and Adventure from Herodotus to Livingstone.* New York: Henry Holt, 1875.

Livingstone, David. *A Popular Account of Dr. Livingstone's Expedition to the Zambesi and Its Tributaries, 1858–1864.* London: John Murray, 1875.

———. *The Life and African Explorations of Dr. David Livingstone.* Unabridged republication of the 1874 edition. New York: Cooper Square Press, 2002.

Petula, Joseph M. *American Environmental History: The Exploitation and Conservation of Natural Resources.* San Francisco: Boyd & Fraser, 1977.

Sanborn, F. B. *The Life of Henry David Thoreau.* Boston: Houghton Mifflin, 1917.

Thoreau, Henry David. *The Maine Woods.* Boston: Houghton Mifflin, 1884.

———. *The Variorum Walden.* New York: Twayne Publishers, 1962.

Whicher, Stephen E., ed. *Selections from Ralph Waldo Emerson.* Boston: Houghton Mifflin, 1957.

EPILOGUE

Bramwell, Anna. *Ecology in the Twentieth Century: A History.* New Haven: Yale University Press, 1989.

Griffiths, Tom, and Libby Robin, eds. *Ecology and Empire: Environmental History of Settler Societies.* Seattle: University of Washington Press, 1997.

Kline, Benjamin. *First Along the River: A Brief History of the U.S. Environmental Movement.* San Francisco: Acada Books, 1997.

Leopold, Aldo. *A Sand County Almanac with Essays from Round River.* New York: Ballantine Books, 1970. Originally published by Oxford University Press, 1949, 1953.

MacKenzie, John M. *The Empire of Nature: Hunting, Conservation and British Imperialism.* Manchester, U.K.: Manchester University Press, 1998.

Turner, Jack. *The Abstract Wild.* Tucson, AZ: University of Arizona Press, 1966.

Worster, Donald. *The Wealth of Nature: Environmental History and the Ecological Imagination.* New York: Oxford University Press, 1993.

ILLUSTRATION ACKNOWLEDGMENTS

Grateful acknowledgment is made to the following for permission to use illustrative material:

Photographs pp. 2, 38, 42, 44, 45, 49, 51, 74, 75, 76, 78, 83, 84, 89, 100, 109, 116, 117, 166, 172, 180, 183, 185, 186, 187, 188, 198, 208, 222, 227, 309, 320 courtesy of Peter Stark, used by permission.

Photographs pp. 64, 126, 144, 162, 228, 229, 269, 272, 276, 291, 297, 298, 300, 303, 310 copyright © Joshua Paul, all rights reserved.

Photographs pp. 232, 244, 260 copyright © Cherri Briggs / Explore Inc., all rights reserved.

Map p. 12 copyright © Mapping Specialists, all rights reserved.

Photographs insert pp. 1 (top), 2, 3, 4, 5, 6 (bottom), 7 (top) courtesy of Peter Stark, used by permission.

Photographs insert pp. 1 (bottom), 6 (top), 7 (bottom), 8 copyright © Joshua Paul, all rights reserved.

NIASSA RESERVE
CONTACT INFORMATION

For more information on the Niassa Reserve and contact
information, see the reserve's Web site:

www.niassa.com

ABOUT THE AUTHOR

A National Magazine Award nominee, PETER STARK is a contributor to *Outside,* where he originally chronicled his Lugenda adventure. His work has also appeared in *Smithsonian* and *The New Yorker.* He is the author of *Last Breath* and *Driving to Greenland* and the editor of an anthology, *Ring of Fire*. He lives in Missoula, Montana.

ABOUT THE TYPE

This book was set in Garamond, a typeface originally designed by the Parisian type cutter Claude Garamond (1480–1561). This version of Garamond was modeled on a 1592 specimen sheet from the Egenolff-Berner foundry, which was produced from types assumed to have been brought to Frankfurt by the punch cutter Jacques Sabon (d. 1580).

Claude Garamond's distinguished romans and italics first appeared in *Opera Ciceronis* in 1543–44. The Garamond types are clear, open, and elegant.